THE QUIET CENTER

THE QUIET CENTER

Women Reflecting on Life's Passages from the Pages of Victoria Magazine

KATHERINE BALL ROSS, EDITOR

HEARST BOOKS

NEW YORK

Library of Congress Cataloging-in-Publication Data

The quiet center : women reflecting on life's passages from the pages of *Victoria* magazine.
  p. cm.
 ISBN 0-688-15464-6
  1. Women—United States—Biography—Miscellanea. I. *Victoria* (New York, N.Y.)
HQ1412.Q54 1997
305.4'092'273—dc21   96-40327
                CIP

Printed in the United States of America

First Edition

1 2 3 4 5 6 7 8 9 10

BOOK DESIGN BY JO ANNE METSCH

FOREWORD

G rowing up a girl means making friends with books—
at least, for me and many others like me. I had my hideaways
for reading: the windowseat on the landing above the entry hall,
the narrow backstairs that led to my bedroom. I loved the teachers who taught me to read, the librarians who fed my hunger
with their personal favorites. Whole shelves of books were devoured—all the *Anne* books, the *Little House* series, *Little Women*
and its successors, and anything by Frances Hodgson Burnett.
If a book gave me a good cry, all the better. I was getting a sentimental education through the classics of children's literature.

My tastes changed as I grew older. I turned more often to
biography, autobiography, memoirs. I wanted to know how others had really lived, men as well as women, to understand the
texture of life, its varying patterns, shifting fortunes. Behind
this new taste lay the youthful question: And what am I to do
with my life? I was seeking guidance. (Even the title of this
book comes from advice handed down from the older writer

Sarah Orne Jewett to her younger friend Willa Cather: "Find the quiet center of your own life," Jewett said, "and write from there to the world.")

Memoirs are the distillation of life's lessons. They are experiences "recollected in tranquillity," and they needn't be dramatic experiences. Life, after all, consists mainly in our routines, our rituals, commonplace things that everyone shares. But the memoir writer discovers the mystery in the commonplace. She bites down on a tiny seed and—open sesame!—the essential oil bursts forth, more intense than we could have ever imagined.

When I began my journey as *Victoria*'s first editor a little more than ten years ago, I envisioned a magazine that spoke to a woman's longing for beauty, that reawakened our sensitivity to beautiful things of every variety. From the beginning, I knew beautiful language—*belles lettres*—would be an integral part of such a magazine. When we realized that *Victoria* had indeed struck a chord with substantial numbers of readers, I felt that I could afford to invite some of the best writers to our pages and give them a forum for their innermost thoughts. It would be a place to share secrets, to transmit traditions, to revel in language, and to light up any small corner of life without regard for whether it was sensational or significant or "relevant." I wanted it just to be good.

Collected here is a celebration—a sampling of the best original writing to have appeared in *Victoria* over the past ten years. Many of the writers represented are well known to you; others will be new acquaintances. So take this little book to your chosen snuggery and curl up with friends, old and new. I promise you fresh insights on familiar scenes, a candle in the dark, a friendly word to spur you on home.

—*Nancy Lindemeyer*
Editor in Chief
Victoria magazine

C ONTENTS

Contents

Contents

Contents

CHILDHOOD

HORSE LOVE

Jane Smiley

When I was fourteen, I learned that virtue could be rewarded. My particular virtue—devotion to the care of a horse that belonged to another family—was one that bemused my mother and stepfather, but they rewarded it anyway by buying me the horse as a surprise over Memorial Day weekend. I still remember hearing this news with the most intense rush of pleasure and exhilaration that I have ever felt. We were to be united at last.

I had spent the spring in a solitary wash of dreams. The frightening storm of eighth grade—algebra, unpopularity, the fashion mistake of white harlequin glasses—had calmed to a ninth-grade Sargasso Sea of geometry, a friend or two, weekends unruffled by social activity. My mother had a new baby, which meant she spent a lot of time in her room. My career was walking the paths along the creek that ran below our house and summoning up elaborate fantasies of my equine future, the horse farm I would have, the friends who would visit, the benign landscape of rolling hills and wooded valleys where it would all take place. On Saturdays and Sundays in spite of my broken arm (a P. E. accident at school), I groomed, walked, and courted my beloved, a Thoroughbred mare, dark bay, almost seventeen hands tall, with a sweet disposition and a good head.

I was well prepared by my reading for translation to the blessed realm of horse ownership. The psychological movement of all girls' horse novels follows a familiar pattern: The beloved object is viewed from a distance, perceived to have singular qualities not apparent to the world at large, defended in the teeth of opposition, and finally won. Love is both the task and the reward, though some serendipitous winning of a race or a contest may prove to the world what the girl knew all along. A horse, though neither a boy nor a religious figure, had some of the qualities of both—inherent reserve, large size, and mystery. What you got from horse love that you didn't get from the other kinds was fresh air and healthful and challenging outdoor activity.

We boarded the mare, whose registered name was Rivertown Gal, but whom I thought of as "Her," at a club outside of St. Louis, just north of the Missouri River. The club had twelve or thirteen other horses, but ours was the only boarder, and I was the only regular rider on summer weekdays. My grandfather, recently retired, made the long drive. He told jokes, teased me, caroled the names of the towns, "Gumbo! Gumbo! Gumboho!" the way he had once heard conductors on long-vanished trains call them out. There were songs, too—my grandfather had a legendary baritone. He sang "Sweet Betsey From Pike," or, as we crossed the wide Missouri, "Shenandoah." From the high arch of the dangerous three-lane bridge that spanned the river, I would look down at the bluff-rimmed swirl. It came from far away. Soon it would fling its brown western burden into the blue Mississippi. This was power. Riding with my grandfather in his white Plymouth Fury is a part of this memory I cherish now, though I overlooked it then. His eventful life—star college athlete (Sigma Chi), rancher in Idaho (where he met my grandmother) and Texas, tannery supervisor in Illinois—was enlivened by years of baseball, boxing, tennis, golf, music, and song. It formed the material he shaped for the grandchildren with his storytelling gift. Every day he talked and joked with me, and I only half listened (I was contemplating Her, of course), but even half listening, I soaked up a feeling for an America that he seemed to embody—the outdoor, sunlit world that the great Missouri ran through, a landscape full of good fellowship and adventures brought to a safe and satisfying end.

He would drop me off in the midmorning, pick me up in the late afternoon. The wealth of hours was barely enough for me to live out the intensity of my affection for Her. The cast was off my arm, I was allowed to ride and jump again, all things had come to fruition.

The club borrowed an English ambience in consonance with the available activities there—riding, skeet shooting, bassetting, dining, and whisky drinking. The long drive from the main road to the rambling white clubhouse was dotted with signs whose messages I simply did not understand, like "Hounds Gentlemen Please" and "Dead Slow." Our dead-slow car carried us past them as though past the Stations of the Cross, and I read them as enigmatic prayers that would soon bring me to my heaven.

There were no other riders. The stableman, Ernst, and the housekeeper, Mrs. Rounceville, were the only people I ever saw during the week, and on the weekends I hated the intrusion of others into my world—the bright, ordered woods and fields outside, and the dark, walnut-paneled, book-lined coolness inside, where only pictures of horses and dogs with that cockeyed eighteenth-century look about them hung on the walls.

My riding skills were improving. I could take the mare over little three-foot fences with some style, put her through elementary dressage paces. Most importantly to me, I felt secure bareback, as close to actually embracing the horse as you could be.

The trail descended a long grassy hill from the dressage ring, passed through a gate into a big meadow, then angled into woods—oaks, dogwoods, beeches. Big logs lay over the woodland section, good for practice jumps. Deep in the woods there was a ravine. You were supposed to sit back just a little going down, then lean forward going up.

The woodland trail ended in another meadow that opened out over the river far below. From the top of the bluff, I could see Gumbo in the distance. It was dizzying.

After that the trail wound away from the river, among bushes. The sun shone hot and picked out the underbrush in sharp-edged shadows. June vegetation, varied, thick with life, didn't yet droop dustily in midsummer heat. I swung my legs gently forward and backwards against the mare's smooth sides, and threaded bits of her black mane between my fingers. We had walked, trotted, cantered, walked again, jumped a few logs and fences. I lengthened the reins and let her stretch her neck. I pushed my velvet cap back from my brow. I let Her take some forbidden bites of grass. We slowed down and relaxed. All around us, the trees and bushes resounded with creaks and swishes, birdsong and tiny animal noises. The mare blew out and shook her head. I saw that we had wandered into a blackberry thicket and we drifted to a halt.

The blackberries were ripe, juicy, blue-black, depending heavily from the canes. I could pick them from where I sat on the tall mare, just leaning here and there, reaching for this one and that one. They liquefied in my mouth, quenching a thirst I hadn't even known I had. The mare, stepping from one mouthful of grass or leaves to another, carried me from berry cluster to berry cluster. We ate enough. We ate until my fingers were black with berry juice and her bit was green with chlorophyll, until the sweat on her neck had dried. Then we came around

the thicket into another meadow. I picked up the reins and
seated myself, then gave her a nudge with my heels. We cantered away.

The acres around the club were fully settled, with farm fields
and roads and houses, but empty—the bluffs above the river
were too hilly for the kind of intensive farming done on the
bottom land near Gumbo. Many of the houses were summer
places—uninhabited during the week. The fact that I never saw
anyone fed into my sense of ever unfolding discovery. Every vista
across a meadow, every narrow stretch of trail through the shady
woods was exceeded in beauty and pleasure by the next one.
Viscerally, I felt I claimed this land by riding over it, by gazing
upon it, and memorizing it. Because of love and solitude, I think
my mind was unusually open to the natural world, and I can
still, after twenty-seven years, recall more of these lands in detail
than any other place I've known.

The horse beneath me moved rhythmically, as horses always
do, the ta-dum ta-dum rhythm of the walk especially conducive
to meditative states, and while I looked around, I perfected my
fantasy of devotion: I would take Her to college to be with Her
always, raise Her offspring when she got too old to ride, and
our home in the future world would look exactly like the club.
The serendipitous contest that would reveal her superlative
worth was hazy, but the continuing task of love was vividly
present, its own reward.

When the ride was over, I cooled Her down with scrupulous
care, bathed Her, dried Her, brushed Her, picked out Her stall,
emptied and filled Her water bucket, fed Her carrots and apples,
sat in Her stall and watched Her, crooning. Then, and only then,
did I go and get my lunch from Mrs. Rounceville. After lunch
I picked old novels from the forties and fifties off the shelves
(*The Hucksters* is one that I remember finding utterly baffling)
and in the midst of reading I usually fell asleep on the carpet,
worn out from my devotions.

I have since found myself to be not precisely the person I seemed to myself then, and I am sure the life I imagined as supremely fulfilling—far out in the country, horses and dogs my only companions, devotion to them my only mental activity—would not have suited me. My mother, who knew I had neither the money nor the equestrian gift to pursue my obsession, proved truer in her predictions of my future than I did. Perhaps my parents only allowed me to live out my fantasy on the getting-it-out-of-my-system principle. Even so, they provided me with more than they, or I, knew. Looking back, I think that girls at a certain stage of puberty are filled simply with feelings they long to attach to an object, and their work is to imagine their futures in a way that they have never needed to do as children. The world is ready to offer them answers, mostly of the one-word variety—mother or teacher or ballerina in those days, or lawyer or doctor or writer or executive in these. But in fact these words are only charms that call up something larger and more complex: how a girl foresees living in the world from day to day, how many children she will have, what their names will be, what her husband will look like, what she will wear to the office and where she will go at night, what kind of house she will have and how she will decorate it. Possibly, few of these details ever work out. A feature of middle age is how we marvel at where life has taken us, now that it looks like we are there to stay.

But I don't think dreams are meant to work out. They are based on ignorance after all, on how we respond to the way the world looks before we know what it is like, or really what we are like. It is the act of dreaming that is important, the daily process of putting together a future that a girl can move toward with confidence and desire. If she is lucky, as I was, the adoration she feels will fix itself on a transitional object, on someone or something like a horse, that is present but basically indifferent, something that can be left behind when the girl discovers her need for reciprocity. If she is really lucky, she will find in that time long hours of solitude, so that the fantasies can elaborate and develop on their own, owing relatively little to group ideas or adult ideas about what is respectable, worthwhile, or even possible for a girl like her, for in their detail and their idiosyncrasy is their strength, their power to carry her through the ever-increasing demands and prescriptions of high school and young womanhood. The desire to have a particular future, and the energy behind that desire, eventually translate to the sense of accomplishment and self-esteem that permits a woman to make a life that she is happy to live, however far that is from the life she imagined at fourteen.

When I remember that summer, though, these things are not what I remember, and I am moved to cherish something else above all, and that is the way my horse love attached me to the physical world. I perceived every sensation—the silky smoothness of Her freshly brushed and shining coat, the heavy richness of the grain in the bucket, the sweetness of its odor and the musical sound it made pouring into Her feeding trough, the taste of blackberries, the dappled chiaroscuro of the trail through the woods, the rhythmic, rippling speed, through my body and hers, of a fast gallop punctuated by a leap over a fat log. I perceived every sensation as if I had never lived in the physical world before, as if my own body were new. I laugh now, and say it must have been hormones, but I think the luckiest thing that happened to me was the freedom to feel and appreciate these sensations, to learn to love the natural world, for in the years since, this sense of attachment has proved an unfailing source of happiness and inner peace.

Though I came to writing through reading, I think I came to my pleasure in depicting the natural world by riding over the landscape—seeing it, then entering it, and feeling it in my own self with Her every stride.

Listening to My Mother's Song

Maxine Clair

It is Sunday morning. Five of the nine of us are already born and four are old enough to get ourselves ready for church. We scurry around upstairs in the two-story wood-frame house on Stewart Avenue in Kansas City, Kansas. By now the bathwater comes out lukewarm, and I am fortunate enough to be the first to use this tubful. We share damp towels the way we share clothes, beds, Tootsie Rolls.

Downstairs my mother scrapes the three-legged piano stool across a once-beautiful hardwood floor. She spins the seat, lowering it to suit her. It squeals. She strikes up a chord or two as though an orchestra were there waiting to tune up. She romps though a few bars of "Jesus Is Real to Me" in a hot gospel rhythm, limbering up her fingers. By the time she abandons it, my brother is coming as close as he can to singing the bass progressions.

Then, as I sit in the tub, she begins another song. It is a

melody that halts my hand's busy industry with the square bar of Ivory inside a wad of faded, napless terry cloth.

I love this song, not because its lyrics formed the earliest rote of my Bible verses, but because of the way it pulls at me, bringing something akin to a quickening in my chest, and with it the desire to fling my wet arms in an arc above my head like an impatient ballerina with the urge to pirouette. My mother plays "The Lord Is My Shepherd." Out of a strange self-consciousness, I hold back, humming as I try to focus on my bath. I can hear my brother somewhere between the kitchen and my parents' bedroom, and I suppose that he is looking for the hairbrush; he has already found his tenor line. My sister knows the soprano line best. Another brother, young and eager, sings in a wavery soprano; another, a baby voice, simply belts out gibberish from the playpen downstairs. Then I surrender to the music.

For as long as my mother will play it, we will sing: me, perfectly still in the cool water, my brother no doubt entranced between brush strokes, my sister probably hugging herself, and the baby satisfied that she is one of us. I am ten years old. It will be years before I understand that this is my mother's art, or that the stillness I experience is my meditation on it.

Artistic expression, as I knew it, was what we did at school every Friday with watercolors and heavy paper while a scratchy concerto of "real" music played on Miss Thorton's portable record player. Or it was what we saw once a year when we took Mr. McCallop's school bus across the river to Missouri and on to the forbidding crypt of silence and landscapes called the Nelson Art Gallery.

Since my mother had no formal training, I thought of her music as merely "playing the piano." It was not unusual for her to breeze through a cycle of fifths with some Count Basie number "by ear." Or she could play counterpoint to a Nat "King"

Cole ballad without thinking. Sometimes she sat down, closed her eyes, threw her head back so that her black hair dangled, and she composed what would have been an entire jazz suite right out of her head for the sheer expression of it. If I asked her, "Muddear, what's that?" she would open her eyes and look at me for minutes before she could speak—so caught up she was in the music. Then she would shrug and say, "Something I made up."

And she wanted more. She took a few lessons one summer. They lasted only long enough for her to learn the significance of the bass and treble clefs and that each of the eighty-eight keys has a signature. With several thin books she practiced every day, stumbling at first, then playing the stodgy compositions, embellishing them with her own style until they sounded like real music. I didn't understand her insistence on following all the steps when she could do much better by ear.

One day as I stood in our dining room ironing a pair of my brother's khakis, she played a classical piece she'd been working at, and for the first time I really listened.

Her sheet music was usually situated in the music stand on the upright piano where we were not to touch it. I can see its pale blue cover with the words "Clair de Lune" and "Debussy" in black script. I can imagine my mother opening the cover and smoothing the crease so that the pages lay flat. After weeks of practice, she began with the first halting, simple thirds, then the gradual sequence falling toward resolution, then harmonies exotic, dramatic, absorbing. It came out through her fingers like laughter and she was off, taking me with her.

As I made the passage from girl to young woman, I was essentially unaware of any talent that I might claim. I was aware, however, of the more sophisticated connotations of being creative, and I associated them with being "cultured," a quality directly related to a desirable social status. The fact that the "cultured" were always people of means was not lost on me. We were definitely not "of means."

But there were tap dancing lessons at Miss Lee's in the back room of the beauty parlor. Piano lessons could be had for a dollar with Mr. Rockwell, an itinerant piano teacher who was reputed to be good. These were available, yes, but the hidden costs of tap shoes and piano books ruled out more than a month or two of any kind of lessons.

This isn't to say that I had no creative expressions of my own. In our childhood abandon, we called it by other names. Many an evening we turned the magical curtain of dusk to our advantage. Our corner house sat on the level top of an incline that rose steeply above our brick street. The wide front yard—our elevated, makeshift stage—had only one unobtrusive tree. When, after bearing down heavily all day, the sun began its languorous retreat, the whole neighborhood relaxed on porches and sipped lemonade from practical, quart-sized Mason jars. Miss Settles braiding her hair, Miss Shelton rocking in her glider, Edith and Betty dressed to the nines and stepping out for the evening—they were the audience.

We were the entertainment. My sisters and girlfriends and I paraded costumes made of anything from crepe to crepe paper, and mimicked the sultriness of Miss Sarah Vaughn. Or we penciled in thin, arching eyebrows and did our own versions of Eartha Kitt singing our own made-up chansons. I provided scenarios lifted from any picture show my fourteen cents could get me. And we were acrobats performing "Astonishing Human Feats!" in our own circus, doing back flips, somersaults, and handstands before we ever knew what the word gymnastics meant. Just as we imagined they were doing in cities like Detroit and Chicago, my brother and his friends crooned doo-wop style—Smokey Robinson and the Miracles—under the streetlight after dark. This was play.

Throughout high school I sang with the chorus and church choir, and even performed the snazzy choreography of the majorette squad. But my excursions into the realm of music were simply incidental. I did not pursue any art in a rigorously disciplined way, therefore—I probably reasoned—it was not legitimate.

By most standards I was studious. And since a brilliant mind could not always be distinguished from a hard-working intelligence, I took on the challenge of doing well in school. The math club, the science fair, and the honor society were my objectives.

My mother would have been happy with whatever choices I made for my future—early marriage, skilled labor, college. But this was the end of the fifties, when America bloomed with newfangled automation and industry. According to my teachers, Black America was on the verge of asserting itself in ways few had imagined. They impressed upon us always that a practical approach to career must prevail. I knew that if I was fortunate enough to have the opportunity to work my way through college, I would surely pursue a useful course of study, something that would ensure a living. Certainly not the arts. I intended, more than anything, to seize the opportunity to become something, and with my aptitude for things scientific, I set out to realize my ambition.

I embarked on my life in the usual ways: a challenging and satisfactory career in medical technology, a marriage, four amazing children. Then, in what at the time seemed like a slow-motion explosion of everything I understood, I found myself the divorced mother of four.

In this confusion of meaning and purpose, I began the long process of teasing out my role in the drama that was my life. I developed the haunting sense that a vital part of who I was had yet to be expressed. I needed to speak. Rather, I needed to give myself permission to project who I thought I was, and to see that reflection in the world.

My approach to my dilemma was not so much a rational one as one bolstered by the courage that we all experience in the face of desperation. I will not describe here all the attendant hardships brought on by major life changes. I will say, though, that spring is inevitable. It dreams itself into existence even as winter lays everything to seeming waste.

I had long since acquired the habit of writing in my journal each night before bed. It had been my way of expressing dismay at the life I had created for myself. In my journal I wrote, not in scientific jargon—the staid and functional language of microbiology and hematology that filled my days. I wrote in the language that came most naturally to mind: the sounds and rhythms I had drunk in every day as naturally as I had drunk water. The entries came out in cadences that were like cell memory—certain and involuntary.

At a time when I was desperate to declare myself in the world, the entirety of an impressionable childhood was available to me. My mother, by example, had long since cultivated an artistic sensibility within me. Clearly inspired by emotions difficult to articulate, her style was unique. She modeled discipline as a matter of course. Circumstances and training had had their place, but nothing was ever lost. By virtue of being my mother's daughter, I was inevitably drawn to creative expression.

I began to write. The reward of discovery was sufficient unto itself. But should there be a listening other, I wanted my utterance to do what my mother's hymn had done for me all those years before. I wanted to be so much at one with language that my words would illuminate an idea, or perhaps strike a chime of joy, pluck a string of grief. Up until that time I had kept the Linda Pastan poem "Waiting for My Life" pinned to the bulletin board above my desk. I had mere scribblings at first, but I kept going.

Of the unfolding that comes with commitment, Goethe said it best: ". . . Concerning all acts of creation, there is one ele-

mentary truth . . . that the moment one definitely commits oneself, then Providence moves too. All sorts of things occur that
would otherwise never have occurred. . . . Whatever you can do,
or dream you can, begin it."

Shortly after the publication of my first volume of poems, my
mother called to hear the details of how it had come to be.

"All those words," she said. "How did you think up all those
words and put them together like that?"

"You are a musician," I said, acknowledging something that
neither of us had said before. "I thought up all those words the
same way you thought up a million combinations of notes to
say what you wanted to say," I told her. "The same way."

THE PALACES OF DOWNTOWN

Catherine Calvert

I come from a long line of committed and passionate shoppers, of women who knew their way around a rack, whose arrival home in the afternoon was often followed by a satisfying crackle of bags and tissue paper as they laid their trophies on the bed.

No one was a spendthrift; making sure a dollar stretched was a matter of necessity in some cases, pride in others. But shop they did, with grace and flare and commitment, and I, from an early age, was expected to come along, too.

I didn't really mind. This was a woman's world, and I felt privileged to be invited, initiated even, in those soft-spoken discussions of hem lengths and fabric content. There was, after all, ceremony to a major shopping trip that yielded it a sense of importance beyond simply procurement of, say, new school shoes. Grocery shopping was amusing, but mere utility, and happened every week; there wasn't much in it for me except a chance to cadge some bubble gum and a weary time aligning the canned goods on the conveyor belt. The few strip malls that were opening did for the daily necessities, but still, the ultimate shopping lay elsewhere.

The department store, like church, was Downtown. The department store, like church, was a solid and lofty edifice, built by people who believed in what was purveyed there. I remember a limestone-faced, Art Deco–graced behemoth anchoring a block of this West Virginia city in sober magnificence. It was a twenty-minute ride to get there, and my grandmother would gingerly park the long-tailed Cadillac, and we would emerge, tugging at our skirts, righting, in some seasons, our hats, and knew we had arrived.

Mother and Grandmother marched through the revolving door with purpose, but I began the first of my dawdles. Those plate-glass windows called to me, with their mannequins in poses of improbable grace, displaying who-knew-what delights. Even when it wasn't Christmastime and the mechanical elves were no longer sawing away, there was amusement here, especially if a window were being dressed and the ladies lay about, their limbs naked and disheveled. I looked my fill, then whisked after my mother and grandmother, gauged the moment to dart into the doors, took three or four extra turns for fun, and was ejected into the store.

It took a minute to be oriented, here in the great vaulted space that was the main selling floor. There was hubbub—customers passing languid hands over rows of pocketbooks or trying on a new pair of short white gloves, and clerks who snapped their sales-check books shut and reached for the glasses that hung from pretty chains round their necks. Carpeting kept everything to a well-bred, soft hum, except for the sharp click and wheeze of the pneumatic tube that passed overhead, whizzing the money and slips to the office. And what was that scent? Chocolate from the candy counter and a whiff of perfume and an overall intoxicating fragrance of . . . newness, of unused leather and cloth and such, ineffable, inescapable.

I kept a wary eye on my mother and dabbled my finger in the rouges and watched as she examined some new lipstick shades, then opted for her usual "Cherries in the Snow." She was purposeful, still, checking off items on the list she carried in her purse, then adding a box of Coty face powder to her packages. Shopping trips, with their built-in deadline of supper preparation, meant time must be used wisely, goals accomplished. Little girls knew their role—to stand quietly, speak politely to the friends of mothers encountered along the way, and to smile gamely as one's growth, or lack of it, was commented on by salesclerks who'd known the child since she was born.

The first floor was just a warm-up to the main event—serious shopping during the White Sale (when sheets and towels were actually white) or a trip to Crystal to replace that water glass that slipped last Sunday. Our stately progress through the store was governed by the elevators, on which the operators sang out the floors like so many stops on the railway. (I was particularly fond of Notions.) We finished in the children's department, where feet that had flapped contentedly in summer sneakers were interred in hard leather, and a child was expected to parade back and forth in slippery new soles as mother, grandmother, and salesman debated buckle-versus-tie. (I spent hours examining my bones in the fluoroscope machine, into which you slipped your feet, and X rays, or something like them, revealed the outline of shoe and contents and you could watch your skeletal toes wiggle.)

By now, even the intrepid shoppers were flagging. My rebellion had been quelled along the way with wintergreen Lifesavers, peeled from a pack in my mother's purse and smelling faintly of her perfume. But we were hungry and found our way to the tearoom, where a hostess in a frilly apron would take us to a table near the fountain. Even I got a menu and began to ponder, as my grandmother and mother stirred their ice teas and I waited for my cherry Coke. What was it to be? This was dainty food, lady food, and the color scheme was white—crustless white bread, tuna and chicken salad, a bowl of mayonnaise for one's tomato. Color accents were provided by parsley or by gleaming jewel-toned Jell-O, quivering on a salad plate. After delicately biting into my little sandwiches and crunching the last of my chips, I would confer with them as we ordered one towering dessert—devil's food cake, so dark it had to be dangerous, yellow cake with a blizzard of coconut—and three forks. Mother and Grandmother were dieting.

There was just enough time for the French Room. This was the sanctum sanctorum, the very heart of the matter, where the most expensive women's wear was offered up by silken-voiced salesladies who knew my grandmother and mother well. I balanced on a small gilt chair or examined my back and sides in a three-part mirror, while my mother touched a rustling taffeta dress or picked up a hem to be sure it was handsewn and deep. Finally, at my grandmother's urging, she slipped on a Davidow suit and was her handsome self, renewed, revolving in the mirrors, as they conferred. "Wrap and send it, please," said my grandmother, as my mother smiled, and we were ready to descend, I with my shoes and a white paper bag of bridge mix, to be picked over on the ride home—avoiding those chocolate-covered white cremes—and then shared with the men who waited.

My mother and I still shop together, and it is still one of the best times we share. We're companionable, paging through the hangers at a discount store or a small boutique, seeking out things for each other, and conversation dips and glides, prompted by a hat or a dress, perhaps. Such times transcend the mere accumulation of goods and have more to do with what we think of each other and what we remember together, memories forged in those great stone palaces Downtown.

My Mother's
Open Door

Reeve Lindbergh

I learned at a very young age that my mother, Anne Morrow Lindbergh, was a writer, beloved by millions of readers around the world. But that did not mean I approved. It wasn't until many years later that I became reconciled to her profession, and it was later still when, to my surprise, I made this same profession my own. In the beginning, her literary work meant no more to me than an inexplicable interruption in the mother-child relationship—a sad cross for a sensitive child to bear.

What I disliked most about her writing was that it separated her from me so physically and palpably, by means of a closed door. When she was in her "writing room" in the house where I grew up in Connecticut, we children—my three brothers, my sister, Anne, and I—were forbidden by our father, Charles, to disturb her. I often did this anyway, if I thought I could get away with it, usually at a time when my father was outside chopping wood or was engrossed in his own writing project in his office downstairs. Nobody would think of disturbing *him* when the door was closed and he was tapping away with two fingers on his "manuscript," eventually published as *The Spirit of St. Louis,* the book about his 1927 pioneering flight from New York to Paris, which won him a Pulitzer Prize.

I had no interest in my father's flying or his writing career and resented his attitude toward our mother's. Surely she did not really want to be shut away for a whole afternoon without seeing my face, hearing my thoughts, inspecting my bruises or, in some other way, affirming for both of us the extraordinary importance of my presence in her life.

I knew this was true because, if I knocked on my mother's door, she always answered; and if I entered the room, she never seemed to mind. She would put down her pen immediately and smile gently and ask what I wanted. (See? She *was* concerned about my needs, above all else, I thought triumphantly. What did my father know? Nothing.) She sat in a straight-backed chair by the window, at a desk that was really just a flat table with a blotter on it, and little more. I could see only a pen tray, holding one or two shells or feathers along with the pens and pencils, and an inkwell, and the blue pad she was writing on.

There was one leafy maple branch outside the bright window just to the left of my mother's desk. ("It is important to have the light come in over the left shoulder," she advised me later, when I was setting up my own writing room in my own house.) As she turned toward the doorway, with the light from the window on her face, I could tell she was very glad to see me.

Yet no matter how far away I thought my father was, he would invariably show up at my mother's writing-room door just about this time, looking extremely displeased. He would take me away from my mother's pleasant nest, with its wall filled with book-shelves at one end, and the old soft leather couch, where I was about to make myself comfortable, at the other. He would shut the door behind us and lecture me once again about my mother's creative gifts, about her need for privacy in order to exercise such gifts to their fullest extent, and about my obligation to respect this aspect of her life. Each time I nodded and apologized and told him I would try to do better in the future.

I didn't mean a word of it. How could I? I was using the most basic of instincts to fight every young animal's greatest threat—separation from the mother.

What I did not understand, and am just beginning to comprehend now, is that my mother's work, that product of our separation, would also be my way back to her again. She herself created that pathway, a connection between us that is much deeper and more lasting than any I had ever anticipated in childhood. All I had to do to find it was open her books.

As a child, I did not read my parents' books, ever. First of all, there were no pictures in them, except for the old black-and-white photographs from a time before I was born, or, in my mother's *Gift From the Sea,* a few line drawings of seashells. Boring. Also, I was embarrassed and squeamish about the fact that my parents wrote at all, constantly spilling out their adventures and their philosophies and the most intimate secrets of our lives to complete strangers. To this day, people who have read my mother's *Diaries and Letters* will come up to me and recount the funny things my brother Jon, now a grandfather, said as a little boy at the breakfast table. The difference is that now, in my middle age, I enjoy this experience. Instead of feeling a child's discomfort at sharing my life with the world, I look eagerly to the world to restore to me what was always mine—only I didn't know it.

It is extraordinary to see my mother's words in print now, quoted in a book or an article by someone I have never met. Once, when I was standing in my kitchen waiting for water to boil, I even found her quoted on the back of a box of herbal tea! It is a little like the shock of seeing a familiar face in a crowd on a television screen; but it is more than that, with its reverberations of old intimacies. It is so nourishing, in fact, that it makes me feel as if I have just had a long telephone conversation with my mother herself, although she is ninety now, and in fragile health, and has not had a long conversation with anyone for several years.

I feel the most direct connection with my mother, though, when I read her books myself, alone. I understand for the first time, with a thrill and an involuntary sting behind the eyelids, how very well I know this voice, this spirit. In *North to the Orient*, I am reading the words of the young copilot—about the age my oldest daughter is now—preparing with her aviator husband to fly the polar route to Asia. And I know this young woman— her courage, her hesitation, her shyness, her turn of phrase— even though this particular adventure was over long before I was born.

In *Hour of Gold, Hour of Lead*, I am sharing the unspeakable grief of the mother who has lost her firstborn son, and I feel her sorrow deeply. I have shared other sorrows with her, including the death of my own firstborn son, her grandson, and our sharing created a closeness that was beyond words. But the words bring it back again. I am breathing in and assimilating in my own grown woman's life the quiet wisdom of *Gift From the Sea*. I know exactly who the author was, how she looked and moved, where she sat when she was writing this book and I was knocking on her door. I know now, too, that I was right about one thing in those days long ago. Her door really was open to me, all the time.

MISS BARTLETT'S
QUOTATIONS

Faye Moskowitz

he clipping my cousin sent me from my hometown newspaper back in Michigan told me my seventh-grade English teacher died one night in her sleep. Miss Bartlett was ninety-three years old. Strange the perception children have of adults' ages; we all thought she was as old as Lear, the king she introduced us to one spring day toward the end of the semester. Thinking back now, I'm touched to realize she was barely fifty when she taught us in 1943.

Tiny, slender as a blade of grass in her familiar dark green wool, a clean white handkerchief pinned to the meager front, Miss Bartlett waited for us each morning as if it took our presence to bring her into being. Who helped give me the love of learning I try to pass on to my own students? Miss Bartlett certainly did. If my childhood was preparation for a love affair with words, then Miss Bartlett was the matchmaker who paired us for life.

Miss Bartlett had the only all-girl homeroom at West Intermediate. Something about her soft voice and fragile demeanor, the combination delicate as the tatting that edged her handkerchief, made that seem absolutely right in our eyes. Who could imagine Miss Bartlett mixing it up with the loutish seventh-grade boys we glimpsed in the hallways, the very same boys who starred in our dreams each night? Though I know I dressed like the other girls in blouses with Peter Pan collars and plaid skirts demurely hovering at the knee, I imagine us now as soulful Pre-Raphaelites, clustering around our teacher, our hair flowing, our dresses white and fluttering banners.

Children of auto executives and factory workers, we came to Miss Bartlett. Some of us had homes where books lined paneled walls of rooms set aside for reading; others, homes where the only book might be a Bible, likely as not, printed in a foreign language.

Each Monday morning when we entered our homeroom just before English class, we would find four or five lines written on the blackboard in Miss Bartlett's elegant Palmer Method. Our first task, even before we recited the Pledge of Allegiance, was to copy the lines into a composition book we kept for that purpose.

On Friday mornings we wrote the lines on clean sheets of loose-leaf paper, evidence that we had learned them "by heart." Passages from Shakespeare, the Bible, and Chaucer, verses of Keats and Shelley, Browning, Tennyson, Longfellow, and Emerson: I have them still to conjure up when traffic stalls or sleep refuses to come. "Bartlett's Familiar Quotations," we called them, of course, and even now, I never know when I will open a book and encounter an entire passage buried in my memory, waiting like Sleeping Beauty for my glance to awaken it.

We learned to construct strong paragraphs in Miss Bartlett's class. "Girls," she would say, looking out to the desks where we sat with hands folded demurely in our laps, "you must start with the finest materials. Just as each board must be true and each brick sound when you want a building to last, so each individual word and sentence must be carefully chosen and placed if a paragraph is to inform, persuade, and delight."

She would turn to the blackboard, the inevitable chalk smudge on the back of the green wool. "A carpenter who is proud of his work," she wrote, "pulls out the crooked nails and smooths the rough boards. You must be willing to revise and edit your writing until you are able to say, 'This is my very best.' "

When Miss Bartlett read us "Annabel Lee" or "Ozymandias," we squirmed in our seats, blushing, unable to translate the rush of emotion that filled us, unwilling to hear in her trembling voice the echo of our own inchoate longing for beauty. Still, some of us went home as I did and read the passages ourselves, over and over, until their force blistered the pages with tears we considered our very own secret.

Enchanting as all this sounds, I'm not so numbed by nostalgia that I can't recall the nameless pit-of-the-stomach dread that characterized most of my days at West Intermediate. Miss Bartlett's wizardry couldn't protect me from everything. I studied the popular girls as assiduously as I puzzled out verb tenses, and I don't know what I considered more hopeless: the miracle of awakening one morning as a blonde, or the likelihood of my mother, with her Yiddish accent, being elected president of the P.T.A.

Clearly, I was the perfect victim for one of the more exquisite forms of mental torture ever devised by adolescents: the slam book. Ruth Mary Stock, our class trendsetter, brought the first to school, a small brown spiral notebook in which she had lettered the names of each girl in class, one to a page. With the herding instinct typical of teens, we soon all carried our own slam books. The idea was as simple and potentially cruel as childhood itself. You exchanged books and merely wrote a comment, as terse or as flowery as you wished, on each person's page.

When Miss Bartlett showed us how to diagram sentences, we furtively slipped the slam books under our desks, past woolen, corduroy, or cotton-covered knees, where they rested until the next time she turned to the board and we could slip the little notebooks behind our grammars. While she was establishing grammar skills, we were establishing social hierarchies, and the miracle is, for all the worrying I did about the dreary "O.K."s that peppered the slam book pages marked with my name, I still can rattle off Miss Bartlett's list of prepositions more quickly than I can recall the birth dates of my own children.

In the wider world outside the red brick walls of West Intermediate, a great world war was raging. "Uncle Sam Wants You!" insisted the posters plastered everywhere. "A Slip of the Lip Will Sink a Ship," warned others. But I had a private battle to fight. Each triumph in Miss Bartlett's class, each paper I brought home marked with the precious "A" that seemed to slip so grudgingly from her fountain pen, only served to widen the breach between me and my parents. When my mother spoke to me in Yiddish, I answered pointedly in English. When, with no small show of irony, she addressed me in English, I took it upon myself to correct each flaw of grammar or pronunciation. I was miserable. I wanted "hubba hubba" and "swell" on my slam book pages, and I wanted my parents to speak English just like Miss Bartlett.

And then one day, Miss Bartlett handed each of us girls in her homeroom a handwritten invitation, individually addressed to our parents on square white envelopes. Miss Ruth Bartlett and the seventh-grade English class of West Intermediate School were cordially inviting Mr. and Mrs. Aaron Stollman to the May Festival Program. "R.S.V.P.," it said. Of course I knew about the program; we had been rehearsing for weeks: a scene from

Romeo and Juliet, recitations of "Thanatopsis" and "Evangeline."
A few of us, including me, would be reading original poems.

I stuffed the invitation in my school satchel, already inventing
the cataclysm that would explain the unavoidable absence of my
mother and dad from the festivities. On my way out of English
class that day, Miss Bartlett stopped me. "I do so look forward
to meeting your parents, dear," she said. "They'll be so proud
of you; I'm sure nothing will stop them from coming." And so,
it seems, Miss Bartlett had yet another lesson to teach me.

I must have driven my parents crazy the night of the program.
I can imagine the instructions, the inspections before we finally
left our house. That part of the evening is a blur to me. What
I do remember is sitting with the other girls in a long row of
chairs at the front of our classroom. Our parents sat at our desks;
some of the taller fathers stood at the back.

I looked at my mother sitting at my desk, her eyes only on
me, her hands folded as if she were a student. I thought back,
then, to when I was five, and she first took me to the neighborhood elementary school. I could recall the skirt and blouse
she dressed me in, the red sweater and tam, the wrinkled cotton
stockings held up with round garters she called "little bagels."
What I suddenly understood was the shame she must have felt
about her broken English, the shyness at encountering so many
strangers: the principal, the schoolteachers, the other parents.
We walked hand in hand along the quiet neighborhood streets,
and when my mother let go of my fingers and left me that first
day, her face was a blur, from her tears or my own, I cannot
say.

We moved to Detroit shortly after the May Festival Program,
and I never saw Miss Bartlett again. Still, I thought of her often
when I became a seventh-grade English teacher myself, and I
think of her even now as I teach writing at the university.

Who knows what has become of those other girls in that long-
ago English class. How did their lives turn out? How many of

them heard of Miss Bartlett's passing and felt, like me, that the world she once opened for us had now suddenly and perceptibly diminished?

In these apple-scented fall days, I remember dreams I've had of escaping, of being the first woman to travel in space. And then I remind myself of "Birches," the Robert Frost poem I learned in Miss Bartlett's class. "Earth's the right place for love," Frost writes. "I don't know where it's likely to go better."

I'm happy you went in your sleep, Miss Bartlett. I like to think you were dreaming of fresh faces in a schoolroom and the start of a brand new year.

LEARNING THE

LANGUAGE OF LOVE

Priscilla Dunhill

ixth grade is a time when hurtling your own true love to the ground in a game of Run Sheepie Run can be the highest token of esteem. Love can be signaled both if someone disdains to sign your new autograph book or scrawls occult, illegible messages over five pages. But in the complex annals of grade-school love, one thing is straightforward: Valentine's Day. At the end of the school day, when the red-and-white crepe paper box comes out and the valentines are distributed amid high anxiety and wildly veering emotions, either you get a valentine—or you don't.

So when I got a valentine from Austin Thomas—our class Adonis, unathletic but with an insouciant way with girls—my heart stopped beating. I didn't dare look up from my desk, let alone make eye contact with Him. Nor did I dare open the valentine in class.

I cannot fathom for the life of me why my instinct protected me so flawlessly at such a young age.

I could feel the valentine was heavy with silver sparkles—I could finger the grittiness right through the envelope. It must have cost ten cents, a luxury in a day when even a penny valentine from Woolworth's was a carefully considered expenditure. No one gave homemade valentines (they were considered tacky), and Miss Gould was tyrannical in ruling out comic valentines that could wound or wither.

When the bell rang, I snatched my stack of valentines, stowed them in my book bag, and rode my bicycle home on zephyred winds. Blissfully I was alone in the house and raced to my room. I slid the valentine from its envelope so not to disturb the silver sprinkles, and there lay a giant silver heart, affixed to a paper lace doily. The gilded message read: Be Mine. Shyly, even though I was the sole presence, I opened to the next page. And there scrawled in his schoolboy's hand, Austin Thomas had written: "To the Fattest Girl in the Class from Austin Thomas."

Cruelty knows no boundaries when you are eleven years old. No lover's stab could have pierced more deeply. I put the valentine back in its envelope. I never threw it away, and never spoke of it again to anyone, least of all Austin Thomas.

Well, as all things go in this world, we went on to high school, graduated, sought our fortunes, married well or poorly, reared families, bore our joys and miseries, and met—oh, yes, we did—at our twenty-fifth reunion. Ninety of us, from a graduating class of one hundred, gathered for three courageous days of celebration.

We conferred in advance—to go or not to go? To take spouses or not to take spouses? What to wear? What to bring? Enter the class tennis tournament? With whom? We went on crash diets, got new perms, and perfected our three-day ensembles.

Ohhhhhh—it was marvelous. Simply marvelous, beginning with the first night at the dinner dance at Lake of the Woods. Down the big ceremonial staircase we all meandered two or three at a time, to see and be seen, waving, chattering, as twittery as if we were all at our first freshman dance. There was Jimmy Johnson our class valedictorian, now on the Federal Reserve Board; Mary Jo Claremont, who married into a sober but rich Texas family and last year recanted most of her riches by becoming a Baptist missionary. Jack Branden, our star athlete, had fattened up to become the town's star peridontist. How little we had really all changed! How reassuring . . . how depressing, we agreed.

So on it went. We mixed and danced and answered, in one way or another, the two questions on everybody's mind: 1) How well have you "done"? (meaning money, mostly) and 2) How well have your children done? (meaning what kind of a person/parent are you). Then simply, directly, without artifice, we settled down to the fun of it all: the Old School brass tacks, exhuming memories, swapping jokes, settling old debts, crying over old loves or laughing over new ones.

And suddenly before me stood Austin Thomas, long forgotten, as insouciant and charming as ever, now brindlehaired with a gentle smile, genuinely delighted to see me. We exchanged pleasantries, and then from some primordial ancient sea of hurt, The Matter of the Valentine bubbled up like heartburn, without warning. Of course Austin Thomas did not remember writing such a message, let alone believe he was capable of such cruelty. You imagined it, he said, or have mixed me up with someone else . . . besides, you weren't fat. (Only partly true. I was chubby—yes, fat—no.) And then the thought occurred to me—Cupid's dart at eleven is clumsy. Could he possibly have meant his barb as some kind of a love message? I asked him. He smiled and said he doubted that, and would I like to dance?

The Gift of Memory

Suzanne Berne

ne of my earliest memories is of being bundled up by my mother and taken outside on a snowy January night to look at the stars. I must have been four or five, still small enough for my slender mother to carry. We stood on the veranda of our house in Virginia, a heavy shawl wrapped around us both, gazing over the white fields at the sky as my mother pointed out the constellations she knew. "The North Star is the one constant star in the sky," she whispered, her warm breath wreathing my ear. "Once you find it, you can always figure out where you are." Nestled against my mother, I found this instruction both sensible and enchanting, and I have never forgotten it.

My mother liked to combine enchantment with sense whenever she wanted to make a point. "This is what morning should look like," my mother told us several times one summer, when she woke us before dawn to visit a barrier beach off Cape Cod. She would usher us through the soft gray light to where a silent old man waited to ferry us over in his narrow fishing boat. As

I recall, he met us at the town landing and without a word, lifted each of us children into his boat and later onto the beach. Then my mother would lead the way across the dunes so that we could watch the sun finish rising over the water. We'd sit on a blanket in our windbreakers eating cranberry muffins and drinking hot chocolate from a Thermos, sand filling our sneakers as the day grew brighter. For miles there was no one but us. Deer ran through the eelgrass; sandpipers dashed back and forth at the shoreline, their thin black legs moving so fast they were almost invisible. The breeze smelled of salt and seaweed. "Look," my mother would say, as she pointed to raccoon prints, to a plover's nest lined with pebbles holding four beautiful spotted eggs.

Although I'm not sure she realized it at the time, my mother believed in creating memories for her daughters—a perfect morning, a glimpse of winter stars—bright pebbles to carry from the nest of childhood. It was her way of defining what she thought should matter to us. She wanted her children to love the world sensually, as she did, and to appreciate small, homely adventures. She also believed in participating in any adventure she charted out—wading barefoot in a creek hunting for craw-fish, for instance. I can still recall the cool ooze of mud between my toes, the warmth of the sun on the back of my neck, and my mother, her linen skirt bunched around her knees, wading beside me, laughing at the leaf shadows dappling the water.

Perhaps because of adventures like that one, I've been fasci-nated by early memories and the mysterious way they color so much of the adult world. Ask my mother why she hates yogurt, and she'll tell you about drinking soured milk during the De-pression on her father's farm. Ask why she likes rooms with high ceilings, and you'll probably hear about afternoons spent in the cornfields, a vault of sky above her head.

On my desk is a notebook full of early recollections I've jotted down from the biographies and memoirs I've read. Not surprisingly many of them involve mothers. One of Eudora Welty's first memories is of her mother reading to her as they sat together in a rocking chair, which "ticked in rhythm as we rocked, as though we had a cricket accompanying the story." Colette writes of her mother's garden, brilliant with "burning shades of roses, lychnis, hydrangeas, and red-hot-pokers." Virginia Woolf recalls her mother standing on a balcony in a white dressing gown, surrounded by passionflowers, "great starry blossoms, with purple streaks, and large green buds, part empty, part full."

As I glance through my notebook, what appeals to me about each of these memories is the bit of detail lacing the edges, the imaginary cricket, the burning roses, those passionflowers. These are the stitches that hem past and present together, what we see when looking back. Nostalgia, after all, is our remembrance of focused attention, our romance with the particular. Without the odd glimmering detail, childhood would be a faded blur, lost to us; it might not have happened at all.

Lately I have been thinking more than usual about early memories, because I have a baby now, who one of these days will begin her own remembering. What will she recall first? Probably something entirely unpredictable—the lemony smell of her father's shaving cream, perhaps, or the roar of the coffee grinder. But maybe one wintry night I'll bring her outside to look up at the stars; or maybe one June morning we'll wake up at dawn and drive to the beach, although the trip may not be as thrilling without that silent old man and his narrow fishing boat.

As my daughter stirs in her crib nearby, I find myself planning: On a midsummer evening before bedtime, that hour when it's still light but the world has turned a dreamy blue and no child wants to go to bed, I will carry her out to the pond behind her grandmother's house so she can listen to the peep-peep of tree frogs and smell the pine breeze and watch the fireflies glint under a thumbnail moon. Just before it's time to go back inside, I'll lean down and say—something sensible, I hope. And then it will happen, the enchantment, that strange alchemy that fixes a flash of life into memory, and suddenly the whole scene will be etched, complete, hers forever, and mine, too.

THE TRANSIENT BEAUTY

OF FIREFLIES

Francine Prose

ince I've had children I've come to understand clearly that a kernel of self exists, present all along, in the infant, the toddler, the child, the woman, the mother. So now, when I remember myself on the summer evenings of my childhood—a beanpole of a girl in the painfully short haircut my well-meaning mother thought was chic in the style of a fifties Italian movie gamine—I see a streamlined, early model of my current self. What engaged my interest then was much like what interests me now, and I already knew certain things I would relearn much later. What I saw and heard on those summer evenings were the first whisperings of the voice I would someday recognize as my vocation.

When I tell friends I grew up in Brooklyn, they seem to imagine a grim cityscape of concrete and brownstone, populated by rowdy gangs of streetwise, tough-talking kids playing stickball in vacant lots twinkling with broken bottles. In fact, ours was a neighborhood more like the main street of a small town, with a block of stately trees, manicured lawns, and rather grand old houses. Like most children, we were unobservant and took nearly everything for granted, but even so we understood that our homes were magical places full of small architectural surprises: stained-glass bay windows, narrow back stairs, porches and porte cocheres, dusty attics, and basements that smelled thrillingly of mold and damp and earth.

But those charms were for other seasons. Summer evenings my younger brother and I, and the kids who lived nearby, roamed in a restless little pack from one backyard to another and believed we had endless hours until our mothers called us home. Finally released after a long family dinner, we exploded out of the door, like fizz erupting from a shaken-up soda bottle.

The only houses that existed for us were the ones where children lived, so we ran from yard to yard till we located the other kids, asking their fathers where they were (we all knew each other's parents). Twilight was the time of the fathers, mowing or watering the lawn, and my dad, a doctor, home from the office like the rest of his neighbors, would be in the yard, too. Today, what most often brings me back to those summer evenings is the smell of freshly cut grass and the hiss of the hose in our garden.

A casual observer watching us playing ball or catching fireflies would have thought we were a group of carefree children, entirely and wholeheartedly immersed in whatever we were doing. In fact, we were a buzzing hive of rapidly shifting loyalties, conspiracies, and alliances, of nightly dramas, betrayals, and passions teeming beneath the surface.

Arguments usually started with some dispute about a game. Somebody was cheating or playing fair, a ball was in or out of bounds. The fights were never interesting in themselves, but only in their intensity and in the abrupt, thrilling way you might suddenly discover who was on your side—and who wasn't. The tenderness of the summer air made all this seem highly charged, even erotic, as though a warm breeze were actually passing over your skin.

I was the oldest child on the block. Several boys were just a bit younger; the youngest were the little girls for whom, from an early age, I used to baby-sit. In disputes, the girls were a swing vote; they might side with me or with their older brothers. My own brother, two years younger, would automatically ally himself with me in extreme situations, but on lesser occasions, he and I were not above using the volatile social situation to settle sibling scores left over from home.

We were all physical creatures; athletic skill counted most. I was reasonably good at sports then, though I never have been since. Maybe it was as simple as the fact that I was older and taller. I honestly didn't think twice about outplaying the boys. But after a certain age—maybe twelve—beating the boys no longer seemed worth doing.

Around that time, a boy on the block asked me to go to the movies. I remember it was a film about an attack of giant ants. I knew I was being asked on a date, but I'd never thought of the boy that way. I turned him down, and for months I couldn't look at him I was so embarrassed.

But all these unnerving and vague adult stirrings seemed to disappear on summer evenings. We played until it got too dark. By then the first fireflies had appeared, and those flashing pinpoints of light caught and captured our whole attention. There were always jars in someone's garage, and we fanned out over the damp lush lawns (by now our fathers had gone back inside and the block belonged to the children), sneaking up on fireflies, trapping them in our cupped hands and, with the aid of a younger assistant, tipping them neatly into a jar.

Of course, I understand now what I didn't want to know then: that an insect would just as soon not be imprisoned inside a glass bottle. Even so, I must confess I've allowed my children to catch fireflies in a bottle, making sure they let them go free before any real damage is done. Watching my sons, I'm struck by what I couldn't have seen at that time: what a beautiful sight it is, children moving through the garden, led forward by the rhythm of the blinking light.

Later, an unmistakable scent lingers on my sons' hands and their glass jars. The smell of fireflies—there is nothing else like it. It rockets me back to a backyard belonging to a boy named Dan, who had a green canvas pup tent.

Here the children (there were about ten of us) crowded for an evening of frightening the smaller kids and ourselves by telling scary stories. The greenish glow of the insects cast only the faintest glimmer. We could hardly see one another, we could all have been greenish monsters.

I was the oldest and the scariest, and I told most of the stories. I'd like to say I invented them out of whole cloth—imaginative early hints of my later career as a writer. But the fact is, I told the same stories again and again and again.

That was fine with the other kids. They didn't want to be surprised. They wanted to know what was coming and experience the slow buildup to the inevitable grisly horror. (It's what Alfred Hitchcock defined as the difference between shock and suspense.)

The challenge was in the retelling. I knew I'd been successful when the older kids got very subdued and a few of the younger ones gently but audibly sniffled. I understood that I had exercised far more magic and power than I ever could—or would—receive from winning at dodgeball.

On those evenings I first became addicted to putting words together and to watching a story work. It was exhilarating, like putting a message in a bottle and being there when someone finds your bottle in the surf.

Today I live with my husband and two sons only a hundred miles from the neighborhood I grew up in. It is so unlike the place of my childhood I often feel as if I've traveled a continent—an entire world—away. It's only at rare and blessed moments that the fields and the mountains around our farmhouse recede and I can remember exactly what it was like to be a child on that pretty, cared-for street. Then I can hear the sound of the mothers' voices echoing over the block, calling us home. The voices sound silvery, high—at once beautiful and irritating.

These sudden flashes cannot be summoned at will. They are never cerebral, but always sensory and immediate, triggered by a sound or smell or a quality of light—or the transient beauty of fireflies.

MOTHERHOOD

A Promenade

with William

Judith Thurman

"People hugging." This is William's first observation
of and in the Luxembourg Gardens. It is February. He has just
turned two. We have moved to Paris for the year. "Here is your
new playground," I tell him. The day has a desolate, winter
beauty: Earth and sky are the same *gris de perle.* We are making
our way down a long allée of plane trees, toward a cluster of
shaggy ponies stamping their feet, but they are still far away.
We can see the pitched green roof of the carousel through the
bare branches, but it doesn't seem to be revolving. The tennis
courts are empty, the fountains are dry, the waffle stand is shuttered, the bocci courts lie under a crust of snow, and the only
evidence of life is, in fact, the passionate young couple—if, indeed, they are young—an assumption one shouldn't make of the
lovers in Paris parks. He has buttoned her inside his overcoat,
their lips and noses are pressed together, their bodies sway a
little, the wind mingles strands of their hair. Will studies this

woolly beast with its two fair heads and four slim legs, intrigued but a little doubtful.

There are no rules about hugging in the Luxembourg. Two of you may share a single garden chair, entwined like the figures in a Moghul painting. You may also pull two chairs together to make a sort of impromptu divan. You may strike the classic cinematic pose, bending your lover half backward, in full view of the Senate and its armed guards. You may stop suddenly, in the middle of a path, in the middle of a sentence, to fling your arms around each other, obstructing the passage of strollers or joggers—who will make a silent, uncomplaining detour around you. You may kiss and snuggle at a café table, or perched on the rim of a fountain, or astride a balustrade, or pressed against a chestnut tree, or on a bench inside the children's playground—provided you have paid your five francs' entrance fee, and you have a child with you. You may not, however, take any sort of pleasure, innocent or guilty, onto the grass.

When the trees are bare, the Luxembourg has the air of a vast, vacant, and dust-sheeted summer palace. Even in summer, the precise allocation of space, the maniacal tidiness and symmetry are, somehow, those of an interior—a very grand, very formal French salon where, as a guest, you are invited to have a good time, but where you are also on your best behavior. The Luxembourg, you will note, is a *jardin*. It is not a *bois* or even a *parc*. While dogs are welcome in most French restaurants, they are forbidden in the Luxembourg. Have I ever seen a dandelion? An untidy hedge? A statue streaked with droppings? I don't think so. The tulips grow in perfectly round, weedless, monochromatic beds. The lawns are as smooth as cashmere. And Will can tell you what happens if you dare to dip a foot—even a little two-year-old foot—into one of those inviting, forbidden pools of green. "Policeman blow whistle!" Yes, a *gardien* in a smart blue uniform, with gold epaulets, and a little blue legionnaire's hat, is instantly upon you, scowling under his moustache, wagging his finger. The presumption, under French law, is always of guilt: *"Vous savez bien, madame, que la pelouse est interdite!"* ("You know perfectly well that the lawn is off-limits!").

The Luxembourg is a great rectangle, but its corners are soft—it feels circular once you are inside its gates. A dirt track runs around its periphery—delicious for jogging. You can smell the hyacinths from the rue de Vaugirard and the damp, faintly sour scent of the well turned-over soil, and as you move from sun to shade, the smells change, as does the temperature of the air. If you run on weekday mornings, you will have the park nearly to yourself—everyone French is at home smoking and drinking black coffee and eating butter. The Parisians are weekend athletes. Nevertheless, they pride themselves on their form. There must be some unwritten code about who may *faire le* footing in the Luxembourg, and who must stay home on the treadmill. No one shuffles. No one wears old Camp Minnewaska T-shirts streaked with bleach, cut-offs, ancient sneakers, John Deere caps, or Kool-Aid-colored nylon shorts over baggy sweatpants. You see no flab or cellulite. The muscles are firm, the flesh is rosy, the outfits are chic, and the brows are only a little moist.

Now that the horse chestnuts have unfurled their awning and the shade is thick on the running paths of the Luxembourg, it is William who takes me to the park on Sundays. He knows its landscape much better than I do. He comes here nearly every weekday afternoon with his baby-sitter—or as the French say, defining the romance of the relationship so precisely—his *jeune fille.* They feed the fat, red goldfish in the sailboat pond. They watch the "dancers," as Will calls them, practicing tai chi in beautifully laundered kimono jackets, on the bocci courts. They play in the crumbly brown sand of the world's most deluxe sand pile, which—with its six neat little boxes—must look, from the air, like an expensive tin of shortbread. Was it, I wonder, tucked behind the labyrinth of hedges because the architect of the Luxembourg thought the little ones needed privacy? Or because he thought the inevitable disorder of their games, quarrels, picnics, and toys was unseemly?

I am always amazed when my son nods to someone I don't know: the pony driver, the ticket seller in the playground, an old man playing chess, and shyly says "bonjoo." His French is improving, and he can also say "oh-vwah," *merci* "bowcoo," *pompiers, donne-le-moi, pain de chocolat, en garde,* and *touché.* But will he remember Paris? Perhaps the Luxembourg will figure in his dreams, and perhaps, when he is a grown man, the smells of hyacinths, waffles, and *Gitanes* will jog his memory of it.

In any event, one of the charms of having played in the Luxembourg Gardens as a child is the Proustian glamour of being able to claim that one did so.

THE GIFT OF A NAME

Susan Schneider

I'd always thought that naming a child would be simple. But once I found out I was having a girl, finding a name—the right name—became a quest. I pored over baby name books, sensing that I'd know the right one when I stumbled upon it, but nothing struck me.

My daughter's name had to express a mood or a feeling; it had to be distinctive without being peculiar. It also had to complement her middle name, which I already knew was going to be Augusta—a family name passed down through generations on her father's side. Augusta seemed made-to-order—I loved old-fashioned names—and I decided her first name should have an old-fashioned flavor too. I thought back to novels I'd read as a child. The names Meg and Jo and Amy and Beth in my favorite, *Little Women,* were all too plain, while Sophronia, of *Five Little Peppers* (or Phronsie as she was called by her family) did seem interesting and unusual, though too weighty when paired with Augusta. My mind cast around. Dorothea from George

Eliot's *Middlemarch* seemed too dry, and Gwendolyn from the same author's *Daniel Deronda* too ordinary. Clara and Hannah, nicely traditional in feeling, were pretty but too humble when attached to the queenly Augusta.

A friend of mine, who had the patience to act as a sounding board in my quest for the perfect name, had one emphatic opinion. "No weird names!" she commanded. "Augusta is unusual enough." Maybe she was right, I conceded. After all, my daughter's paternal grandmother had been named Mary Augusta.

But rummaging more determinedly through still more name books, I was intrigued and relieved to find that in the nineteenth century, people became a little bored with the likes of Mary, Elizabeth, and Susannah and began to give rein to their imaginations. Little girls were named after precious stones (Pearl, Ruby, Beryl, Opal, even Emerald and Diamond), and for the first time, flower names (Lily, Iris, Violet, Pansy, Ivy, Azalea, and Hazel) became popular. Nicely poetic but too whimsical for my purposes. Other popular horticultural names of the day, such as Olive, Myrtle, and Fern, sounded old and grumpy. Eighty years from now, Myrtle might suit my dowager daughter to a T, but being called Myrtle the Turtle in the first grade probably isn't the most pleasant formative experience a mother could wish on a child.

I kept searching. A hundred or so years ago, people were rediscovering forgotten names like the Anglo-Saxon Edith, Ethel, and Audrey. (Too stern, I decided.) Thanks to Alfred Lord Tennyson's "Idylls of the King," the Arthurian legend—and Guinevere—became fashionable. Tennyson was also responsible for the rejuvenation of Enid and Vivian and Elaine and Maud. I loved Maud, but my sensible friend pronounced it weird and austere. And besides, she pointed out, little Maud's fellow first-graders would be sure to call her Mud. Not funny to us, but to a six-year-old, a quite witty play on words. If you like traditional names so much, she added, why not the gentler, more feminine

Charlotte, or Maria, or Henrietta? How about Emmaline or Sophia?

Those were lovely, I admitted, but none was exactly right. I wanted something really different. I recalled Rowena from Sir Walter Scott's *Ivanhoe,* and I dusted off my college Shakespeare and rediscovered Juliet, Rosalind, and Viola. But no, the name awaiting my daughter still eluded me.

Coming across a biography of Florence Nightingale in a box of old books I'd bought when the local library was cleaning out its ancient attic, I briefly considered Florence.

It had dignity and grace. But again, it seemed too mature and perhaps carried too many associations of goodness and virtue for a child to live up to. I also learned from the same biography that Florence had had a sister named Parthenope. I had no trouble rejecting that—too ridiculous.

Yet in that same box of old, forgotten books, I found a novel, written earlier this century, about a wealthy little girl named India Allen growing up in the nineteenth-century American South. I loved the name India, and more than that, I knew *this* was it. It had the virtue of being exotic as well as old-fashioned, and it complemented the mature stateliness of Augusta. And India stuck. When I somewhat fearfully told my sensible friend that I'd found the name, her reaction astonished me. Her face lit up. A self-described British Royal Family buff, she said, "So you're naming your daughter after India Mountbatten? Good choice!" I barely had the heart to tell her I'd never heard of India Mountbatten and was even secretly a little disappointed that she'd gotten to the name before I did!

India Augusta is four years old now, and to her the name is nothing special. But to other people it is. Most often, they want to know "where it comes from." I have been told that my blond, blue-eyed daughter doesn't look like an India, and I have been asked if I once lived in that country or if I'm a follower of Eastern religions. The answer to both questions is no. One woman I met on a bus informed me that India was the name of her favorite soap opera character—a very wicked woman apparently—and wanted to know if I was a fan of the same soap opera. Again, no. A friend of my mother's first reacted by saying, "Oh, my, where did you get that?" then added cautiously, "Well, now, it's certainly a fine name. A name she'll grow into."

But the most interesting reactions by far are from the Southerners I infrequently meet. My fictitious "India" from the novel I'd unearthed turns out to have many real-life Southern counterparts. In fact, it seems that India had been a very common name for women in the nineteenth-century American South. "Why, I had two Aunt Indias down in Alabama," one woman told me. "And I haven't heard that name in years." And a young male librarian, hearing me whisper to my daughter among the children's books, told me, "India was my favorite name when I was growing up in Georgia. I tried to persuade my sister to name her first daughter India, but she thought it was too old-fashioned." Very politely, he inquired, "Are you from the South by any chance?"

Sorry to disappoint him, I said we weren't, but I secretly wondered if I might not have some long-lost aunties of that name lurking in my past. When a friend, a *Gone With the Wind* buff, asked me if I'd named my daughter for India Wilkes in the novel, I stopped and thought seriously. Certainly, I'd read the book at least twice when I was a child. Perhaps the name had been buried in my memory, only rising to the surface now. I could picture myself poring over my dog-eared *Gone With the Wind,* coming across the name of Ashley's sister and wistfully imagining such a strange, lovely name belonging to me. But really I don't remember.

Coincidentally, my daughter's two best friends have "place" names too—Sydney and Raleigh. Recently, I met a six-year-old Asia in the park. Raleigh's mother isn't from North Carolina and doesn't have any idea why that name suited her daughter so perfectly. "I didn't have to think about it," she said. "I just knew that if I ever had a little girl, that's what I'd call her." Her comment struck a chord with me. I too, had probably known all along. A child and its name become entwined so quickly that now it's hard to imagine my daughter as anything but India. I'm convinced names do wait for people, and sometimes there's just no telling where the names come from. But that's part of the fun and mystery of naming a child. For the mothers of Sydney, Raleigh, Asia, and India, naming our daughters was a chance to be a little poetic—to step beyond the ordinary and give our daughters something beautiful and special right from the start.

A Desk for

My Daughter

Gardner McFall

When I was nine, and about to enter fourth grade, my mother surprised me by giving me a desk. She bought it for seventy-five dollars at an outdoor auction, and I dimly recall the rap of the auctioneer's gavel, signaling that the circa-1900 fan-front, slant-top desk was mine.

It was oak, a smooth honey color, stained just dark enough to "look important," according to my mother. The leaf opened to become a solid writing surface. The cabinet held three recessed filing slots, a letter holder and, in the center, a space for items like glue and tape. Above that was a drawer, which soon enough held my crayons and collection of seaweed mounted on index cards.

The desk had two larger drawers below that bracketed shelves. At first I put stuffed animals on the shelves and, later, books. On the front, the keyhole's brass plate, which I loved instantly, was fancifully etched with a bird flying up toward a crescent moon and a tree tossed by the wind. And it came with a key that worked. Open or closed, the desk was a marvel. But the most marvelous feature couldn't be seen at a glance, as I discovered the day it was moved into my room.

Seated at it, I removed the small center drawer from its slip, and, as I did, another drawer fell down from above—a secret compartment accessible when eased down its slanted tracks. Not even the auctioneer had mentioned this secret drawer. I thought my desk was the finest in the world.

From fourth through twelfth grades, I worked at this desk, writing my first poem, reading letters from the friends separated from me by our transient military life, and writing to my father when he was overseas. I filled out my college application on its sturdy leaf and, more than once during those years, put my head down on it and wept about some now-forgotten matter. For a child in a Navy family, pulling up stakes every two years was hard, but my desk anchored me. It became a kind of repository for all my young selves and lives. It was a constant.

Even after I left home twenty-five years ago for college and a career, I still returned to the desk periodically, storing there the mementos that charted my course: college diploma, love letters, a wedding-gift record book, the first magazine that published my poems. This summer I cleaned the desk out in anticipation of giving it to my eight-year-old daughter, about to enter the third grade.

This afternoon we are standing outside our apartment building in New York waiting for the desk to be delivered from Florida. All day she has been anticipating its arrival. I hardly know what it means to her; she hasn't ever asked for a desk, but she's as excited as if awaiting her best friend.

When the van finally appears, she leaps up and down, yelling, "Mommy, it's here!" and something inside me leaps, too. The driver, a Jacksonville antiques dealer and family friend, greets us, slides open the door. I see my desk, wrapped in blankets, sandwiched between a highboy and a bedroom bureau. It looks tiny to me, but I know that to my daughter it is enormous.

With my husband's help, the driver maneuvers it up to our apartment on a dolly. After he's gone and my daughter and I are in her room, the desk in its corner, I put my arms around her and say simply, "My mother bought this for me when I was going into fourth grade, and now I want you to have it, because you're going into third."

She gives me a gripping hug and bounds off to put her treasures away—pencils in their holder, diary in one of the file slots. She stands the painted bookends made at summer camp on the top ledge. As I turn to leave her to this greatest of pleasures, she calls after me in an emphatic, rather grown-up way, "Now life's getting organized!"

But I know it's herself she's beginning to organize, along with her crayons, markers, sketch pads, and collection of bears soon to be installed on the bottom shelves. Should I tell her about the secret compartment, I wonder, halfway down the hall, and what I kept in it—beach glass, Beatles cards, things too small or precious to be kept anywhere else? Should I point out the key or the little bird flying up to the moon?

I decide not to. I will let her find them and make of her desk what she will. I like to think that one day in the next century, she'll give it to her own daughter and say, "Your great-grandmother bought this desk at an auction. It has many secrets and charms. See how many you can find."

SWEET WILLIAM

Judith Thurman

My sweet William is a handsome four-footer with big feet, hazel eyes, and a cowlick. Unlike his mother, he can't wait to get weighed in the morning, hoping, as he puts it, to "turn fifty." He must have heard the expression in a different context. Turning fifty is my next hurdle. Will has just cleared seven.

Seven is called the age of reason, something I haven't explained to Will. But I think he knows. At six and three quarters, he seemed to have a foreboding that his next birthday would mark the end of an idyll of innocence, romance, and savagery—his little boyhood. It was endangered by such new responsibilities as real homework and chores and by such new privileges as using the computer and collecting an allowance. Will has begun to lay out his own school clothes for the morning and to fuss with a spray bottle and brush over what he charmingly calls his hairdo. He's able to laugh at himself, or at least at his younger self. And suddenly, he is too tall for us to swing him between us when we walk, or to carry up the two flights to bed. "I'm afraid," he told me one night, "that soon I won't want to sleep with Tiger anymore." I didn't tell him that I was steeling myself for that moment, too.

Will got Tiger when he was five months old, and they were the same size. We have a picture of them, both wearing stripes, Will laughing demoniacally and shaking his new best friend by the ears. Since then, he has permitted other animals—Stripey, Fuzzy, Curly, Caspar, Chester, Oinky, Getwell, Dredd, and Secret—to share the privilege of his bed and favor, but Tiger has never lost his primacy. His embroidered nose has been worn away, his sleek bright coat has faded to the color of stale taffy, and his whiskers have thinned out with age. Will's devoted Great-aunt Charlotte has restuffed Tiger several times, the last time rather too generously, and he is no longer the lithe young cub he once was. But to me, Tiger has transcended his thingness: Will's love has conferred a soul on him.

That extraordinary laugh Will greeted Tiger with seemed to come from a much older and deeper place than his infant body. It was as if he were recovering a forgotten truth or pleasure rather than discovering it. I heard the same laugh on the morning that Will pulled himself up on wobbly legs in the tub, pointed to the faucet, then to his own nakedness, and exclaimed: "Boy!" I heard it the moonless summer night Will got his first flashlight. He turned it off, then on, then brandished it defiantly—mythically—at the powers of darkness. Then there was the day I called out to him, "Where is Will?" and he answered triumphantly, "Mommy, I am here. I am here!" He had figured out the first person: He had found himself.

When I look at Will, I see my tender little boy, but looking into his own mirror. Will sees an action hero, a martial artist, a macho man, a road warrior, a tough guy, an hombre. Of the nine friends he invited to his most recent birthday party, eight were boys and one a girl, which is the approximate ratio at the moment of the yang and yin in his character. He has long since stripped my old dollhouse of its frills and converted it into a garage for his emergency vehicles.

Vehicles, the flashier the better, have always been his signature passion. In fact, when he began to speak, Will referred to himself as Wheel. He was not quite two when my friend Max brought him a spectacular model car. He immediately opened the hood, examined the motor, and made ecstatic revving noises. "What do you say, darling?" I asked. "Ferrari," said Will.

I can't think of any exercise healthier for the middle-aged heart than life with a little boy. Before I had one, though, I'd never expected to be the mother of a son. I was myself an only child, the devoted daughter of a devoted daughter, and I'd grown up in a world of women. My sedentary and dreamy mother was only too happy to encourage my passion for dolls, reading, pastels, the piano, empathy, and other decorous and mostly solitary pursuits. The incautious and rowdy world of boys was a foreign country to her.

When I left home for college, it was Mother who carefully wrapped up my collection of Madame Alexander dolls, my "Baby Coo" with her handmade layette, and that heirloom dollhouse which is now a garage—all for the grandchild whom she blithely assumed would be a girl. Will arrived three weeks before her death. I brought him to the hospital so she could hold him—so we could marvel at him together—and she understood the blessing of his otherness better than I did. "When I see you look at your son," she told me, "I feel that you will make a more lucid mirror for him than I made for you. You won't be so tempted, or so afraid, to see in him your own reflection."

Sometimes, though, I am tempted. I'm thrilled, for example, that Will, like me, loves the smell of old books. I am perversely proud to say that he has my tin ear; that we both snore loudly and, when we sleep in the same room, in unison; and that we're similarly vain and distractible. Will shares some of my most fundamental predilections: for order, puddles, Cheetos, shaggy dogs, iambic trimeter, white chocolate, wood smoke, being tickled, navy blue, even numbers, and snow. It moves me indescribably that he puts his stuffed animals to bed exactly the way I tucked in my dolls. They get the cozy, secure inside places close to the wall, while he sleeps on the drafty outer edge—maternally.

Last year Will and I were reading our bedtime story when we came upon an old Chinese proverb: "A parent owes a child two things: roots and wings." I paused to give him a meaningful kiss, and Will was intrigued to see me so impressed by the book he had picked out. "What does it mean?" he asked.

"It means," I began, "that my job is to give you all the things roots give a tree: Food to grow on, and the balance that comes from strong attachments. [And here I kissed him again.] But that's not enough. I owe you wings, too, so that one day when you're ready and willing, you'll be able to fly away."

Here Will snuggled closer in our big brown reading chair. "But suppose I don't want to fly away?" he whispered.

Neither of us knew it, but Will was already feeling that obscure ache in his being which means that wing buds have begun to sprout. He was learning to swim; we took off his training wheels; he started playing soccer and chess. Suddenly, he could read and write. Under my plate or pillow or inside my shoe, he would occasionally leave me little memos, valentines, or teasers: "Guess who? Boo! Will to Mom: I love you."

For me, language has always been the ultimate source of complicity with another human being. That's another thing I haven't explained to Will, but I think he knows. Just before his seventh birthday, he gave me a wish list, painstakingly printed and illustrated. Under the picture of a shaggy black puppy he had written *roots*. And under the picture of a bright red two-wheeler he had written *wings*.

GRANDMOTHERS

MAY YOUR LIFE BE
ONE SWEET SONG

Susan J. Gordon

keep my grandmother's autograph album on a shelf near my desk. When I hold it in my hands, I imagine her exchanging this velvet-bound book with other thirteen-year-old girls many years ago and writing "forget-me-not" on the corners of its gold-edged pages—the wishes, hopes, and dreams they had for each other as well as for themselves.

"To Esther," wrote Clara, "Long may your life be, in happiness and in ever lasting joy." "Live—not only exist," declared Biance. And Anna, another classmate, said, "May each minute, each hour of your life be a golden holiday."

The album is small but almost regal in its richness. The pages are thick, although they crumble at the edges and most of them have pulled away from the binding. To a young girl growing up on the Lower East Side of New York City, this book was probably a treasured possession. I often wonder what prompted my grandmother to save this album through years of marriage, the births and raising of children, widowhood, and then the ten years she spent taking care of my brother and me.

When I was a child, I loved to look through this book. I knew it was special, even before I could read the words, because it made me realize that once, a very long time ago, my grandmother—that white-haired lady who loved me so, whose hands were roughened and yet soft at the same time, whose arms and legs often ached with arthritis, whose eyebrows could be raised imperiously when something irked her or someone disregarded her instructions—had once been as young as I, dreaming about the future, and wondering what it would hold.

I would imagine Esther and her friends purchasing their albums in neighborhood stationery stores. Graduation time was coming, and the girls eagerly recorded their names and brief philosophies of life in each other's books. Wishes for romance and love were counterbalanced with images of independence:

> You may fall from a tree-top
> You may fall from above,
> But the greatest fall you'll ever have
> Is when you fall in love.—Beatrice

The albums were also brought to school, where teachers added their comments, using the opportunity to praise these budding individuals and spur them on to heights unknown. "I trust your success here may be a stepping-stone to successes in your future," noted one. Another quoted Shakespeare, reminding my grandmother, "This above all: to thine own self be true. Thou canst not then be false to any man."

Did some of these writers sense that the albums would be permanent, that their words would be read in the far-off future? Perhaps that's why classmate Dora wrote, "In memory's casket, drop one pearl for me," and Joanna said,

Remember me when you are happy,
Keep for me one little spot,
In the depth of thine affection
Plant a sweet forget-me-not.

After that brief season in the sunlight of school graduation, the albums were placed on shelves or tucked into drawers where they remained until the owners crossed other thresholds of life. Within five years, my grandmother married and moved away, and she took the album with her. She married a man who owned his own business *and* his own horse and carriage! Within ten years, he switched to motor cars, they had three daughters, and they moved to Manhattan's Upper West Side. But the Depression of the 1930s brought hard financial times. My grandfather died, the three daughters got married, and my grandmother moved to a much smaller apartment. Her life was probably pretty quiet for a while, that is, until my parents divorced and my mother came back home, bringing my brother and me with her. She found a job, and my grandmother took care of us while she worked.

Fortunately, she was the kind of parent a child could live with. In cramped quarters, she never made us feel restricted. Did I want to paint? She set up the bridge table for me, right in the middle of the living room. Did I need to be alone for a while? No place was off limits. She was exuberant and energetic, tackling the challenges of caring for us with optimism and confidence. She cooked, she cleaned, did the laundry, the baking, and the sewing. She quizzed us on our lessons and insisted we do well in school. Whatever dreams she may have had for herself at that time, she put aside. But maybe we were always part of her dreams. And maybe the best thing she could have wished for was the chance to raise children again.

That's why "granddaughter" is to me one of the sweetest words in the language. It means to be loved by someone unconditionally. Even the sound of the word evokes splendor: GRAND daughter.

Today, memories of my grandmother are a part of my children's lives. She's with us when I read to my children, sing to my children, and teach them how to bake and sew. She's near us when we're all together, laughing about some silly joke or story. And she's near me when I'm all alone, wishing I could help a small child who is unhappy, and wondering what I've done to make her feel that way. "As long as you love your children, and make sure they know it, everything will work out," I hear her saying. "Love—and family—are the most important things."

Now, it's another school year, and Edward, my eight-year-old son, has purchased his first autograph album. This event required a visit to three nearby stationery stores, until a wine-colored leatherette album was selected. The pages are edged in gold.

"Would you sign my album?" he asks me when we get home. "You'll be the first one."

"I'd be honored," I tell him, and we sit down together at the kitchen table. I look at Edward and wonder, what can I write? Big thoughts swim through my head, and little ones surface too. He is my firstborn child, named after my grandmother, Esther. I remember how he looked last Halloween, and how he sings when he gets dressed in the morning. I remember how he walks slowly on his way to school, and then races home each afternoon. Will he save this book for a long, long time? And one day, will his child read it too?

What do I wish for him, what do I hope his life will be?

"May your life be one sweet song," I write, stealing this prayer from "Augusta," who wrote it to his great-grandmother back in 1903.

"I like it!" Edward exclaimed. And as I watched him walk away, I was sure I could hear him humming.

COLLECTING
GRANDMOTHERS

Whitney Otto

During college I used to abandon my books on Sunday evenings to go ice-skating. I'm not sure why, but I preferred to go alone—maybe because I was so clumsy on the ice, maybe because I just enjoyed the solitude. In any case, I was not alone long, since the children who skated on Sundays, ranging in age from seven to eleven, quickly befriended me. They invited me to their birthday parties, gave me tips on how to improve my skating technique, chatted with me as we circled the rink, and introduced me to their mothers. They said, "Mom, this is my friend," when referring to me.

I once asked one of the kids, an eight-year-old named Travis, how old he thought I was. We were resting on one of the benches next to the ice; I drank cocoa while he sipped coffee.

"Are you sixteen?" he asked.

I shook my head.

"Are you thirty?"

I realized that for kids, age is pure abstraction; they have little use for chronology and, with regard to companionship, respond to something else, something inside a person that is ageless.

At seven years old I had two best friends: One was my age and the other was in her early seventies. The one in her seventies was named Apple and my parents often drove me from Pasadena to Burbank to spend weekends with her. Apple was a friend of the family, of course, but we had a special friendship that existed outside that one. I was just as happy to spend time with her as I was with my other, younger friend. Our conversations seemed to me just as lively, our interests shared, and boredom simply did not figure into my time spent in the company of this woman ten times my age.

It is possible that I was more predisposed toward a friendship with a much older woman because I hardly knew my own grandmothers. With too much time and distance between us, I felt only a vague affection toward them and could never rightfully claim to know them. I only knew what was said about them.

But I knew Apple. I knew that she loved the feeling of climbing into a bed with cold sheets. That she liked people to be straightforward with her. And that it did not distress her to live by herself.

On Saturday evenings we stayed up past midnight watching *The Fabulous Fifty-Two*, often discussing the movies shown, which Apple enjoyed without being entranced by them. She liked Audrey Hepburn, Claudette Colbert, and was convinced that Clark Gable was an awful man since his relationship with his first wife seemed wholly opportunistic. We disagreed on this point because I had a crush on Clark, although when she informed me that his teeth were false I momentarily had to rethink my affections. I had once, inadvertently, seen Apple without her teeth. It would have bothered her had she known, since she often maintained that "some things are private."

She taught me to roller-skate and play jacks and solitaire. She allowed me to take my first puff of a cigarette. Apple smoked exactly three cigarettes a day and never once did I see her exceed that number. So when I asked to try it, she handed it over to me, told me to inhale. Of course, I did not like it much and so that was that.

She talked as well as listened and rarely moralized; as with the cigarette experimentation, she let me discover things on my own. As she was born in the 1880s, in New York City, her childhood was very different from mine and we would discuss it at length. It is possible that those conversations provided the foundation for my love of history, for viewing life as difficult and great. Apple always treated my questions with respect and truth; truth, I learned, was most important in her world. Along with humor (hers sly and smart), along with love.

She kept a photograph of J.F.K. in the Oval Office displayed on top of her television set. Being of Irish descent herself, she took his presidency as a source of pride. To her he was always "my boyfriend." His assassination rendered her silent and angry.

About twice a month Apple and I climbed into her black 1959 Rambler and drove out to the Movie Retirement Home in Woodland Hills. Her sister-in-law lived in a small, cheery bungalow with a paper-trained parakeet that spent most of its time outside the cage. Apple's real name was Ethel and her sister-in-law was also Ethel. The two Ethels were widowed.

I would sit on the floor, half-listening to the conversation, as I leafed through the other Ethel's scrapbooks from her days as a silent-movie star. At sixteen she had portrayed Jane Eyre in the film by the same name, an occurrence I found thrilling since Jane Eyre was one of my favorite characters. A day with Ethel was almost like hanging out with Jane herself. The scrapbooks were wonderfully made, published on oversized glossy sheets and full of stills taken by the studio photographers. I was the only kid in my grade school who had ever even heard of the actor

Francis X. Bushman, let alone able to recognize him. Not only was I familiar with a number of lesser-known stars, but I soon had favorites. My other best friend, the one who was my age, shared television with me; the Ethels shared the silent screen and the early years of movies.

When Apple and I walked to Tony's Market, we always stopped by Apple's friend Billie's apartment to ask her if she needed us to pick up anything for her. On our return, we would sit in her sunny kitchen, Apple and Billie talking and drinking tea. Actually, Billie did almost all the talking and Apple listened as closely to her as she did to me.

One night Billie had us over to dinner and watch television in her rarely used living room. We never went to Billie's at night, nor did we venture out of the sunny dinette area of the kitchen. I was more interested in the dated decor of Billie's living room than the TV program. With the exception of the television, we three could have been spending an identical evening in the early forties. The entire evening felt strange and timeless.

"Why doesn't she go to the store herself?" I once asked Apple.

"Oh, Billie doesn't leave the house. It makes her uncomfortable."

A few years later, after Billie had died, Apple and I were driving south, past Long Beach. Apple pointed in the direction of the airport and said, "Billie used to fly in and out of there all the time."

"Where did she go?" I asked.

"Here and there. Sometimes to air shows. She was quite an aviatrix."

I thought of Billie sitting in the well of windows in her bright kitchen, in view of her weird, anachronistic living room, too afraid to venture outside, alongside the image of a new, younger Billie who flew airplanes. And I could not link the two at all.

Apple had a gentleman friend who occasionally "escorted us," as he said, to dinner. His name was Charles and he was always marvelously dressed in jackets, scarves, and hats—unusual clothing for the arid Southern California climate. We went to the Tam O'Shanter, The Chronicle. He had been married three times but engaged four.

When Charles was a young soldier in World War II, he met a girl, the teenage daughter of a well-to-do family. They fell in love and when they became engaged, she took him to a rather large room in her parent's house, where he saw enough furniture, lamps, rugs, linens, china, cookware, silver, and home decorations to fill a small house.

"What is all this?" he asked, only to be told that she had been "collecting" since she was a little girl. Her parents indulged her because she was a sickly child. The young woman ended up dying suddenly, months before she was to marry Charles.

I asked Charles why she had all those things, and he replied, "I asked her that same question. And since no one had told me about her difficult health, her answer only made sense to me much later. She said, 'So I can live forever.'"

Of course, I loved that story. I loved all their stories and understood, from an early age, that "elderly" people have the best tales to tell. Their respective lives seemed, to me, as enthralling as any fiction. I also knew that elderly women need not be kooky or crotchety, that between these two poles existed as wide a range of complexity as found at any age. And that older women are generally not silly gossips with little respect or desire for privacy. Nor are they mean. Or crazy.

Not long after my college ice-skating years, still in my early twenties, I worked in an office with a number of women in their sixties. I often talked about them to friends, one of whom came to meet me for lunch one day. I introduced him around and after we left he turned to me and said, "Those women are old!" Something, I guess, I neglected to mention. Perhaps because they did not seem old to me, as Apple and her group had not seemed old to me; they were ageless.

Again, I found myself listening to the stories of their lives, past and present: Two had worked in munitions factories during World War II; one, a child of the Depression, still bought far too many pairs of shoes; another purchased her first house in Hollywood for $1700; still another had survived the London Blitz.

They still spoke of their husbands as if the men were recent boyfriends—that is, with humor and affection. They were all wonderfully, romantically inclined. And if there was marital misery at home, no one publicly confessed it; it must have only sounded in private.

I am often asked if the women in my novel were based on my grandmothers or women I grew up around. The answer is no, they were not; they are invented. They have their own, not borrowed, lives. However, the observations I made as a girl stayed with me: That life is rich and varied throughout all years; that fundamentally our changes are small, we tend to be who we always were, albeit a bit more experienced; that the body may change but the heart remains the same.

Now writers often tend to write about what they long for— certainly we all have very specific concerns that permeate our work. So maybe this is one of mine: The stories of older people, particularly women, who are not embittered by the world, not defeated by it. As if this is achieved with a sort of goodwill or bravery—not unlike the way in which many people consider their grandfathers as heroes or something along that line. The lives of these women (Apple, Billie, Jane, the ladies in my office) contained occurrences large and small; the meshing of personal and global history. I admire this acceptance of life, not as "survivors" but as people who simply lived their lives. It is impressive that this good cheer comes from people closer to the end than the beginning of their lives: It is one thing to be hopeful at twenty and quite another to be hopeful at seventy.

That is what I learned from all these grandmothers, who were not of my own blood, but who taught me, without knowing they were teaching, of agelessness. And, of course, they had the best stories.

Surely the one thing I will miss in the course of my own aging is the narrowing of the gap between my age and theirs; a child of ten discussing the world with a woman of eighty.

At Grandmother's Table

M. J. Andersen

My maternal grandmother was a champion accumulator, legendary in our South Dakota town for her impact at auctions and thrift sales, and in our family for never dropping by empty-handed. A few years ago, it fell to my Aunt Mary and me to ready her possessions for sale—a job anyone who had seen Grandma Tait's house would have shuddered to contemplate.

I set aside three weeks that November and flew home to do nothing but sort and box. But by Thanksgiving Day, when Aunt Mary and I had hoped to be done, mountains remained.

By the middle of the first week we had already turned punchy. Just opening drawers and looking into closets made me feel faint. Many of the possessions I doubt Grandma herself had seen in years. Our work became an archaeology of the soul, the layers of things testifying to Grandma Tait's unruly aspirations and changing enthusiasms. She painted pictures with oils, collected stamps and coins. She kept everything. We sorted through paper dolls, hats and hatboxes, and enough vases to stock a florist's shop. I counted more than sixty throw pillows.

But Grandma's great love, as we had always known, was dishes. They were everywhere: in kitchen and bathroom cabinets, in the basement and the attic, under the beds. Fancy plates were stacked three deep on the dining-room plate rails.

One night, exhausted and stretched out on the living-room floor, I noticed a cabinet under the TV that we had overlooked. Inside was an entire set of Limoges. We laughed until we were tearful. Grandma's formal china, familiar from holiday dinners, was a Hutschenreuther set, beautiful violets on a white background. Where and when had she ever come up with this gold-rimmed Limoges with its pale-green flowers?

Most of the things in Grandma's house were destined for auction. To speed our work, Aunt Mary and I designated the large dining-room table the "maybe" table. Anything we might want to keep or give to relatives but were not sure about, we placed on the maybe table. That way, we would not stop to agonize over each thing. As the days passed, it became loaded with dishes. There were candy dishes and relish plates, handpainted hot-chocolate sets, Tom and Jerry mugs, a punch bowl, dessert plates decorated with fruit. There were flaming-red liqueur glasses brought home from Venice, and Delft pieces from the Dutch foreign-exchange student our family hosted when Mary was in high school.

There was Wedgwood, Roseville, Fostoria, and Nippon; cut glass and milk glass, Depression glass and etched glass. There were butter pats from the old set once used down at the Masonic lodge. (How did she get her hands on those?) And the Limoges.

As the accumulation grew, it became somewhat easier for us to release our darlings into the boxes bound for auction. What we contemplated keeping surpassed sense. Both of us already had dishes of our own. And as my father observed: How many plates can you eat from?

Still, in the process of sorting through Grandma's things, a self

I scarcely recognized as mine began to emerge. Aunt Mary had always loved what she called "stuff," but I tended to panic when stuff crossed the threshold into clutter. I liked order; Grandma, a true daughter of the Victorians, thrived amid profusion. *Needing* so many dishes was not the point; the essence of her collection was exuberance, a pure unbounded delight in the things of this world.

I knew quite young that Grandma and I were decided opposites; we mixed as ill as bone china and Bakelite. Yet in those weeks of sorting, I felt free to draw near her, in a way I never could when our clashing personalities met. For the first time, I could experience the pleasure she had taken in what she used to call "my pretty things." I appreciated, too, her fierce need to fill her life, in a place where there was always too little going on to suit her, and where the starkness of the landscape disagreed so violently with her sensibility. She longed for culture and manners and social distinction. Perhaps she thought teacups with handpainted roses would force all these things to bloom.

As it came time for me to return east, I knew I would never see the like of this accumulation again, and that in some ways I would always mourn the dispersal of Grandma's heroic assemblage. There was a bid for immortality here that was as great, in its way, as the pyramids were in theirs. And who would honor it, I wondered, if her small, dispersed family did not?

Reader, I kept the Limoges.

I saved a few other things too: the periwinkle water glasses I remembered so well from Thanksgiving dinners; some small silver trays; a white creamer, German, with a calla lily on it.

Aunt Mary got a kick out of my belated succumbing to Grandma's things, though perhaps all along she expected it— knew this lust for dishes was genetically encoded, and that there would be little I could do. But I hope Grandma knows, too, somehow, that I came to her table at last. And that on those long days of sorting and laughing, her daughter and her granddaughter celebrated her life.

"SICK-ABED ON TWO CHAIRS": PUDDING COMFORTS

Sylvia Thompson

When I was little and what my grandmother called "sick-abed on two chairs" she would comfort me with pudding. My grandmother was very fond of pudding, and as I grew older, it crossed my mind that she wasn't always that sorry I was indisposed.

Coughs and sniffles and the usual childhood distresses were the occasion for her sweeping into the bedroom with a tray crowned with something warm and wonderfully scented. My parents' lives were such that much of my girlhood was spent in my grandmother's house—lucky me. Born of the children of pioneers in 1884 in California's Great Valley, my grandmother was a woman whose cooking was the perfection of American plainsong. I thrived on it.

My earliest memories of Grandmother's pudding are intertwined with my recollections of the books I was reading while "sick-abed." Leaning against a tumble of pillows and furrowing my brow over the plights of the orphans in *The Five Little Peppers and How They Grew,* I spooned up creamy, golden rice pudding with rose sauce. The rice had simmered in milk in the oven for hours and hours, which gave it a honeyed glow. And the color and fragrance of the sauce were reminiscent of Reine des Violettes, my grandmother's old French rose.

A bout with chicken pox brought forth raspberried bread-and-butter pudding with nutmeg sauce. In keeping with her stylish-but-saving ways, I half-expected, when I turned a page of *Little Women,* to find that Marmee had made one for Meg, Jo, Beth, and Amy—with raspberries Laurie had brought over from his garden. The determined optimism of those plucky girls and that pudding, with the reviving pungence of its nutmeg sauce, made my itching tolerable.

A disastrous spill while roller skating was the occasion for a feathery chocolate pudding. An English friend had given my grandmother a sleek white pudding bowl for steaming. Deep, yet of an intimate size, it was just right to serve one chocolate-fancying grandmother and one miserable little girl. Although few cooks steam puddings nowadays (it seems more of a nuisance than it really is), my grandmother knew that steaming keeps a pudding moist. Spooning up clouds of ephemeral dark chocolate and whipped cream, I liked to imagine that if Aunt Polly had made such a treat for Tom Sawyer, Tom might have stayed home instead of dashing off after Huck Finn and making everybody nervous.

Then there was Delmonico pudding. Inspired by a recipe in a nineteenth-century cookbook, my grandmother sliced fresh peaches over soft custard, slathered them with meringue, and baked the concoction just enough to color the meringue and warm the pudding. At that point I was in high school, at home nursing something or other and devouring *Gone With the Wind.* My grandmother had moved East by then, but by happy chance, she was visiting. Delmonico pudding was just what the doctor ordered! Oh my, yes. If Scarlett had had her wits about her and had baked Delmonico pudding with Tara peaches for Captain Butler, he might well have given a damn.

Time passed and I stayed healthy. Then in the freezing February of my sophomore year of college, I went to Paris. Near the end of reading *Madame Bovary* I caught the world's worst cold. I longed for my grandmother and the comfort of pudding.

When the lovely woman who ran our *pension* (she was both a grandmother and a wonderful cook) asked if there was anything she could do for me, I smiled. In a trice she presented me with one of the most satisfying puddings imaginable: plump prunes steeped in port and caught between crisp, puffed, brown layers. It was not unlike Yorkshire pudding, except the center was creamy and faintly flavored with orange. As this pudding is traditional in the Limousin, I wondered whether Emma Bovary would ever have tasted it. Poor thing; it would have soothed her frazzled nerves.

Of course there are real, not fancied, puddings in books. In *Beauchamp's Career* written in the nineteenth century, George Meredith exulted in ". . . our English pudding, a fortuitous concourse of all the sweets in the grocer's shop . . ." Indeed, Queen Victoria's handwritten "receipt" book was filled with puddings— her favorite "sulebubble" (syllabub) was made with equal parts cream and milk, flavored with orange water and white wine, sweetened with sugar, and foamy with beaten egg whites. "If you will have it of a red color," she noted, "put in clarett instead of white wine." There was a grandmother!

And now I am one, with small grandchildren who give hints of being bookish. I so look forward again to the company of the five little Peppers, Meg, Jo, Beth, Amy, Tom and Huck, and in my turn, to watch as the children "sick-abed on two chairs" spoon up my pudding comforts.

CHEERS FOR THE

QUEEN MUM

Catherine Calvert

*S*he walks slowly to the great gates, her small feet teetering in their size four and a half high-heeled shoes, her head crowned by a hat like a peony, her face full of humor and smiles that reach to the eyes, while children, grandchildren, great-grandchildren bob in her wake. She bows to take a handful of posies from a little girl, and a boy rushes up with a full bouquet, the crowd smiling, too, as she walks among them, and the band plays "She Must Have Been a Beautiful Baby." Elizabeth, the Queen Mother, is celebrating her birthday, as she lives her life, with informal charm and a graceful regalness illuminated on her ninety-fifth birthday (August 4, 1995), with the glow that comes from her unique place in British hearts.

Cecil Beaton wrote in 1953 that she is "the great mother figure and nannie of us all." In a time when, as in the forties, enemy bombs dropped, or, as in the eighties, royal gossip bomb-shells exploded, she remains the unruffled rallying point for those who find the family—as well as fairy tale—of a royal dynasty part of the very point of national identity. In June 1995, when the veterans of World War II assembled in London to commemorate the fiftieth anniversary of VE Day, it was the Queen Mother, tremulous but unbowed in her salute, who caught the eye and the heart. Those who'd endured those years remembered the fluting voices of the royal family on the radio, full of courage and good cheer, and the mother who refused to have her children, the young princesses, evacuated. Even those born later recognized that here was more than a mere ceremonial figurehead, but the very embodiment of a generation who knew its role, and filled its duty, all flags flying. Her accolades affirmed that she, who describes work as the rent we pay for the position we occupy in life, "knew her job and performed it well."

Certainly she didn't set out to be queen. Born the ninth in a family of ten to the Earl of Strathmore, she was the much-petted last daughter reared in a handsome Queen Anne house in Hertfordshire and at Glamis Castle, her tall and turreted home in Scotland. She was a pretty little girl, all smocks and ringlets, tutored in the dancing and music and poise appropriate for her class. By the time she was launched in society, eyes were on her, taken with her light spirit, her energy. As "Chips" Channon, politician and diarist, wrote, she was "well-bred, kind, gentle and slack . . . always charming, always gay, pleasant and smiling, mildly flirtatious in a very proper romantic old-fashioned Valentine sort of way. . . . She makes every man feel chivalrous and gallant towards her."

When the shy and stammering young Duke of York met Elizabeth at a ball, he was immediately attracted to the girl with the bright blue eyes and began to pursue her. ("You'll be a lucky fellow if she'll have you," said his father, George V.) They danced in London and through long Scottish evenings, Elizabeth in a "rose brocade Vandyck dress with pearls in her hair," and walked in the moonlight while Bertie courted her.

But she said no, no again, each time the timid prince asked her to marry him. She was only twenty and unsure she wanted life in the quiet palaces of St. James. After two more years of Highland balls and London theater evenings, Bertie asked for the fourth time. And she, laughing, is said to have responded, "If you are going to keep this up forever, I might as well say yes now." And so, in a drift of silk and lace and white roses, she was married.

"He is a man who will be made or marred by his wife," her mother had said. And there's little doubt that part of the public's respect for Elizabeth comes from her successful undertaking of this marriage—and the slow transformation of Bertie from awkward prince imprisoned by his shyness and stammer to the man who grew more comfortable in his role and mastered his speech when he could rest his eyes constantly on the encouraging face of his wife.

By the thirties, two little girls, trim in white gloves and matching coats, had joined them. The York family seemed the very epitome of a royal family—and a dramatic contrast to Edward, the Prince of Wales, with his paralyzing appetite for other people's wives.

His abdication, when Bertie was transformed into King George VI, and Elizabeth donned her crown, was as much family tragedy as constitutional crisis. The steel in her character glinted: She accepted the duties of her crown ("the intolerable honour"), but blamed her husband's early death on the onerous tasks he had to assume. And she never forgave the Duchess of Windsor for the events that transpired. (Wallis's rancor against Elizabeth raged lifelong: the Duchess's mouth twisted as she dubbed the queen "Cookie" for her seeming cook's taste in hats and handbags and blamed her for the lack of money and honor accorded the Duke.)

When thirty-nine-year-old Elizabeth walked into Buckingham Palace as queen, she began the making of her legend. A country still struggling with the Depression and hearing the wingbeats of approaching war loved its new queen with her polished children and smiling face. Neither a stunning beauty, nor a fashion plate, she wisely turned to Norman Hartnell, a young designer, who made dresses for her based on Winterhalter's crinoline-filled paintings of the young Victoria. Photographer Cecil Beaton, also at the start of his career, began to create portraits that captured the public's imagination—and his own.

Their first sitting occurred in July 1939, when Beaton, who had thought "how dreary and dowdy to have the Yorks on the throne," was transported when he met Elizabeth. Her face was "very dazzling, white and pink and the complexion flawless." They spent the day finding new settings around the palace gardens, as Elizabeth changed from a crinoline of gold and silver to tulle with spangles "like a fairy doll." The pictures of her piquant profile and billowing skirts became the making of a public romance; we still expect to see her in colors taken from an herbaceous border and hats with a life of their own. Through the brave years of the war, when she and the king spent every day in Buckingham Palace, even as it took a direct hit, she was a perfect queen, from hat on high-held head to impeccable shoes. To see her in stark black at her husband's funeral was to reinforce the shock of her loss.

She was just fifty-one when he died and could have retired to her rooms and her garden. (She wrote a friend that she was "engulfed by great black clouds of unhappiness and misery"; that sorrow is "small and selfish" but "it bangs one about until one is senseless.") But she had another whole lifetime to live, becoming the reliable patron of charities, her eyes sparkling as she dived into crowds or took the controls of a jet, or cheered for one of her horses as it rounded the curve for home. And that zest is just what we love, that firm grasp on life that seems to make her ever interested, ever surprised by what for many of the royals seems mere toil.

If we perceive her as lively, it's no doubt, because she is. She has her own courtiers, mostly unmarried men who are good company. She fills her tables with artists, musicians, and wits as well as those who like country pursuits and racing. She collects contemporary art and reads constantly and widely. "She is never, never bored," says her private secretary and, indeed, seems as happy going to a premiere in tiara and gloves as visiting a youth group's judo demonstration. She treasures the country life, especially in Scotland at her own Castle of Mey, the only house she's ever done up on her own. Her constant stream of visitors know to expect a weekend of stiff drinks and charades in the drawing room after long walks. She's close to the Queen, sharing an interest in corgis and colts, and is particularly fond of the Prince of Wales. She is religious, conservative, and protective of the family and its place in the world.

This private image reinforces the public face, a winning portrait of the world's granny, pouring out the champagne and beckoning anyone with a good tale to tell to sit next to her. (The Queen has been quoted as saying, "You know, I do work awfully hard, but Mummy has all the charm.")

It is Cecil Beaton who puts it best. "Of course, there is something of the great actress about her, and in public she has to put on a show that never fails, but it is her heart and imagination which guide her. She will always say just the one thing that puts people at ease and makes them feel a glow of happiness, because she understands and appreciates the reality of any situation—whether it be tragic or gay." And that, finally, was what the cheers were about that birthday, for the small woman, straight-backed and at her ease, who did her duty and always managed a smile.

SISTERS

FOREVER ENTWINED

Susan Minot

here was always a blurring between me and my sisters. Where did one sister end and the other begin? Over the years we've studied the differences between us with an attention bordering on the manic, not really questioning the peculiar assumption that we were more alike than different.

There were four of us. One was darkest, one the tallest, one the youngest, one the most nimble. Our qualities were measured in relation to one another. There was one who could dance best, the one we thought prettiest, the one who knew most about the world, the one who made us laugh.

There was always a sister around. Never to be thoroughly alone is both a curse and a blessing. We cut one another's hair and painted one another's nails. On uneventful afternoons we drifted around the house, ending up in convulsive laughter. I remember making daisy chains, I remember being whacked with a wet washcloth.

We put on plays. My younger sister still resents being made, as the third sister, to play the witch. We dressed up, arguing over who got to wear my mother's bed jacket with the pale blue ostrich feathers. When we became interested in photography we put our baby sister in a tutu and posed her beside an Easter lily. There was no question of her saying no.

We shared bedrooms. After I'd slept beside my older sister for a while, I switched and moved in with my younger. Both of them talked in their sleep; they told me I did, too. During feuds, we marked down the center of the room, dividing our sides. Off the rug, the wooden floor was neutral area so you could get to the door.

I learned from my sisters of the outside world. Who else would outline the way one behaved at a party? When my older sister came home from spending the night at a friend's, she would tell every detail. "Okay, first we got out of the car. Then we went into the kitchen where her brothers were . . ." We'd lie on one another's beds and listen to everything.

One eye was always on a sister. We began our Christmas lists, trying to think of things. The eldest, more discerning, was writing intently. We fell back on a sure thing: whatever she asks for.

Once, on an August afternoon, I slipped through a pier railing, falling to the water below. My older sister, at age five, was so affected by the accident, she hurried back to her room, changed into pajamas, and climbed into bed.

The history of sisters is one of imitation and competition. We followed one another in summer work programs, in getting our ears pierced, in learning to drive. We also barricaded our doors and learned to keep secrets and attempted to forge identities apart from our family. Outside friends were part of this. When one sister had a friend over, I hovered nearby. Everything they did was fascinating. "Go away," my sister would say. They were making milkshakes, they were swinging in the hammock. I hid behind a tree, longing to be where they were, and when it was my turn to have a friend visit, I'd tell the sister lingering near the door, "Go back to your own room." It was only fair.

Property was important, as in "Who said you could use my pen?" or "That's my hair band!" It was only right there should be absolute equality between us. "How come you get to have a new bag?" "Susan got to go first last time." We were jealous. Why did the hat with the pom-pom look so much better than my striped one? Because Dinah was wearing it. When Carrie wasn't home I'd wear her sweater and feel like a new better person. Having lost it for weeks, I'd find my favorite blue jean jacket crumpled up in the bottom of Eliza's closet.

Clothes remain a constant subject for us. We still give one another hand-me-downs. Having lost our mother fifteen years ago, we mother one another. We buy extra pairs of earrings. We understand the subtleties of each person's taste: "I got some of those wide pants." "Okay, I see what you mean." I am no longer surprised to go to a party and meet my sister there, dressed in pretty much the same thing I'm wearing.

We are standing on a lawn on a pale spring day. The ocean down the hill is silver. We stand stomach to stomach, my sisters and I, planning the house. Around us are thrown sweaters, our brothers' hockey sticks, shoes, a rake. We mark the kitchen with a plastic bat, the bedrooms run along the garden border. You be the mother, I'll be the father. We make decisions with eerie goodwill. An hour later we will be pushing one another out of the place-where-I-was-sitting in the TV room or hoarding the last chocolate Ring Ding, but for the moment we are in harmony.

Thirty years later we can plan a dinner for fifty in a day, a wedding in a week. We began making dinners at my older sister's first apartment in New York—where we all lived at various times—cramming mismatched chairs around two or three tables. In the kitchen we communicated in code.

"Where's the—?"

"Here."

"Did you—?"

"I got it."

The men watched baffled. Someone made a remark about a four-headed hydra.

We were least close as teenagers. It was time to venture out on our own. We found a world where people did not immediately get the joke or automatically understand what you meant by a glance. Yet even as we sought to discover ourselves and where we fit in, our wardrobes remained interchangeable and our friends continued to intersect.

Our lives are relatively separate. Still, we can choose the right clothes to bring back to a dressing room. If we're traveling together, there's minimal negotiating about who stays with the bags and who buys the tickets. We do it in sign language. We visit one another's houses and apartments. I now expect to see the identical bedspread on her bed and that she too has found that new shampoo.

With my sisters I am presumptuous. I feel I know what's going on in their heads. Of course, I don't. But I bet I'm closer to knowing than anyone else. Sometimes I have the sensation of living three additional lives. I have felt this sister's happiness and this one's frustration. In my dreams I have their hands, I am fighting with their boyfriends, I'm pregnant. Our memories have become collective. Was I there that summer during the hurricane? Well, one of us was.

Once I rode to the hospital with my older sister on the tailgate of a station wagon over padded white roads after a great blizzard. She had broken her wrist falling in the snow. They tried to separate us when we changed cars—there was a sort of volunteer taxi service—but I stuck with her to the waiting room. She would have done the same for me. When I was twelve I broke my leg skiing. As I lay delirious on the slope while a ski patrolman fumbled with a splint, my sisters were crying out, "Leave her alone! You're hurting her!" They were not altogether wrong.

I've watched my sisters have babies, get married, watched them get awards, diplomas, sacraments. We know one another's soft spots with the radar of the blind. Sometimes trust has wavered—we can make one another furious—but our loyalty remains firm.

I call my sisters from the city, from the country, from abroad. I always know where they are. In the background I hear my nieces singing, pens scratching invitations, sirens sounding, a baby crying. Carrie's scissors are cutting—she's a decoupage artist. Eliza is away from her desk and I get her voice mail, the voice sounding oddly like mine. When she calls back, we talk about movies or boys or writing, with office phones ringing beside her. Dinah calls from her car phone on the way back from the movie studio. Work is exhausting, the girls are fine. No detail is too small to relate. We have both just bought the same coat, and for a moment I wonder if I've made a mistake with the black. She's gotten it in green.

I call my sister and hear water running three thousand miles away.

"What're you washing?"

"A sweater. You?"

"Laying one out to dry."

ALICE AND CHARLOTTE

Judith Thurman

From their retirement until they died, my parents lived with my mother's younger sister. The success of this arrangement surprised the three of them, the two sisters most of all. They could not have been more different.

My mother had a passion for order, solitude, lists, bad weather, crossword puzzles, smoking, daydreams, and grammar. She told me proudly that when *Ulysses* was first published, she had punctuated Molly Bloom's soliloquy. It was she, naturally, who taught me to write, and I have never had a more ruthless editor.

Music made my mother anxious: All the channels on her radio were set to the news. Nature left her indifferent. She mistrusted spring, loathed summer, hated to go out, and she would, I think, have been happy living in a burrow, immaculately clean with a bank of telephones, kept at the temperature of a deep freeze, and furnished in shades of brown.

My aunt never married and engaged in some form of social

work all her life. Her political idealism did not prevent her from loving expensive hats, and I still have, in its box, one of her satin toques from Lilly Daché. When her parents died, she became an intrepid traveler, always game to camp on a floor or to climb the nine hundred steps of a bell tower to see the view. She lived alone then, in a studio that was full of plants and charming old things—a desk, a sewing table—that she had refinished. It was she who taught me to swim and to ride a bike, who took me trick-or-treating dressed as Gene Autry, and who would later come to visit me in my "hovels," as she liked to call them: a garret in London, a walk-up in the East Village, a Tuscan farmhouse with no plumbing. She was, with her sister's unselfish blessing and unjealous gratitude, my model for independence.

Alice and Charlotte were born and grew up on the street in Manhattan where I now live. When I cast my vote for president last November, it was in the turn-of-the-century brick school where they learned to read, and that still has separate entrances—obsoletely decorous and guarded by stone lions—for girls and boys.

To the east of Second Avenue, the fine mansions of old Yorkville still had their mews. To the west, in the shadows of the elevated train tracks, there was a lively neighborhood of brownstones and tenements. At the end of winter, they were visited by itinerant ragmen and knife sharpeners, each of whom had his own cry. The housewives beat their carpets in the backyards, and in summer families slept on their fire escapes. There was no traffic: The cobbled streets were a playground for the children. The Ruppert brewery, near Gracie Mansion, still made deliveries in a cart drawn by Percherons, and so did the icehouse. Boys—and tomboys like my aunt—hitched rides on the ice wagons and, in the heat of August, scavenged for ice chips. Commerce was the province of the mom and pop shops that gave credit and sold sweet paprika and fresh poppy seeds, embroidery thread, essence of violet, fanciful little marzipan cakes, kerosene, dried mushrooms, pipe tobacco, exotic teas, and pork sausages. On weekends, the dance halls of Eighty-sixth Street—vast and innocent—were filled with hardworking immigrants in fancy headgear, who waltzed to the music of gypsy violins.

My grandfather had a bakery, a very good one. He had done his apprenticeship at the Hotel Sacher in Vienna and had delivered breakfast rolls to the emperor's palace on his bicycle. He was amazingly dextrous and could shape his croissants, which were called kipfel, two at a time, one with each hand. My grandmother's specialty was strudel, so thin you could read the newspaper through the sheet of dough. She told me, smiling, that the secret to great cooking was a pound of butter for every course. Like all Hungarians, she loved finery. Twice a year, she had a dressmaker come to the house, a Madame Sottile, from Palermo. They would spend a companionable week sewing, listening to the opera on the radio, and drinking linden tea. When she found a bargain, my grandmother bought her daughters white silk by the bolt, and while Madame Sottile did the cutting, she crocheted the trim for nightgowns, slips, and the camisoles they called "fairy waists" (Ferris waists) that were fit for a princess.

Alice, my mother, was named after the boat in a Hardy Boys adventure novel that her older brother, Wesley, happened to be reading when she was born. Charlotte was named for the heroine of Goethe's *The Sorrows of Young Werther*. Three years had passed, and Wesley's taste in literature had improved. He was, by then, an apprentice baker himself, but also a lover of poetry, a champion swimmer—he dove off the piers of the East River with Johnny Weissmuller—and a figure of great, even terrible glamour to the girls of the neighborhood. My grandmother fretted over these adventures, amorous and natatorial, and so did "baby

Alice," who learned the fine, feminine art of worry, her sister liked to say, in the cradle.

Alice was the stoic in a volatile, drama-loving family. She was plump and dreamy, with eyes like two black currants and the skin of a bisque doll. Her sister made much more strenuous claims than she did on their mother's love, and her speciality was goodness. As a little girl, she had suffered meekly through Charlotte's colic, and then through Charlotte's rheumatic fever, and then through her violin lessons. "I got so mad at her saintliness," said my aunt, "that I smashed the violin over her head."

By the time Charlotte was old enough to be a real playmate for her, Alice had given up jumping rope and playing "Rover, Rover, come over" on Eighty-second Street: She had discovered her brother's library. Reading became her refuge and remained so. She ate and read and ate and read, though by sixteen, miraculously, she shed the cocoon of her baby fat and emerged as a beauty. I have a picture of the two sisters from that era, on the beach at Sea Cliff on Long Island, where one of their aunts ran a hotel. They are both wearing the slinky, square-cut knitted bathing suits of the twenties. Alice is small, pale, and voluptuous. Charlotte has bobbed hair, a freckled nose, and the body of an athlete. Indeed, she was swimming two miles a day in the Atlantic. "I couldn't decide," she once told me, "whether I wanted to be Douglas Fairbanks or to marry him."

My grandparents moved to Boston when Alice and Charlotte were in their early twenties. It was there that my mother met my father, a young lawyer, and Charlotte—after working in a settlement house—embarked on her career in the civil service. When they were in their sixties, they all found a quiet, houselike apartment with a fireplace and a back porch in a suburb on the trolley line.

If my father had any misgivings about living with his sister-in-law, he never voiced them. His new role, as a chaste pasha—

waited on by two pugnacious houris—suited him all too well. He had never learned to drive. He had also never learned to boil an egg or wash a dish. He never shopped, even for his own clothes, and my mother took care of all their bills and taxes. From time to time we tried to convince him that a pair of good leather shoes no longer cost twelve dollars, but we gave up. In a restaurant, he rarely looked at the menu, letting Alice order a steak, hash, or a piece of veal for him. He had grown up with six bossy, loquacious, maternal older sisters, and he found it quite natural that in his home, at least, he should be babied.

In the early years of their ménage à trois, my aunt and father were still working. They were both morning people—unlike Alice—and revoltingly cheerful at an ungodly hour. They were up before dawn, and by six-thirty she had dropped him at his office on the way to hers. Before they left, she inspected him to make sure there were no egg stains on his tie and that he wasn't wearing odd socks. His mandarin unworldliness always shocked her, but her fierceness seemed to act on him as a kind of tonic. He accepted her scoldings as the gift of devotion they really were. And once in the car, driving through the sleeping suburbs with the moon setting, they would put an opera into the tape deck, and turn up the volume. Music was a bond, and more than that: a source of fraternal complicity between them.

Alice considered that her sister and her husband had their jobs and she had hers: the house. The two women shared the chores, but Alice orchestrated them. She had trouble with stairs, so Charlotte was allowed to carry the laundry to the basement and load the machine, but she couldn't do the executive job of sorting it. The electric broom, said Alice, was like a dog, faithful only to one master. It was she who clipped the coupons, ordered the cupboards, kept the accounts, managed their savings, and made the shopping lists. Charlotte was eventually permitted to push her own cart at the supermarket, but only up and down those aisles Alice had assigned to her. They fought about money, each of them trying to force more of it on the other.

Alice and Charlotte had never resembled each other, but as the years passed, they began to. People confused them at the bank and on the phone. Each of them exacted a sacrifice from the other, and adjusted to—forgave—the one she had made. Charlotte gave up her wanderlust, then her work, and most of her old friends, and submitted with better grace than I could ever muster to the loving tyranny of my mother's managing and dependence. Alice gave up her precious and perverse invisibility. She exposed herself to Charlotte's light.

My father was, in this household, like the center pole of a tent: structurally essential but impassive, and it sometimes seemed to me that the real marriage was between Alice and Charlotte. I was wrong, though, and naive—as children often are about their parents' romance. One morning, when Charlotte was in the kitchen making him a second piece of French toast, my father had a stroke and died. My mother discovered quickly and with profound surprise that she couldn't live without him. She managed to survive just long enough—seven months—to hold my newborn son, her only grandchild, in her arms.

Three old friends living together have to die in some order. My parents would have felt they did it right. Only Charlotte, who was nearly eighty when she "broke camp" and moved back to Yorkville, could have lived alone again, in a studio full of plants, and run after a little boy. She protests it isn't fair—to my father, to Alice—that she gets to "hog the joy." But I know my father would have been glad: his sense of justice was his finest quality. And I know my mother would have been grateful. She would have given—she has given—her sister's last great love, for this child of mine, a blessing.

TELLING THE

STORY OF SISTERS

Catherine Calvert

S he is four, a sunny, blond, and bright-eyed child with the sort of sweeping lashes that had passersby cooing over her from birth. I am six, skinny and snaggletoothed, and shy as a mouse. She has the bed by the window, the blonde-haired doll, and a new pair of cowboy boots. I hate her.

She is seven and I am nine, and we are about to enter our fifth school in a childhood marked by moves. It is a large, red-brick building, solid as a fortress, and a torrent of children, all unknown, caper and shout in the schoolyard. We, our new shoes squeaking, our fresh-pressed dresses crisp about our knees, stand frozen by the fence. And we shift our new lunch boxes to the other hand and grab on to each other. I love her.

We are in our twenties and living far apart. Sometimes we'll go for weeks without talking or writing, bobbing in our separate lives, one married, one on her own. But then will come the phone call, at night when the rates are low. "The most amazing thing happened today," she'll say, and we'll be off, racing with the energy of feelings understood. And I love her.

Those of us with sisters know certain truths: Here is the person with whom we are as familiar as our fingertips and at the farthest poles of fathoming. She's the one in our lives who'll complete the sentence as we speak it, share the memories, the household language. Even when the relationship is one tinged with rancor or rubbed by rivalry, the bedrock lies below. Once, we were two portions of the whole that is a family.

Certainly this relationship has its portion of mystery, something that is intriguing to explore in one's own thoughts or by reading books that turn on the subject. For children, there are fairy tales to discover—"Snow White and Rose Red," Hans Christian Anderson's "Little Mermaid." As soon as reading is fluent, most girls find their way to *Little Women,* which seems to be the book that best captures sisters living together, even if they are unnaturally good. (Though not always. Naughty Amy certainly has her fits of temper.)

Just as in life, literary sisters are cast into roles, polar opposites of goodness or creativity, shyness or calm. The portrayal of sisters lets a writer explore all the faces of woman, like turning a crystal so different facets illuminate. What would Jane Austen be without a clutch of sisters flitting and plotting in such books as *Sense and Sensibility* or *Pride and Prejudice?* As with *Little Women,* each sister occupies a different point on the compass of human behavior.

For the Victorians, family love had the force of romantic love. Edith Wharton explores the pull of both in her newly republished *The Children.* She introduces a passel of brothers and sisters, presided over by fifteen-year-old Judith Wheater. A lonely bachelor is ensnared by the delights of this odd little family's life, unaware that he is drawn, too, to Judith and her "fitful beauty." Wharton deftly tangles the threads of emotions with a thorough look at society's foibles.

While Victorian writers often created sisters who seemed like pasteboard figures, contemporary writers tend toward fully inflected portrayals. One of the best is Gail Godwin's *A Mother and Two Daughters*. The daughters in question are Cate, who has chosen to flout convention, and Lydia, who has framed her life narrowly. Their return home to North Carolina for their father's funeral sets up the old patterns of fury and love. "There are things life expects of you," Lydia says, "and there are things you have a right to expect of life. You just have to learn which is which. And get yourself organized." Over time, the two learn to follow Godwin's rephrasing of Montaigne's challenge to "deal gently and justly with one's family and oneself."

There is a more subtle exposition of the sisters' tie in Shirley Hazzard's *Transit of Venus*. Orphaned, Caroline and Grace Bell travel to England from Australia after World War II. Their loves and lives are the center the novel revolves around. Shirley Hazzard's immaculate prose, which details personality, countryside, and plot with ease and grace, is masterly, so one is immediately drawn into her observations of the times and places the girls inhabit. "You could see the two sisters had passed through some unequivocal experience, which, though it might not interest others, had formed and indissolubly bound them. It was the gravity with which they sat, ate, talked and, you could practically say, laughed. It was whatever they exchanged, not looking at one another but making a pair. . . . Because they were alike in feature, the contrast in colouring was remarkable. It was not only that one was dark and one fair, but that the one called Caro should have hair so very black, so straight, heavy and Oriental in coarse texture. Grace was for this reason seen to be fairer than she was—as she was judged the lighter, the easier, for the strength of Caro. People exaggerated the fairness, to make things neat: dark she, fair she."

Those who learned their sisterhood in a large family, in a tumble of sisters and brothers like so many puppies in a box, will savor the humor and be moved by the tragedy of Susan Minot's novel *Monkeys*. Clearly, her ear was informed by her own memories of sisters discovering their similarities and their differences. Finding one's special place in a family is difficult in the awkwardness of adolescence, as Sophie discovered. "Her sisters came home [from school] for vacations, threw big parties, remembered funny stories. Things were a certain way and Caitlin and Delilah were that way along with them. If she had been dropped down in the jungle Sophie would have felt more at home." The novel is amusing and short, encompassing little details of life in a family of seven children. All that makes domestic life is sketched in quick strokes—even the event that shakes the family's foundations—and the true voice of childhood rings engagingly here. Caitlin and Sophie, Delilah and Minnie intertwine, come together and break apart, in the dance of the family.

At home, and in these books, we are convinced again of the power of sisterhood. "We wove a web in childhood, a web of sunny air," wrote Charlotte Brontë, who surely knew the joys of sisterly devotion, the web with its filaments of fidelity and joy and memory, that bind us still today.

PLACES OF

THE HEART

A BELL-REGULATED EDEN

Phyllis Theroux

When I was ten years old, our family moved from San Francisco to Marin County. It was an upwardly mobile kind of move that everybody was supposed to celebrate because now we owned a house instead of renting a flat. But I grieved for the dense, crosshatched map of alleys, squashed together apartment buildings, and laundry lines that had been slipped out from under me as deftly as a place mat. Now all I saw—through the plate-glass windows of an L-shaped ranch—were bare brown hills rising behind a man-made lagoon. It was during this period that I realized California and I were not suited for each other over the long haul.

This is not to say it was a complete mismatch of soul and geography. I never tired of watching the morning fog gather like bright cotton behind Mount Tamalpais before spilling down its flanks in thick sheets of batting. A grove of eucalyptus trees seemed full of angels. In fact, it still does. Long before I knew I was a writer, I tried to capture California in words. But most

of the time it felt too big with too little in it to satisfy my need
for slightly overstuffed civilization. To compensate, I read stories
about nineteenth-century English schoolgirls who drank tea and
wore knee socks. You couldn't even find knee socks in Marin
County. The weather was too warm.

The first year in Marin County I went to a public school
distinguished by good landscaping and bad teachers. As I recall,
I excelled in one subject, tetherball. Then something quite unexpected and wonderful happened. My grandmother decided to
take my life into her hands.

That Grandmother could do anything with anybody's life,
given her utter inability to manage her own, was not particularly
surprising. When possessed by a clear enough vision, she could
rise above the agoraphobia and depression that ordinarily nailed
her to a wing chair and act in a very decisive way. This time,
the vision that got her dressed and driving across the Golden
Gate Bridge to Marin County was a worry in disguise. If somebody didn't take action fairly soon, her granddaughter would
wind up permanently unrefined.

Grandmother was a snob without supporting papers, which
is not to say that our family was entirely without brilliant moments. We could point to a couple of distinguished ancestors to
prove that we weren't all riding the rails to nowhere. But in
Grandmother's mind we were what I later realized was an ox-
ymoron—California aristocrats.

How, she demanded, did my parents think the intellectual
and social skills I would need later on could ever be gotten in
a paid-for-by-taxpayers public school? My parents, who used paper napkins and had five other children to think about, said they
didn't know. Grandmother did. Wrapping her good pearls and
a fox fur around her neck, she got my father to drive her across
the bay to Dominican Convent in San Rafael.

Surely, she told Sister Kathleen, the convent's lower-school principal, the nuns would be interested to know that her own mother had attended Dominican while it was still a finishing school in Benecia. Oh, is that so, replied Sister Kathleen, who did, indeed, appreciate these kinds of genealogical details. After an hour of similarly pointed allusions, Grandmother emerged with what she had come for—a place for me in their sixth grade on full scholarship. Thus with the nod of one wimpled head, my life was instantly upgraded from tourist to first-class. It was just in time. The following year, my grandmother died.

According to the list of uniforms the nuns sent home, a Dominican girl had many different occasions to which her wardrobe needed to respond: gym tunics, summer uniforms, winter uniforms, dress uniforms, going-to-the-city uniforms, aprons. I found this deeply thrilling. After a life of too much time on my hands, I was finally headed toward jam-packed days. As importantly, wearing a uniform relieved me of having to reinvent myself every morning, while silently proclaiming me, like a tiara, as being part of something larger and more prestigious than myself—a feeling the convent's motherhouse underscored.

In 1951, the year I entered the school, San Rafael was a rather nondescript town that ended without ceremony at a cluster of Rotary and Kiwanis club signs on the outskirts. But the convent, painted pale yellow with a red-tile roof, was a splendid Victorian contraption of turrets, walk-ways, bay windows, and porte cocheres. A wide apron of stairs led to the second-floor main entrance and the entire motherhouse rose above the palm trees on Grand Avenue like a protective, organizing principle. Built in 1889 for $100,000, the nuns raised the money through their usual spiritual-extortion method: novenas.

This made Father Louis, the nuns' confessor in San Francisco, nervous. Perhaps prayer might not be enough. He wrote a letter to their superior, Mother O'Donnell, instructing her: "Have seven candles burning steadily during the novena. Purchase the candles and send the bill to me." In twenty years the mortgage was paid in full.

This feat of faith says something about candles, novenas, and the Virgin Mary as banker. But it primarily attests to the logic that powered all the nuns' major decisions. They had the vocation to educate, and since it was God Himself who had given them that vocation, He was duty bound to give them the means to honor it. Again and again, He did.

By the mid-1950s, Dominican was a fully developed fiefdom, attracting students from all over California, Mexico, Hawaii, Central and South America. Latin American families often sent their daughters to Dominican, knowing they would be strictly chaperoned, although the layout and life of the school left us with little reason to leave.

Academic and residence buildings were laid out amongst ten acres of gardens planted with olive, cedar, and fruit trees. Next to the swimming pool and tennis courts was an elaborate summerhouse, covered with wisteria. A dozen hawthorn trees surrounded the central courtyard. There were hockey fields, a riding rink, separate music and gymnasium buildings.

I stayed at Dominican from sixth grade through senior year of high school, but it never seemed too small to me, which is not to say that it was large enough to make me happy. No piece of real estate can do that. But I knew (as I was to know once again as a new mother) that I was in the midst of a blessing that could no more remain than I could, once my allotted number of school days was done.

My grandmother was right to assume that the nuns would knock a little politesse into me. We learned how to curtsy, write Oscar-winning thank-you notes, use a calligraphy pen, and be trilingual in the "Hail Mary"—English, French, and Latin. These accomplishments have not had much cash value in my postconvent life. But being able to live for a sustained period of time in an orderly, cohesive universe continues to be of inestimable worth to me. It was in this small, bell-regulated Eden that life first began to make serious sense.

Beyond the precincts of the convent, adults drank too much, Elvis Presley was heading toward stardom, and a lot of hot misbehaving was going on at drive-in movies near the Miracle Mile. None of this touched us directly, although I wondered how I was going to get from Hawthorn Court to the bleachers of a Cal-Stanford football game—miraculously transformed into a coed who knew the score.

What I did know was that once inside the convent with the cool, polished-wood floors, there was little to physically remind me that I lived in the twentieth century, much less California, which was only a dusty backdrop around an oasis. The outer world was kept at arm's distance, giving me inner time to catch up. Then, as now, I strongly believe that an all-girls' school strengthened my capacity to live in the outer world later on.

I am told that before entering Dominican I was an overly talkative child who made more noise than other children. This is probably true. Oddly, I remember feeling full of words that had no way to get out. But soon the words began to organize themselves like notes within a stanza—a metaphor that comes easily to mind since the school was soaked in music. We were never more than thirty minutes away from hearing or singing it.

We sang Gregorian chants for Sunday mass. There was a separate, elite Schola society. Once a year, the school came together for a song festival. At Christmas the nuns serenaded the students from the motherhouse balcony. We sang spontaneously and unselfconsciously, whenever a soprano could find an alto, and last year, at the funeral of my college friend, Barbara, that instinct to sing reemerged.

At her graveside, five of us, all convent educated, instinctively placed our hands upon her casket and sang *Tantum Ergo* as the coffin was lowered into the ground. The impulse to sing stays with me, although, thankfully, the ersatz nineteenth-century schoolgirl has almost disappeared.

An argument could be made that the nuns did not prepare us well for the future. By teaching us to see life in the broadest possible context (and what could be broader than the Mystical Body of Christ), evil was reduced to a faint margin around a brilliant picture—a view the motherhouse, rising into the bright blue California skies like a theme-park castle, reinforced. We were taught that the best way to deal with evil was to go to confession and make a fresh start of things.

As for how the nuns taught us to regard ourselves as women, the message was mixed. The role models nearest (and dearest) at hand were the nuns themselves. They led merry, man-free lives in a society of other capable women. The curriculum was as heavy on history, mathematics, and science as any private boys' school around. But the not-so-hidden trajectory was aiming us, first and foremost, toward the goal of being good wives and mothers.

It was traditional for graduates to return with their fiancés to receive the nuns' approval. Then on their wedding day, they would often come to Dominican with their husbands after the ceremony for a prehoneymoon blessing. And when the children arrived, they too were presented for the nuns' blessing and, later on, an education.

Are these customs out of date, sideswiped by all those non-maternal arenas of accomplishment that women need encouragement to try? Reader, you are asking the wrong writer on the wrong day for what may be the politically correct answer. As a parent who has played to mixed reviews for years, I don't think anybody ever knows enough to prepare the next generation adequately. We can only pray that we do not misuse what little we do know. And the nuns prayed continually—or at least this is how I remember them.

We revisit those places where we experienced love, as pilgrims return to holy places, to be reminded, restored, and reaffirmed by them. Several years ago, when visiting my mother, who lived near the convent in northern California, I decided to risk disillusionment and return.

Both the nuns and school (later renamed San Domenico) had long since moved to a larger piece of property in nearby San Anselmo, but the original motherhouse and convent high school, still owned by the order, were nearly untouched. The hawthorn trees that had created soft drifts of blossoms in the courtyard every spring had all died, which saddened me. And the study hall, that long, polished room of tears, was now a dance studio full of mats and mirrors. But in all other ways, the convent was no different than I remembered, and I could easily imagine it instantly refilling with noisy, bumptious girls who had just rushed off campus for a few minutes for a fire drill. Even my old practice room in Angelico Hall had a half-filled bottle of Skrip ink on top of the piano. Had I been the last person there?

For several hours I walked around the grounds, taking pictures of the only "people" left, the various saints and angels who gazed over my shoulder from their garden pedestals. Two months later, the past went up in flames when a housepainter misused his blowtorch in the motherhouse. When the first tongue of fire grabbed the ancient wood, it was a done deed.

The community of San Rafael gathered all afternoon across Grand Avenue and watched the town's most elegant landmark fly up to heaven in sparks. There were no injuries, but the townspeople wept alongside the nuns as if they were watching a beloved relative being consumed upon a pyre.

Seventy-three-year-old Sister Virginia took the upbeat position. "This just means," she said to an *Independent Journal* reporter, "that we start over. We have done that before; we started from scratch in eighteen eighty-nine. We can do it again." Undoubtedly, the nuns will do it the same way they have always drilled holes into Heaven, through spiritual extortion. More candles will be purchased. New novenas will be made. The sisters did, however, cover their heavenly bets with earthly insurance. That, plus a fund started by the townspeople of San Rafael for the sisters' welfare, has launched them once again.

The core of the novena's nine consecutive days of prayer is steadfastness, a virtue I entirely lacked when I first arrived at Dominican as a turbulent, disorganized twelve-year-old with an amorphous desire on my mind "to be great at something." I had no idea what that something could be. Nor, during the seven years I was at Dominican, was that ever clarified. But something else, never articulated until later, was ensuing.

As educators, the sisters consistently held us to the task of learning to distinguish between what was a truthful, beautiful thing and what was not. The academia was rigorous, but in the long run it was not an intellectual knowing they bestowed upon us as much as a certain knowing of the heart.

What we knew most of all and what was, in effect, our trump card—to play against the sisters, themselves—was that they prayed for us. Steadfastly. On a day-and-night basis. They were nuns. They had to, an imperative I found deeply consoling. My life was not only in my own inexperienced hands. We are all connected, an insight that was first taught to me against a backdrop so vivid that I would be sure to remember it. Many times since, it has been reaffirmed.

Porch Swings, Old Novels, and

Memories of Summers Past

Catherine Calvert

*T*hough many a house has sheltered me in the course of summers past, one memory serves to tie them all. It's early afternoon and all is sweet peace. Just a shift of the pillows sets the porch swing swaying gently—pillows covered in faded chintz with the slight musty scent that attests to their long winter's nap in the shed. The book lying tented across my chest is slightly musty too, foxed with the brown spots of age, since it was left downstairs in the bookcase thirty or forty years ago. You may be sure there's nothing in it to tax the brain: It's a romance and Cressida and Percy are settling their futures over a game of tennis. But I shall simply revel in the pleasures of the present, listening to the burr of the lawn mower down the road, watching the hornets busy themselves with their nest, biting into the slice of lemon I've fished from my iced tea.

Ah, the joys of a summer place! Unlike year-round houses filled with serious furniture and serious concerns, this is the house that transcends utility, that summons up the joys of summertime when you cross the threshold. Shuffle off your shoes and pad across the cool floors, search out the porch (there has to be a porch with the traditional blue-painted roof). Count the beds, with their white counterpanes and sagging springs—all is as it should be, as it was, and ever shall be.

The proper summer house exists out of time and has a sort of parallel life to our own workaday existence. I've been lucky in living in some of the classics—breeze-swept houses by the sea in towns where generations of voyagers have spun out their summers under the maple trees. Whether turreted Victorians or restrained eighteenth-century houses with center halls, they had much in common. You'd pry the door open, as it stuck from winter's dampness, and be met with that curious scent of past summers, compounded of damp bathing suits and Sunday morning bacon, dried wildflowers forgotten in vases, and sofa cushions that had seen too many wet towels. The floors were usually broad expanses of painted boards, so welcoming to sandy feet, with dust kittens rolling about under the furniture, testimony to haphazard housekeeping.

Everyone would claim a bedroom, searching out the one with the mattress that least resembled a hammock and longing for the sound of the sea singing in the ear at night. The kitchens and baths were mere utility—if that. Many of these houses were old, having belonged to families who'd farmed potatoes in the neighborhood for two hundred years. If they were content with a toilet that rumbled and a stove that spit, surely these city folk could make do. And who planned much time inside anyway, when beach and meadow summoned?

Summer houses serve as the last repository for many families: Grandmother's parlor suite sits next to a 1950s plywood table, and always wicker squeaks under its layers of paint, a protest, perhaps, against generations of spring spruce-ups. Any decorating scheme is as much a matter of memories as of material possessions.

Making our house our own was always easy. We could add what we liked—and subtract. Sometimes we'd spend the first few hours hiding the owners' plastic lobsters, fake fishnets, and seagull mobiles in a deep dark closet to allow a clean sweep for our time there. There was always the delicious sense of being temporary, of freedom never known at home. Drape a Marseilles spread over the sofa, swap the lamps around, drag the softest chair into the landing that overlooks the lake—all is permissible, all is comfortable. The point is to put one's stamp on the house and settle in.

As June faded into July and then August, each house would become more and more ours. Our accumulations grew, the sum of summer days. Someone would gather a bucket of irresistible shells, as pink as the first light of morning, and scatter them along the mantelpiece. There were always tomatoes ripening on the windowsills and handfuls of berries found on country lanes. A seagull feather was dropped on the duck decoy, and wildflowers filled every jelly glass, shedding their petals on the table.

Books mounted on every surface. My favorites were the long-forgotten lode in every bookcase, the frothy reading of previous generations, school stories and adventure tales, courtly romances and memoirs of the Spanish American War—all to be gobbled, as they had been originally, while we were ensconced in the porch swing.

We'd line the sideboard with jars of beach plum jelly from the Ladies Beautification Committee Fair and hang a watercolor of a rose discovered at a tag sale—and consider all of it quite beautiful indeed (if anyone had paused to look in between dashes to the tennis courts or bike rides to the beach).

The most important piece of furniture in the house was undoubtedly the dining room table, which was large, square, and surrounded by ten mismatched chairs that wobbled when discussions grew animated. Dinnertime was precious, and not a few morning hours were devoted to driving to the lobster pound and idling in the farmer's market, hefting the green bundles of basil, or eyeing the corn with the concentration of a connoisseur. At twilight, an intrepid friend would crouch, under cover of rising mists, and scratch through the neighboring field for forgotten potatoes. After that, the whole glorious pile of provender would be cleaned and steamed and served, with rivers of butter and some herbs, to the impatient table. Conversation dwindled as everyone ate, the only arguments rising over whether this was, in fact, the best corn all summer, or whether lobsters should be plunged into cold or boiling water. Then the evening would spin on, as the fireflies flashed through the screens, and everyone talked through the night and felt the glow of sun-warmed skin and good friendship.

Thinking back, I realize that the only time I ever really looked at any of our summer houses was on the last day, just before I turned the key in the lock to go home. My ostensible mission was to search for anything forgotten, but that final survey was always poignant. The house had never seemed so tidy— already the tides of family life were receding. I'd walk from room to room, looking at and then lowering the windows and pulling the shades. In the kitchen, I'd reach for the bouquet of wildflowers, then leave it there, knowing it would surely wilt on the journey home. But I would seek out one last shell from the mantelpiece to carry with me, my fingers searching its cool, smooth contours, a shell as empty, and as beautiful, as that tall old house by the sea.

MEDORA'S STORY

Susan Minot

'd been on Route 94 for hours, having crossed the border of Montana into North Dakota, when I spotted a sign for Chateau de Mores in a town called Medora. In Wibaux, the last town, there had not even been a restaurant. It seemed an unlikely place for a chateau in the midst of red buttes and sandy cliffs. I took the exit. At first amused when I saw the clapboard house on the open hill, I soon grew charmed by the story of the house and by the spirit that seemed to sweep through its airy rooms. Though now a museum, every corner still bears the unmistakable touch of its mistress, Medora de Mores.

In the late summer of 1883 a young woman disembarked the recently completed Northern Pacific Railroad at a stop near the Little Missouri River in North Dakota. She was twenty-six years old, five feet tall, and dressed with great elegance. She had brought with her dozens of trunks, each holding an outfit of a skirt, petticoat, vest, corset, and silk shoes. Among her luggage were hand-stitched linens, bedclothes, silk comforters, rare china, silver teapots, rugs, curtains, and even a wooden covered bidet. One of her cases had built-in velvet compartments for a sixteen-piece silver vanity set. She was bringing it all to her chateau.

It was not a proper chateau with turrets and stone arches and a gravel drive. It looked more like a large farmhouse and was painted a pale blue with tomato-red shutters and trim. Here in the Badlands, twenty-five miles east of the Montana border, the buttes are striped with sage, and rainbows rise like smoke from the horizon. The land is bare except for the cottonwoods along the river, which rustle during the dry summers and freeze during the harsh winters. The chateau was used only as a summer residence.

It was called a chateau by the local residents, most of them employed by the man who owned it: Marquis de Mores, a Frenchman who'd started his own cattle and meat-packing enterprise in this untapped land. When he started building a town here, he put up two hotels and a general store, a town hall and a church. On April 1, 1883, he smashed a wine bottle on the peg of a tent and christened the town after his bride, Medora.

Marie Medora Von Hoffman was the daughter of Louis A. Von Hoffman, a wealthy German-born New York banker who called himself, with no particular claim to nobility, "Baron." Medora was educated in New York and France, and it was in Cannes in 1882 that she met the marquis, her future husband, Antoine Amedee Marie Vincent Amant Manca de Vallombrosa, whose family was of Spanish descent. He'd distinguished himself in military schools, despite a reputation for outrageous high jinks.

After the two were married, they sailed to America and spent a sweltering summer at the Von Hoffman estate on Staten Island. That fall the marquis immersed himself in finance and, while he learned a great deal, grew restless in the confines of an office and looked to the West. His wife shared his adventurous spirit and supported him when he set off.

In the early days he met with hostile frontiersmen who resented foreign intrusion, and in a standoff battle he killed a man. The marquis was eventually acquitted, but when riding about the country dressed always in a red shirt and high boots he was, according to one observer, "armed like a battleship."

The woman who stepped off the train at the Little Missouri stop did not appear to be of the frontier. She had abundant hair swinging to her waist and delicate features—a thin mouth above a set chin, curls at her forehead, and deep-set eaglelike eyes. Though raised in sumptuous circumstances, she took to the raw and beautiful landscape, alternately described by reporters at the time as the "lake-gemmed, breeze-swept empire of the Northwest" or "a vast frigid desert." The name "badlands" came from a phrase used by the French explorers of the eighteenth century, *mauvaises terres.*

Medora loved to ride over the land sidesaddle, an eagle feather bent in her hat, wearing a simple long dress with a ruffle at the neck, a belt of gun shells around her narrow waist. She went on hunting expeditions with her husband, who maintained she was a better shot than he—this from a man who was rumored to have shot every type of animal in the area and who once, bored with shooting, decided to—and did—kill a bear with a knife. The marquis's servant reported how Madame shot a deer bolting from the bush, then immediately felled another that followed. On these trips Medora brought along beds, china, and silver. After one expedition, the hunting coach carried in six bears, four of which had been killed by Medora.

A son and a daughter were born those first two years—Medora returned to New York for the births—and she turned her attention to making their summer residence in North Dakota comfortable. The house was built of white pine, shipped from

Virginia, Minnesota. Beveled posts supported a large wooden porch that wrapped around two sides of the house and shaded wicker chaises filled with large pillows. Inside, the floors were covered with Oriental carpets and the windows hung with heavy curtains. A large square fireplace at the center of the house served four different rooms.

Medora's bedroom was downstairs. Her walnut bed canopied with lace and red velvet was foreshortened, in the style of the times. (One slept propped up to prevent contraction of tuberculosis.) A matching walnut tray with tapered legs was brought in for her breakfast. After her long hair was brushed each morning, the brushes were cleaned and the hair saved in a linen bag stitched with Medora's name. These strands were then used to make Madame's hairpieces.

Her husband slept in the room next door. In the twin bed beside him was his personal valet who dressed him and managed his clothes. The man who fought cowboys and knifed bears wore expensive silk underwear and custom-made shirts from Madison Avenue. Each downstairs room had doors that opened to the adjoining rooms and onto the porch. Though there were precious heirlooms from across the Atlantic, the house had a simplicity and airiness throughout.

Bead-and-board wainscoting lined the small staircase that led upstairs to a wide open hallway with eleven bedrooms where the servants and children slept. There were twenty servants— personal maids, a doctor, nannies for the children, a butler, chambermaids, a laundrywoman, and a cook. Some maids were employed in the dining room only. Outside were gardeners, a stable boy, and Medora's private guide.

The front rooms upstairs were guest rooms (for his in-laws, the marquis had built a brick house in town), and the guest beds were draped with lace and mosquito netting. Tall windows looked out of each all-white room to the dry, sand-striped bluffs. On each table sat a washbowl and pitcher and linen towel. Tin washtubs with tilted backs were a particular luxury. The beaded headboard of one bed matched the pattern on a mirrored bureau. In the children's room a lacy net suspended by a star of six crossed wooden slats cascaded around a crib. The children's toys lay about—crude wooden carts, colored block puzzles, and a little leather pug dog.

The kitchen was the same size as the dining room. The servants ate off ironstone dishes stenciled with a brown-and-white flower pattern. Mock stained glass, made of colored paper, kept privacy between the paned doors. Through the butler's window passed great platters of beef and game to the dining room, where bottles of French wine were passed among rare blue-and-white china.

Many guests were entertained at the chateau. Counts and dukes traveled from Europe, attracted by the hunting. Young Theodore Roosevelt, who had graduated from Harvard a few years back, bought some land nearby and was a visitor, sharing with the marquis a passion for sport and politics. Medora played the piano, and with the windows and doors open to the porch the guests would dance in the hot Dakota night, sipping iced champagne from crystal glasses.

The books around the house were in many languages— French, German, English. Medora herself spoke seven languages. In the front flaps of these leather-bound books Medora sometimes jotted down household expenditures. The woman who would spend an easy $750 at Tiffany's noted that the price of cauliflower seemed "dear."

Medora was an accomplished watercolor painter. Sitting under a canvas umbrella down near the river she painted her house and surrounding landscapes. Among her paintings were seascapes of Cannes, a tangled forest, and a study of a yellow rose.

After two summers in North Dakota, it became clear that the meat-packing venture had failed. With a million and a half dollars lost, Marquis de Mores moved the family back to Europe, where they had residences in Paris, southern France, and Switzerland. The marquis continued his adventurous life, making expeditions to Indochina and North Africa. It was there in the desert in 1896, at thirty-six, that he was murdered by tribesmen. Medora believed they had been hired by political rivals but was never able to prove it.

But the family had kept its holding of nine thousand acres in the Wild West, and caretakers looked after the house. Gertrude and J. W. Foley closed off the upstairs and the front rooms and slept in the de Moreses' linen closet. For fifty years the house was maintained. Mrs. Foley described "a rare relic room, showing memories of de Mores, his wife and children, de Mores's saddle, gun, hunting boots, bearskin coat and chaps, his packing bags, hunting coat, pack saddle, his French stiletto, ammunition and loading outfits of various kinds including exploding bullets (for he loaded all his own shells), sporting goods of all descriptions and curios, Madame de Mores's saddle, bridle, whip, spurs and riding habit, her white box and bathtub. We have the children's things that have been here all these years—baby wicker cribs with lace canopy, satin eiderdown quilts and embroidered pillows, French baby bathtub, children's books, dishes, silk hose and kid shoes, baby dolls and the large baby buggy."

In 1903, seventeen years after her departure, Medora returned to North Dakota with her three grown children so they could see the town their father had founded. She threw open the doors of the chateau and extended invitations to everyone in the community, and once again there was drinking of champagne on the wide porch. She and her family stayed for six weeks and never again returned.

During World War I Medora transformed her house in Paris into a hospital and worked there as a nurse. As a result of an injury she suffered at this time, she died in 1921 at the age of sixty-five. The chateau was left to her son Louis Vallombrosa, who donated it to the state of North Dakota as a museum in 1936.

Today one can visit the Chateau de Mores in the middle of what is now Theodore Roosevelt National park. The orange brick chimney, all that remains of the packing plant, rises like a monument at the edge of the town of Medora. Trains still chug through. The brick house built for the Von Hoffmans is now a doll museum with a doll cutout fence surrounding it.

The chateau sits above the town. A dry wind blows across the porch. Inside are remnants of the high life. Off the kitchen one small room is filled with rows of empty wine bottles, their labels brown and mottled. The dining room table is set with the blue-and-white china and finger bowls of colored glass. Medora's sheet music still leans on the piano. In her studio, an easel holds an unfinished watercolor, and on her writing desk is a picture of an elegant friend in white and a painted fan. A row of tree ornaments hangs from a shelf, colored balls dangling from tin candleholders. There are old boxes from New York stores and faded folding chairs. In the marquis's room, a fencing mask lies tipped on the bureau. In his office, a great black safe is painted with a river landscape and the inscription: "Sold by M. A. Bigford & Co., St. Paul, Minn."

In the relic room still are heads of deer, antelope, mountain ram. Old trunks are open showing compartments and straps, the paint trim flaking with age. Throughout the house are scattered old bills and order forms for household items.

Upstairs the netting draped over the beds has yellowed, but the rooms are as light and airy as before. Rocking chairs with dark accents in the blond wood are graceful and still. There are chamber pots and old spectacles and tortoiseshell hairpins. A row of hooks, black against the white walls, appears beside a filigreed tin matchbox holder, for lighting the oil lamps. In the children's room a pleated smock and a white bib lie across the bed. On the canopied crib is a pale blue-and-white coverlet with an embroidered ribbon containing the words of a German prayer: "May God protect your sleep with dreams of angels."

THE SITE OF
FIRST DREAMS

Janette Turner Hospital

*I*t was never just a house, it was where the world began, right there at 30 Station Street, Ringwood, in the city of Melbourne, Australia. There were wide verandas on three sides, gables, stained-glass borders on the living room windows, figured glass on the front door, a riotous garden with the scent of camellia, gardenia, and wisteria careless in the air.

It was a Federation house (built, that is, around 1901, the year of Australia's graduation from the status of British colony to its federation as an independent nation), the kind of house now much sought after and fetching prices unimaginable to my grandparents who scraped together a down payment in 1918, just as the First World War was ending. Grandpa Morgan was a railway ganger and Grandma Morgan had been the stationmistress at a railway siding to the rural northwest of Melbourne. The railway was their life, but now they wanted city schools for their brood of five sons and one daughter (my mother), and they found a house in what was then still the outskirts of Melbourne, opposite the railway line.

My mother was four years old when they moved in, and four was exactly the age of her second child (my little brother David) when she moved out. I was seven and can remember that momentous moving day, the tearful farewell to my grandparents, my father not long demobbed from the Second World War, my second brother Adrian just a baby-in-arms, all our possessions loaded into an old Bedford van for the thousand-mile trek to the north. In the steamy subtropical city of Brisbane (where I lived between the ages of seven and twenty-four), my father was to open an office for his company. We felt as though we were setting out for the edge of the world. Like all emigrants, we preserved an image of the place we had left. We cherished it as an icon. We made annual pilgrimages back. And so the Ringwood house, the house of the first seven years of my life and of many subsequent holidays, was always home for my mother and has always occupied huge territorial space in my own country of recall.

The front gate was directly opposite the Ringwood Railway Station, and trains rumbled across the tracks of my earliest dreams, prophesying travel. Faraway places threw shadows on my bedroom wall. Strangers got off the trains, walked over the footbridge from the station, and stepped into our lives. For Grandpa Morgan had magnetic powers—he exerted some sort of irresistible pull. He remains a legendary figure in memory, he lurks in my books: Morgan Morgan, ex–gold miner, former railway ganger, and in retirement, gardener extraordinaire. Trowel in hand, earth on his boots and fingers, his sumptuous dahlias rising around him like pin-tucked suns, he would glance up at the heads that bobbed along the top of the high white picket fence, flick, flick, flick between the palings, and it was instinctive with him, deep in his Welsh miner's blood and his railway ganger's soul, to offer greetings. "G'day, mate," he would nod. "Nice weather for a spot of leave." He had a voice like the bass melody of a Welsh hymn; with his sons, my uncles (all away at the front or in essential services), we had an all-in-the-family Male Voice Choir.

I would watch the way the tips of fence above the privet hedge made people switch themselves on and off, on off, on off, as they moved in blinking stripes until Grandpa spoke, and then they stopped. They leaned over the top of the gate. They chatted. They came in to inspect the dahlias. Often, they wore uniforms. They spoke somberly of the bombing of Darwin, the blackout, the curfew, Japanese submarines in Sydney Harbour, embarkation dates. Grandpa Morgan offered his dahlias and a listening ear.

So. In the beginning, it was never just a house.

In the beginning there was the war, there was black paint on the figured front-door glass (for the blackout, to foil the Japanese bombers), and there was wisteria, cascades of it, lavish cataracts of it.

It spills over the side veranda railing, the one that begins at my bedroom and marches straight as soldiers and airmen on parade to the front veranda steps. There the veranda makes a smart turn left, eyes front, chin up, left, right, Uncle Morg in khaki spats and his digger's hat, my father in his Royal Australian Air Force blues, the war kept out by the picket fence, left right, left right, front door and bay window to my left, Grandpa's roses on my right, here's the corner where the living room fireplace is, mark time, leeeeft . . . turn! quick march, past MummyandDaddy's bedroom window (though Daddy doesn't sleep here, he is Away, he is in the RAAF making parachutes that will float like dandelion fluff between the Japanese planes). Only Mummy sleeps here, in MummyandDaddy's room, and sometimes Auntie Ann when she visits with my cousin John because Uncle Morgan is also Away. He is in Egypt (so Auntie

Ann thinks from the letters, though Uncle Morg has to write in riddles, that's a rule, on account of the Germans and on account of the Rats of Tobruk).

It is difficult now to sort out the memories that belong to the time when my father was Away from the time when he Came Back. When I think of the Ringwood house, my father is both There and Not There all the time. But certainly, my mother and my grandparents were always there. Those first seven years seem to me a period of undifferentiated happiness, when I was queen of a large domain. The wraparound veranda was endless, a playground for all seasons. I remember the beat of rain on the bull-nosed iron roof, a sound rarely heard now but still capable of catapulting me straight into bliss.

Beyond the veranda was Grandpa's kingdom: the lawn at the back of the house, the vegetable garden, the cottage garden of shrubs and flowers, and most important of all, the dahlia garden, set apart and demarcated by hedges, a place to wonder at.

Beyond all this manicured space was the "chook house"—our Australian idiom for a chicken coop; a cockatoo in a cage, famous for saying, "Hello, cocky!" when spoken to, and infamous for taking a savage bite from my three-year-old hand; Grandpa's work shed; and then the jungle, a great tangled unkempt wilderness of a place through which my little brother David and I blazed secret trails to hidden cubby houses and caves. I have often thought that this rank space behind the sheds, full of the lure of the primeval and the unknown, had much to do with my later love of medieval literature, with my instinctive interest in Beowulf's dark world of dragons in the fens. Our private jungle seemed without limits, and unknowable. And yet, I have come to realize with astonishment, the entire property—house, garden, sheds, jungle—occupied a bit less than half an acre, and the "wilderness" must have been a minuscule twenty-five feet by twenty. I know this, and yet I cannot believe it. I can close my eyes and smell nettles and feel the swish of tall grass above my head as David and I listen for tigers. Grandma's call from the kitchen is dangerous miles away.

Time curves, Einstein said. Distance and space are elastic. This seems plain common sense to me, or to anyone who, after long absence, has traveled back to the site of first dreams. The places of childhood contract for each year away, it's a geometric regression, I am sure of it.

If the jungle was my own magic kingdom and the garden was Grandpa's, Grandma's place of sorcery was the kitchen. Ah, what a place! One whole wall was a warm recessed cave, lined with firebrick, occupied by the cast-iron wood stove, a black dragon of a thing, certainly alive, breathing steam through its nostrils and flame through its many mouths.

I remember the deft way Grandma would hook the iron lever into the cooking openings: lifting a black-iron circle, letting the fire leap from the belly of the stove, throwing in some more wood chips, slotting the cover back into place, moving one pot over it, edging another farther away. What an art form it was, regulating the heat on those old monsters. Stoves had personality in those days. They had to be fed and cleaned and cared for. Their ashes were removed every night, their diet was the first task of the day. They had to be spoken to and treated with respect. They had to be known intimately, their idiosyncrasies understood, their peccadillos indulged. They knew their own mistresses and answered only to them. As I write of this, forty-five years later and a hemisphere away, my room fills with the fragrance of fresh-baked bread and cinnamon rolls and the delectable crackle of roast chook. Kettles whistle, pokers gleam, Grandma Morgan croons softly to the stove and lifts the corner of her apron and uses it as potholder to move a cauldron full of lamb and fresh garden herbs.

Water, in a great kettle, was always on the boil and the bricked cave above the stove was foggy with steam. There was no hot running water, and no electric water heater either, until my father installed one above the kitchen sink not long before we left for Brisbane. I can remember the steady relay of pitchers and kettles to the bathroom, across a covered lobby from the kitchen.

The bathroom: There was a tub with clawed feet and a huge mahogany dresser with a black-spotted mirror and a marble counter on which stood a great enameled washbowl. For the children, I remember, there was a stool. When I climbed onto it, I could just see my face in the speckled mirror. My mother would pour a kettle of boiling water directly onto the bar of Velvet soap in the enamel washbowl and the steam would rise and stroke my cheeks.

There was, at the foot of the bathtub, an ancient dragon of a heater, cousin to the kitchen stove, a cylindrical construction of gleaming chrome that went right to the ceiling and through it, an object treated with the utmost caution and respect. Rituals for lighting it were so shrouded in risk and secrecy that I never actually saw the incendiary act. No one except the fire lighter himself (either my grandfather or my father) was permitted in the bathroom during the fearful task. I do remember that the ritual involved long newspaper tapers fed into the dragon's mouth, and that the mouth belched and was given to small explosions.

There was an outhouse, of course, an exotic thing, a place of mystery and adventure beyond the vegetable garden, beyond the lawn, under the spreading plum tree. Last thing before bed, someone (usually Grandpa) had to take me "down the back." Grandpa would stand outside, under the plum tree and the stars, and whistle "Amazing Grace" or "Men of Harlech" or some rousing Welsh hymn to reassure me while I sat on the smooth pine bench in the dark. There was no light in the outhouse; only the glow of Grandpa's presence, the smell of the plum tree, the sharp tang of the box of sawdust from which one scooped to cover one's traces.

See, Grandpa would say, one hand holding mine, the other pointing, as we walked back up the garden path. We navigated by the stars and the light from the kitchen window. Do you see? Grandpa would crouch down and point, and my eyes would follow the line of his arm. There's the Southern Cross. And those are the two pointer stars. First you look for the pointers, and then you can see the cross.

Writing now, I am startled to recall that not until 1961, after Grandpa had died and Grandma was alone in the house, did her children club together to have a flush toilet installed, to have the bathroom properly plumbed and properly joined to the house, to replace the old copper with a washing machine. I do know that Grandma loved the ease and comfort these luxuries gave, but I also know that until they were provided, it never occurred to her—vibrant, seemingly tireless, deeply contented and joyful as she always was—that she was in any way deprived. Do I pine for exhausting laundry chores or nightly backyard trips? Not exactly. Yet sometimes I find myself wondering if it isn't we who are a little deprived. It is certain what we gained in convenience, we lost in enchantment.

If I wander about the house—past the ice chest, past the mahogany sideboard and into the dining room—I can finger Grandma's intricate crochet work and hold her Royal Albert china up to the light. It is formal, elegant, scattered now through the dining rooms of married grandchildren around the world.

I can see those grandchildren still, my many Morgan cousins, underfoot and everywhere, in the living room, crowded around Grandpa's chair in front of the fire listening to stories, crammed into the big bay window watching the trains, chasing each other around the veranda. At birthdays and at Christmas, the kitchen, the dining room, the living room, the wide verandas were always brimful of aunts and uncles and cousins, and that time is still paradise to me, it comes back instantly with the smell of plum pudding.

Oh, plum pudding! It was Grandma's speciality, a monster of a thing wrapped in an old sheet and steamed in the copper, a little round world full of plums and dates and raisins and sixpenny bits, all drowned in custard. Of course it was crazy, reproducing a Dickensian Christmas while the down-under sun peeled the paint off the iron roof and the thermometer registered 100 degrees Fahrenheit in the veranda shade. It was crazy, but that never occurred to us, and we wouldn't have cared if it had. I believe the trains in Ringwood Station came to a halt purely to catch a whiff of Grandma's plum pudding. It was divine.

The Ringwood Railway Station and its footbridge are still right where they always were, but the house is not. In 1965, the year of my marriage, Grandma Morgan moved to Brisbane. She moved into my Brisbane bedroom when I moved out, and the house in Ringwood was sold to the neighboring Methodist Church. For some years it was used as a hostel for recent immigrants, and I liked to think that our family ghosts offered peace to those new arrivals. It was not until 1985 that I was back in Melbourne again, and I made my pilgrimage the first chance I got.

Shock.

Where the house had been was now a parking lot.

I felt as though a part of me had been hacked off with a cleaver. I was afraid of disgracing myself in public, I was afraid of sobbing, I was afraid of alarming the people mechanically entering and leaving their cars. And then, heedless, I began to pace the parking lot. Here's where the jungle began, I thought. Here's where the dahlias were. And oh, here's the plum tree, a miracle—still here, still here!—beneath which Grandpa stood and whistled Welsh hymns while the Southern Cross kept guard.

Last year, 1992, marked the fiftieth wedding anniversary of my parents (February) and my own fiftieth birthday (November). I found myself in Melbourne again, a visiting professor at a university in that city, and I gave my parents (who still live in Brisbane) a trip "home" as a golden-anniversary gift. Pilgrimage. My husband and I (who have lived far away for many years, mainly in the United States and in Canada) drove my parents out to Ringwood. It is no longer a suburb on the outskirts; the city has long since engulfed it and spread far beyond. My parents and I walked between cars in the parking lot that used to be 30 Station Street, locating the outhouse and the chook house and Grandma's stove. We stroked the great plum tree that had seen it all. We believed we could detect the bumps where the veranda footings had been. And the veranda posts and spindles and finials raised their ghostly selves and promised: The past cannot be destroyed while memory lasts and love preserves.

My Mother and Mendocino

Phyllis Theroux

ifteen years ago my mother decided to simplify her life. Putting into storage everything that wouldn't fit into the back of her car, she left Carmel-by-the-Sea, California, and headed north to another town barely bigger than the cabin she rented in it. Mendocino.

Mendocino has poppies, whales spouting off the headlands, and a small collection of Victorian-era cottages on a bluff overlooking the Pacific. My mother loved it at once.

"I can lean outside my kitchen window and look at the ocean and pick blackberries at the same time," she wrote to me.

"Guess what?" she reported in another note. "On my morning walk yesterday, I saw a deer standing on the headlands, knee-deep in fog."

My mother has an artist's eye for these kinds of physical details.

Soon I had a small stack of exultant letters from her—filled with important developments involving sunsets and abalone shells and thick mats of nasturtiums that hang out of weather-beaten window boxes. Finally, I could not stand it any longer and decided to see Mendocino—and my mother—for myself.

In one important way, my mother's life and my own have gone in opposite directions. At sixteen, her parents put her on a train in New York City and sent her out to visit an aunt in Santa Cruz, California. She never came back, having fallen in love twice over—with the uncrowded, sunburned hills that rolled down to the sea and with my father. My life has inclined the other way.

From an early age I dreamed of escaping California, which seemed like nothing surrounded by nothing, unless you wanted to make a case for Nevada, which I still find hard to do. I longed for Manhattan towers, not redwood trees, solid ground, not earthquakes. And since the age of eighteen, when I went east to college, I have lived my life on the opposite coast, with short visits and long telephone calls being enough to make up the difference.

Then, around the same time my mother moved to Mendocino something entirely unexpected happened. I began to miss California with the deep atavistic longing one can only feel for one's childhood home—or one's mother. The timing was serendipitous. Because I am the oldest of six children, and time alone with my mother was rare, my trip to Mendocino was my first opportunity to have her all to myself.

She is a small, silver-haired woman with Gallic features. ("I think my nose would do very well in France," she once commented.) Every year she pares a few more pounds off her now quite birdlike frame, which is slightly disconcerting; it is difficult to watch one's mother dissolve in increments. But she still walks with the light step of a young girl, wears Kate-Hepburn-in-the-country clothes, and is full of schemes for as yet unmarketed ways to combine capitalism with creative fulfillment, like starting a mail-order lotus bulb company. Her eyes are her best feature—wide and doelike, the eyes of a dreamer.

"I don't know," she once confessed to a friend. "Maybe my ideas are just pie in the sky."

"No, they aren't," he protested. "You just need a longer fork."

I had been in Mendocino only one hour before I understood why my mother was there. The town was full of "long fork" people—poets and potters, sea-urchin divers married to dowsers. My mother, who had lived for years as a proper housewife with a station wagon and a 1950s husband, exulted in the freedom to live as herself.

I understood something else as well—the value of having a mother who had not stopped taking chances and looking at life with delight. It was comforting to know that I was not at the head of the parade, that there was an older, wiser woman moving in front of me. And now she lived in a town that was as comfortable as her own sneakers. With its brilliant light and sea-scrubbed air, Mendocino was the right place for her to be.

I came to stay for two weeks. We devoured every minute of it, but slowly, like a delicious loaf of bread, one day or slice at a time. We took long walks by the ocean, sat up late at night talking, spreading out our lives, like a set of expandable blueprints on the kitchen table. In between I slept, made blackberry pies, and thought of new questions I wanted to ask, like "How did the relationship between my mother and her mother differ from our own?"

We had never had such a long, uninterrupted row of days together. And we spent a lot of them talking about the past, stitching together our separate memories, creating one quilt out of two lives. In a culture where many mothers are too busy to be mothers until their own daughters are grown, I felt fortunate to have been given a reprieve—and a town as well.

Mendocino has become almost as much a part of me as my

own mother. I return often to be recharged. I fill my eyes with wild poppies, blue herons, and the Pacific Ocean, and I fill my soul with the kind of light and hope that only a mother who continues to dream can provide. It takes about a year to empty them. Then I head west again.

THE TANGLE AND THE BOG

Suzanne Berne

wice now, I have almost gone back to visit my grandfather's summer house in North Chatham, Massachusetts— a shady, quiet place I dream of on long bus rides and on warm nights when I can't sleep. But each time I've turned around just as I've gotten close, worried that what I might find there could diminish what I remember.

From the first, my grandfather's house provided a green latitude I have never known anywhere else; it seemed a place of met needs, an impression I realize now that he cultivated, the way some people cultivate English accents. I used to imagine that our whole family would be stranded at his house someday and all our wants would be perfectly satisfied. Living alone year after year, perhaps my grandfather imagined the same thing.

Around the house curled a carefully tended lawn, unfolding in back to display a mown expanse, separated from the apple trees and blueberry bushes by ornamental brick walls and trimmed privet hedges. Stone benches scattered here and there.

The lawn was pleasant but unambiguous, good for a game of statues, occasionally good for spotting a mother quail in the evening toddling earnestly across the grass with a line of chicks, little thumbs in tow. Mourning doves gave their sad wooing call from deep inside the apple trees: "Be-be-loved," they seemed to cry, "be-loved."

On the north side of the house grew an uncut thicket of wild grape, blackberry, sumac, scrub oak, and poison ivy. This wilderness, so closely neighboring the manicured back lawn with its roses and hydrangea bushes, enticed and seduced me: It suggested secrets, peril, the romance of being lost. I remember this part of my grandfather's land being known as the Tangle. Through the Tangle he had cut paths, narrow, prickly paths that required shoes, even socks—paths that wound through the overgrowth like tunnels.

My grandfather would strike out ahead of me with his cane and his brown leather walking shoes, while I dangled behind flirting with the idea of disappearing forever a hundred yards from the patio where my parents sat drinking their minty iced tea. The paths must have been cut in only two or three directions, but I remember winding through them for hours, losing my grandfather around a bend, finding him beside a hemlock tree, losing him again when I bent to examine a cracked robin's egg, a few thin field mouse bones. What had happened here? A flash of teeth, a blur of wings. The leaves stirred and rustled around me.

That disappearance could be quixotic and impermanent was only part of what I discovered at my grandfather's house. Exploring the far end of the Tangle one day, I came upon a dense stand of scrub pine that descended sharply into a margin of blackberry bushes. If you persevered, fending off thorny branches and sliding down the incline, you tumbled out, as unexpectedly as Alice from her rabbit hole, into a wide, watery expanse of flooded cranberry bog.

Cranberries had not been harvested there for more than ten years by the time I first saw it. A small wooden shed stood to one side, still containing, I imagined, rakes, trowels, and rotting hemp baskets. The bog itself was entirely transformed. Instead of resembling a marshy field, it had become a shallow, oval pond with a little path winding around the edges, cattails bristling at either end, ringed by sedge and shadbush, hidden from roads and houses by a thick band of pine and scrub oak. In the early morning, when a primordial mist steamed up from the bog, bitterns cried—a lost gulping sound. Gazing at the water I saw tadpoles skitter into the reeds, freakish of shadows. Wildflowers stippled the banks, woven into the grass and the reeds. Midges swarmed over the bog's surface and swallows dipped over the water in the evening.

A strange, soggy, teeming place, the bog was a world of busy self-absorption. It implied that one should have an activity. For my tenth birthday I asked for binoculars and spent hours spying out grackles, finches, titmice, even once, in a streak of brilliant blue, an indigo bunting, all of which I recorded in a green notebook titled "What I Have Seen." Woodpeckers drummed distantly in the woods. I practiced whistling bobwhite calls.

The only human being I encountered regularly at the bog was an elderly woman named Mrs. Johnson who lived behind a breakwater right on Pleasant Bay. In the mornings she might be seen carrying a small wicker basket, wearing sneakers and a faded sun hat. She gathered beach grasses, berries, and wildflowers to use as dyes for wool she carded and spun herself. Mrs. Johnson reminded me of a witch. The benign kind, who lived peacefully in the days when people got their medicine from the fields and hills, their clothing from animals, their entertainment and occupation from the weather, the water, and the land—but still a witch. She had a witch's fine eye for economy, collecting what most people would hardly notice. I romantically imagined her house as a driftwood lean-to decorated with tiny bleached bird skulls, seashells, and salt-spray roses, furnished by ship-wreck, thatched with eelgrass and dried seaweed.

Whenever I came upon Mrs. Johnson she was usually bending over a clump of sedge or a stalk of goldenrod with a pair of clippers in her hand, her basket on her arm. She wore cardigans of her own design, knitted from her own wool. Once, when she invited me to tea at her cottage (disappointingly neat with chintz-covered easy chairs), she showed me tapestries hung on her walls, woven with the colors of our bog. She must have been around seventy. I still think of her as much older, as someone who knew everything about the bog, who had seen the cran-berries, had seen what was there before cranberries. What were witches, after all, but people who knew more than everyone else?

And Mrs. Johnson, with her loom full of grasses and weeds, was the first artist I had ever met. A true artist, who transformed the colors of her walks into something she could touch, read, give away. Memory hung enchanted on her walls, woven from the sea, bogs, hurricanes, floods, summers with no rain: For sev-enty years she had watched winter turn to spring turn to sum-mer turn to fall. And she had kept all of those things. I left her cottage with a sense of panic I didn't understand for years.

Scrambling back through the blackberry bushes, through the scrub pines and back into the Tangle's labyrinth, I always paused for a moment to adjust myself before bursting out into full view of my grandfather's house. The worlds of the Tangle and the bog had their particular behavioral demands. They were not the world of carefully mowed lawns and iced tea on the patio, to which I had to return if I wanted to be fed. And a certain recognition of this difference was required. The bog and the Tangle were districts where I could be as uncomprehending as I needed to be. The lawn demanded more calculation. I had to explain, for instance, how I had managed to get pine needles in my hair and mud on my blouse, why I had missed lunch and the cousins' visit. Before going into the house I caught my breath. The lawn was zoned for scrutiny and display, for evasion and excuses, not particularly for watching.

Once, not long before he died, I asked my grandfather why he hadn't cut down the Tangle and made it into lawn instead. He said, "Because I needed a few paths for walking, that's why."

I wondered about his answer for a long time before I realized what he meant. A path is a way through. It leads somewhere not distinguishable from the point of departure. You begin one place and journey to another, a different place from where you began. A path is a story you walk. If everything can be seen easily, what's the need of a path? My grandfather knew. Everyone needs some paths, some stories, otherwise no one could go anywhere.

It still seems to me that my grandfather's house was a place of met needs: I had it all in one place—shelter, exposure, company, wildness, industry, drama, mystery. There has been nowhere I've lived since that married the elements of the world so nearly. Or at least this is the story I have followed, perhaps a story my grandfather left for me to find.

Which is why, now long after his land was sold to a developer, I am afraid to go back. What if ornamental brick walls ring the bog? What if my grandfather's paths are now trim yards and neat doorsteps?

Lately I have been weaving together memories for myself, memories of walking, memories of bog light, the slide of reeds against my calves, the marshy, salty wind that blows pine needles onto the grass. All into stories to be saved, hoarded. Here is one more.

This moment I was just visiting my grandfather's house, fingering the cracked bindings of books in the living room bookshelves, smelling the musty smell of damp rugs and old pine walls, tasting salt. Feeling the grass from the lawn turn from tender carpet beneath my bare feet to sharp stubble as I step into the mouth of the Tangle. Watching the late afternoon sift into the cattails at the eastern edge of the bog, a breeze skimming the water. Evening is coming on. The trees fill with last calls. A gull screams overhead. Light turns blue. My heart is riven with the impossibilities I planned to accomplish at ten, at twelve—the love I planned to have, the brilliance, the soar. There, still.

Oxford in My Time

Caroline Seebohm

*I*n my day at Oxford, there were five male undergraduates to every one female, a ratio that would make any maiden's heart beat faster. Mine was hyperactive for the full three years I was there. (Oxford's undergraduate degree course takes three years, unless you are studying Classics. The school's thirteenth-century founders no doubt thought three years were enough in that heady atmosphere, and they were right.) When I was there, most of the male undergraduates were two years older than the females, having spent two years in the National Service after leaving school. Thus the men not only predominated, but they were also older, more sophisticated, more—*experienced*. What was a poor girl to do?

Easy. Sit in the Bodleian Library with one's books and wait. The invitations were slow to take off at first, as the candidates squared off, whispered to each other, estimated potential. My first, I recall, was slipped under my Oxford equivalent of a Trapper-Keeper notebook with such sleight of hand that for a moment I did not realize what had happened. I opened the slip of paper carefully, feeling sure my cheeks were betraying my inner turmoil. "Let's meet for coffee at four this afternoon at the Cadena," the note said in an almost illiterate and arrogant scrawl, the affectation of Old Etonians. I looked around furtively for the sender, who was by this time back in his seat and gazing nonchalantly out the window. Fair, nice eyes, good chin, all right for starters. I gave him an almost imperceptible nod, which, I was pleased to note, provoked in return a gratifying rush of color to the cheek.

Thus one became a fixture at the Cadena, a second-rate cafe above Carfax, the central hub of the city of Oxford. Notes would fly like Wagner's Woodbird song between the desks of the Bodleian, directing us women to further adventures. Coffee at the Cadena soon progressed to tea and crumpets and, later still, champagne, in the glorious college rooms allocated to the male undergraduates of the university. Of the twenty-two men's colleges at Oxford in my time, Christ Church, New College, and Trinity were the Big Three in terms of social and aesthetic desirability. Balliol was the choice of intellectuals, where along with the crumpets would come heavy discussions about Nietzsche, Kant, and the "meaning of meaning." Worcester had the best gardens as well as a strong theatrical bent for those destined for the West End stage. We never entered Queen's, in spite of its handsome facade fronting High Street. Queen's men seemed all to be geographers, regarded universally and inexplicably as the lowest form of intelligent life.

No one spent much time in the neo-Gothic or red brick institutions assigned to us gender-latecomers. The women's colleges, built in the late nineteenth-century when women started being admitted to Oxford, were typical of Victorian and Edwardian architecture, rarely inspiring the spirit to poetic expression as did the four-hundred-year-old masterpieces inhabited by our male colleagues. (Women were finally admitted as members of these hallowed bastions in 1974.) Yet even our colleges had some form of rating. Mine, Somerville, was considered bluestocking (I was surely the exception that proved the rule). Lady Margaret Hall contained the debutante types, and St. Anne's, St. Hugh's, and St. Hilda's never attained rating status at all in those ruthlessly discriminating days.

The high point of each of my three years was the Commemoration Ball, or Commem—the June party that ended the summer term. Commems were held in different colleges each year, and the colleges chosen went all out to make their party the biggest, grandest, most memorable anyone had ever attended. Tents, champagne, food, music, punting on the river, dancing till dawn with the undergraduate you had fixed your hopes on all year long—this was the pinnacle of the Oxford experience. Never mind that your particular partner's only dance step was a rhythmic stomping on your satin pumps, or that your student of choice preferred to throw up in flower beds instead of bringing you breakfast at sunrise. Walking through the floodlit quadrangles of Christ Church, St. John's, Lincoln, or Magdalen, with stars above, music in the sky, scented flowers in the air, you knew you were in a private magical world that would never be yours again.

Matthew Arnold called Oxford "that sweet city with her dreaming spires." Sweet indeed. As for an education, well, I may not have benefited much from the books I studied, but the friendships I made have lasted to this day. Thanks to Oxford, I learned how to stay afloat in a punt, how to toast a mean crumpet, and how to tell a Balliol man to get lost. What better training for life could there be?

A GENTLY

HAUNTED HOUSE

Susan Schneider

oon after my daughter, my friend Jessie, and I moved into the bottom half of a four-story Victorian house on a busy street in Jersey City, I noticed we occasionally received mail addressed to Elaine Hoos.

Our landlord enlightened us: Elaine and her sister, Mignon, had lived in our house their entire lives. A portrait of a rather stern-looking gentleman, which we found in a closet, proved to be the sisters' father, who had been mayor of this city at the turn of the century. This struck us as an interesting piece of lore, but what we came to realize was that the Hoos house, as we began calling it, was . . . well, not exactly haunted, but certainly inhabited in some way by the two sisters.

All three of us have perceived this in our own ways. Jessie, a friend of twenty years, is deeply intuitive. In the front parlor, which is now her bedroom, she once felt something brush her cheek, ever so softly, as she awoke one morning. She swore to me it wasn't her cat, Obie, who usually sleeps with her. She also senses that one of the sisters favored the front parlor as her sitting room. (It is a beautiful, high-ceilinged room with an ornate marble fireplace, a carved medallion, and a brass chandelier; a tarnished brass picture hanger in the shape of a snake was left on the molding, as if a picture had just been taken down.) "The sisters are here," Jessie assured me. "Of course, it could just be my feeling that this is the sisters' world. But I think they're holding onto it in some way."

My daughter, India, takes off her shoes in the parlor because she doesn't want to wake up the "nice witches sleeping downstairs." She isn't exactly scared, but sometimes I catch her listening intently as she tiptoes past me in her socks. She's had two birthday parties here, and the house has accommodated the stampede of children through its spacious rooms. I've wondered if the presence of a little girl echoes the childhoods of the sisters—India is certainly the first child living here in seventy or so years. I like to think that Elaine and Mignon find her, and the children who visit us, invigorating.

I may not have had any actual encounters with spirits, but I do feel as if I'm a guest in this house, with the sisters my hostesses, graciously offering me temporary shelter. Old people in the neighborhood told us how years and years ago, the sisters hosted musical evenings here, with the doors between back and front parlors thrown open. One sister (we don't know which) was known for her exquisite piano playing. Neither sister ever married, although the story is that one (again we don't know which) had been disappointed in love.

These tales all enhance the idea of their presence, as do other gentle little reminders. On the very day I sat at my completely modern computer to write about the house, a circular arrived, addressed to Elaine Hoos. It's been months since anything for Elaine has landed in the mailbox, I thought. Why this day? Out of curiosity, I opened the envelope; it was only a form letter from a realtor looking for prospective clients. I strongly felt the real message was: Remember us.

We do remember them, and we think Elaine and Mignon are pleased to have us in their wonderful house. We also feel we are in some way connected to them. Jessie and I are more like sisters than friends, and in this house we seem to be carrying on a tradition of close ties between women. Both of us feel protected, or watched over, by the sisters—and we want to return the courtesy for as long as we are their guests.

Shortly before we moved in, our landlord cut down a tree in the front yard to make way for a parking place for the upstairs tenants. People in the neighborhood say, shaking their heads, "That tree was special. It was the only old tree on the street. It set the house apart." One elderly woman says the tree had been planted to commemorate Mignon's birth, while another tree in the backyard was for Elaine. The one out in back is still flourishing, making the loss of the other seem even crueler. In the sisters' house, we sense their sadness. The astonishing thing is that, over a year later, people in the neighborhood are still heartbroken; it is as if something alive and vital, bridging past and present, had been removed from our midst.

This old house on Summit Avenue will always belong to Elaine and Mignon. And the past. But we can be good guests and guardians while we are here; we can, in small ways, make up for the loss of their tree. Last summer, while reviving the backyard garden that had gone to seed, Jessie replanted a rosebush her mother had given her shortly before she died. Both of us hoped against hope that it would take. It did. Those big, pale yellow blooms in the once neglected garden were a fragrant, living sign that the spirits of a beloved mother and two unknown women whose house we occupy are present, and at home with us. It seemed to be their gift back to us for nurturing the house—something alive and beautiful, keeping us connected, as the old elm did, to other times and to people who lived before us.

MEDITATIONS AMONG THE PEONIES

Susan Allen Toth

*I*t is a chilly, showery April morning at our cabin. Tucking dirt-stained rain pants into my bright-green garden boots, I adjust my soaked rain cape over a shirt that is already damp and clammy. I don't bother putting up my hood—the first gust of rainy wind would only whip it off. As I head toward the door, clutching the newly arrived box of daylilies, my daughter Jenny looks at me in disbelief. "You're going out there, *now?*" she asks. "Out there in the *rain?* Can't those plants wait?"

On a hot July afternoon, I spray mosquito repellent over my shirt before I slip into it. Then I lather the smelly stuff over my face and neck. Already I'm starting to perspire a little in my jeans, but I swell up so much with the tiniest nibble that I don't dare change to shorts. Glancing out the window at the bright sun, I jam a once-white canvas hat on my head. Jenny looks up from the sofa, where she is reading. "You're going outside in this *heat?* Are you nuts? Can't the weeding wait?"

Yes, I want to tell her, maybe the weeding can wait. But I can't. Of course, Jenny wouldn't understand. She is not a gardener—at least, not yet. Now a studio-arts major, she has recently begun painting landscapes with intense concentration and fervor. Loving color, line, shape, and texture, how could she not someday want a garden?

I see why Jenny thinks I'm a little crazy. When I first started my garden on a wooded Wisconsin bluff overlooking the Mississippi, James, my architect husband, measured out a trapezoidal plot, about eight by fourteen feet, near the house. "I'm not going to have much of a garden," I told him, "because we'll mostly be here only on weekends and vacations, and I don't want to bother."

But I had not perceived the insidious effect of suddenly having so much space. In the city houses where I'd lived before marrying James, I had always been restricted to modest backyard gardens. Now, however, I could go berserk. It did not happen all at once. At first I confined myself to the laid-out plot. But the following fall, I decided to put some daffodils just beyond the edges of the garden. When I no longer had any room for new plants, I began extending my boundaries. As I dug and excavated, foot by foot, the garden grew larger. A mown meadow, a weedy prairie-grass bank, and a small wild clearing soon blossomed.

Last spring James finally spoke up. "Susan," he said, with a worried tone that makes him sound almost angry, "this has got to stop. I love your garden, but I absolutely don't want to work in it, and you know it's impossible to find anyone else around here to help. You're already out there from morning to night. Enough!"

But for an avid gardener, there is no enough. I know what will happen next winter, when the first specialty-grower catalogs arrive in the mail. Looking at my frozen, snow-covered garden, I'll easily convince myself I can fit in a few new irises, peonies, or daylilies. In the catalog from Gilbert H. Wild and Son, Inc., in Sarcoxie, Missouri, the copywriter composes brief, but absolutely irresistible, descriptions of hundreds of different daylilies. I want them all. "Pink Taffy . . . Under sun this apricot pink self mellows to smooth orchid pink with a glowing tangerine heart; raised orchid ribs." "Oakleigh . . . Rolled back pale peach with orchid overlay under cloudy day." "Heather Green . . . Clear apple blossom; vibrant green lightens some but holds throughout day." Who could resist an apple-blossom daylily? An orchid overlay? A glowing tangerine heart?

I am a greedy gardener, but I am not just obsessed about acquisition. I enjoy the whole sensuous process—digging, preparing the soil, mixing peat moss and sand into my clay soil, planting, mulching, fertilizing, even pulling weeds. In spring, as I lie in bed at night, planning what I'll do the next day in the garden, I am sometimes so excited I have a hard time falling asleep.

Tomorrow, I think, I'll uncover the peonies. I'll cultivate around the daylilies, rake in some bonemeal, and trowel out any weeds that have sprouted during the winter. Then I'll prune the dead wood on my shrub roses. Perhaps I'll even have time to attack that garden path by the shed: It is so overgrown it has almost disappeared. I imagine sinking my small Dutch hoe into the soft earth, turning up and tossing away intruding clods of grass, neatly slicing a new edge, and finally pitching fresh wood chips over the rescued and widened path. I can hardly wait to bring the garden back to life again.

Part of my deep pleasure in gardening probably comes from my instinctive belief that I am somehow clearing away chaos to make room for order. Where weeds and tangled grasses once flourished, I can make daylilies bloom. In a scrappy patch of tall grasses where I once hesitated to walk, fearing poison ivy, prickly bush and burrs, soft wood-chip paths now gently lead me in and among clumps of flowers.

I know Thoreau's pride and delight when he wrote in *Walden* that he was "making the earth say beans instead of grass." Except I want to make the earth sing, and I want it to sing in colors. For I am clearly not a gardener with much sense of structure. I know that a garden is supposed to have bones, a firm sense of delineated shapes. Before creating Sissinghurst, their famous English garden, Harold Nicolson and his wife, Vita Sackville-West, thoughtfully planned each section. They considered geometric boundaries, sight lines, and balanced proportions. Within each section, they discussed together just what plants to place where. When Nicolson laid out spring plantings in small squares around a row of lime trees, he first drew infinitely detailed sketches on graph paper, specifying each primrose, each tulip, each clump of bluebells, each daffodil. The result—as I saw one sunny April morning at Sissinghurst—was breathtaking.

My own garden simply grew up around my feet. I have few principles of design—except More Is Good, and Even More Is Better. Insatiably curious about new plants, I add them recklessly. This is easy in early spring, when the first green shoots seem quite small and manageable. Later, as growing plants elbow and rustle against each other, I have to search for a bare brown spot of earth. Could I jam some purple coneflower in here? Where could I transplant my burgeoning lavender sea aster? Should I make room by getting rid of this pathetic lupine, which only managed one feeble stalk of bloom last summer?

My attempts at design have to allow for a tender heart. I hate uprooting plants. Although it never resembled the picture in my catalog, my failing lupine had once flourished aloft several dense pink spikes of flowers. My solution was to give the aging plant one more chance, moving it to a semiwild section where it could expire unnoticed. I wrote sympathetically on its metal marker, "Pathetic Lupine." It repaid me by briefly reviving into a final bloom before it sank into recycling on the compost pile.

Although I tend to ignore perspective, balance, and other elements of basic design, I delight in a bright scarlet monarda or a sky-blue iris or a black hollyhock. I intellectually understand the place of foliage plants in a garden—hostas, ferns, artemisia—but I cannot love them as I do plants that unfold or burst or flame into lavish color.

Every summer evening when we are at our cabin, James and I take a short stroll after supper around the garden so I can point out each day's new bloom. We pay as much attention to a single velvety-purple delphinium as if it were a whole English perennial border. During the daylily season, we marvel at the subtle differences of each flower: lemon-yellow shading into a green throat, golden streaks highlighting ruby-red petals, ivory ribs against soft apricot.

Sometimes color seems to spill over into fragrance, as if the two floated into the air together. In spring, James and I take turns bending over our peonies and breathing deeply. Their hauntingly rich, penetrating perfume is indistinguishable from the cherry-red or candy-pink or frosting-white blooms. No wonder one catalog describes a peony named "Raspberry Sundae" like this: "Take a heap of vanilla ice cream, liberally apply raspberry topping to drip over petals, and this variety appears." It takes more than one sense to appreciate a peony.

But perhaps I am most struck by the tiniest flowers. A gardener spends a lot of time on his or her knees. (Kipling knew this when he wrote: "Gardens are not made,/By singing—'Oh, how beautiful!' and sitting in the shade.") When I am working a few inches from the soil, I have a chance to admire the randomly creeping clumps of Myosotis, old-fashioned forget-me-not. Myosotis is profligate with minute blue flowers, each with a yellow eye that shines like a speck-sized sun. The blossoms are so intricate that it is almost impossible for me not to think, when I see this small plant, of the complexity and beauty of the rest of the natural world. Although I nurture this Myosotis as best I can, I did not create it, and I alone do not make it grow. I do not believe it would be easy to be both an atheist and a gardener.

Meditative time is rare in my life, and that is another reason I treasure my garden. Once I am in my muddy jeans, inching my way along a closely examined strip of earth, I am so far from my telephone that even if I could hear it ring, for a few moments I might not remember what it was. As I dig, pull, pat, and firm the soil around my plants, I think of very little except what I am doing. Perhaps I wonder if this sprouting hollyhock will be pink or red, or whether I should yank out more intrusive evening primrose, or where I could wedge in another white phlox. But mostly I just keep working.

Working in a garden has a timeless quality. Inside my house, I am uneasily aware that the living room I've straightened today will be messy tomorrow. The beet-orange soup I spent an hour to concoct will disappear even sooner. But in my garden, although my plants will bloom and wither away, they will return given decent weather, loving care, and luck. As a gardener, I become part of a process.

Sometimes, when the cold wind begins to bend the last faded mums to the ground, I find myself in a last-chance flurry of planting. My order of daffodils and tulips never arrives early enough, and as James builds a fire indoors, I huddle in the garden with my sharp-edged bulb planter and a bag of bonemeal. My fingers are sometimes numb with cold, and my back hurts. But I am happy.

As I sink my last bulbs into the ground, I always remember E. B. White's preface to *Onward and Upward in the Garden.* This collection of gardening essays by his wife, Katharine S. White, was published several years after her death. Recalling how she planned and directed the final laying out of her bulb garden, E. B. White concluded: "As the years went by and age overtook her, there was something comical yet touching in her bedraggled appearance on this awesome occasion—the small, hunched-over figure, her studied absorption in the implausible notion that there would be yet another spring, oblivious to the ending of her own days, which she knew perfectly well was near at hand, sitting there with her detailed chart under those dark skies in the dying October, calmly plotting the resurrection." E. B. White knew why gardening can't wait.

HOUSEGUESTS

Kim Waller

Because the lilac was in bloom, and I was browning stew meat, I opened the front door wide to let the sweetness of lilacs waft through the house. In the country, this is risky. You never know what will wander in, from bees to raccoons.

One weekend, a high-pitched bickering coming from the dining room turned out to be a pair of barn swallows perched on a corner of the table, avidly debating the pros and cons of nesting right there. She was all nervous complaint; he was all patience. Obviously, the house didn't measure up: In a blue flash, they veered out the back door as expertly as they had shussed in the front.

This weekend, as I turned the meat in the pan, our neighbor's aggressively friendly red setter, Vixen, danced in, muddy-pawed and sopping from a dip in our pond, wriggling her hindquarters with the pleasure she knew her visit would bring me. What was I cooking that smelled so good? Despite her assumption to the contrary, Vixen is not my favorite dog. "Out!" I yelled, flapping a dish towel. "Out of the house! Go home, Vixen." Theatrically heartbroken, she slinked out, and I shut the door, sadly, against her and the lilacs.

Dogs—even Vixen—are smart enough to know whose house is whose. Not so, we've learned, with the other tribes whose names are legion—blithe creatures of wing and paw who year after year colonize our old farmhouse in the Connecticut hills without so much as a "May I?" They don't pay rent. They don't carry in firewood or scrub the floors. But they do labor for a living within our walls, which were built some two hundred years ago with the intention of separating man from nature.

Try telling that to a field mouse when the first cold snap at the end of August fills it with warm thoughts of home—specifically, our home. The autumn we bought the house, I encountered my first mouse, a pretty thing with sparrow toes and a pale belly, who, late one evening, scurried past my chair on its way to the kitchen garbage pail. Believe it or not, I thought it was cute.

Within weeks, the little mouse was eight little mice. They got unmannerly, even giddy. My husband firmly believed that, in the days between our weekend visits, they settled themselves in our fireside chairs in mouse slippers and read the paper, diving into hiding only as our key turned in the door. In self-defense, we enlisted another part of nature: We got a cat. Well-fed and spoiled, she was a failure as a hunter and, now that she's ancient, doesn't even try. I still uncover neat little mouse-hoards of pilfered birdseed between the guest-room mattress and box spring. I sweep them up with a pang. So much labor, so much racing back and forth between rooms, went into storing this small provender. (Mice, I recently learned, are almost as denatured as cats: They thrive because we provide them with nice warm houses.)

At least they venture out in summer, when the fields are fat, though I suspect that even offspring born in the grass are genetically imprinted with memories of our guest room. Certain insects, however—particularly the aptly named houseflies—seem to have hatched, bred, whizzed, and died for countless generations entirely within our hospitable walls. They are not there, then one warm day they are, dotting the windows like nervous punctuation marks, their drone of longing aimed at the real, inaccessible world beyond the glass. I have come to believe that their ancestors (who in 1795 undoubtedly knew the builder's cows intimately) gave them eternal deed to our walls and floorboards. Alas for them, they abide forever in Plato's cave, crawling across their own shadows. And who am I, I sometimes wonder, to be vacuuming them up? Or, for that matter, stuffing knotholes in the back-porch beams to discourage the wasps who choose to live there?

The flies, at least, fulfill a purpose. They feed the spiders. Or, looked at another way, the spiders—who can refestoon a dusted table leg in an hour—serve the purpose of catching flies. It appears, at times, that our house is host not just to city friends who bring crusty loaves and nice wine, but to a whole ecology of tiny squatters living off each other under the roof we call ours, as at home as toads in a garden.

To me, the spiders seem harmless and amusing. Particularly during the iron months of winter, when little else stirs, I find myself feeling companionable toward one or another of them. I read; it weaves, it waits. It doesn't ask what I'm cooking or expect to be petted. The fire burns down. Then along the walls, a little scurry. What does the mouse know about this old house, I wonder, that I do not? It lives in another, interior house I cannot enter, amid webby lathing and wandering pipes. The mice get impatient, I think, when I read late. They are waiting for me to turn off the light. They are waiting to reclaim their territory.

Well, so did we, the spring my husband decided to reframe the windows and insulate the walls of a downstairs bedroom.

He returned one weekend, sleeves rolled up, to find a fat robin nesting serenely on top of the table saw. To nature, I guess, all things are nature. There was nothing for it but to declare the lying-in room off limits to humans and noisy tools, leave the windows unsealed, and await the blessed event. Eventually, three clumsy, speckled babies got launched. Theirs, at least, was a short-term lease.

As is ours, I realize—certainly as compared with the age of the farmhouse's chestnut posts, cut long ago, before the blight that eradicated these lovely trees from New England. A house made of wood is organic. A house made of old wood, a house that's known a few roof leaks and needs some clapboards replaced, undoubtedly harbors spores, bacteria, and larvae whose tribes I can't begin to name. I can dust, vacuum, and spray, but the minute I come in with an armload of flowers from the garden, I know I'm only kidding myself about our proprietal claim, filed as it may be at the town clerk's office. There's sure to be an earwig wandering out of the phlox, an ant I didn't see on the peony bud, who takes off across the carpet like Magellan setting out across the seas.

So we battle for our living space ("Shut that screen door!" I call, as the kids run out after dark. "The moths are invading!"), but not too hard. In an old country house, as on an old planet, it all comes down to a matter of sharing.

R I T U A L S

''Tell Me a Story''

Madeleine L'Engle

Quite often people come up to me and say, "Let me tell you about my family. Wouldn't you love to write about it?" I say, "No, that's your story, and you have to write it. If you don't recount your family history, it will be lost." Honor your own stories and tell them too. The tales may not seem very important, but they are what binds families and makes each of us who we are.

"Tell me a story," I would beg my mother.

How blessed I was to be born into a family with a tradition of storytelling. My mother was a Southerner, and after the terrible War Between the States, all that her family (like many others) had left were stories. Their houses had been burned. Much of the land had been salted so that it could not bear crops. There was no money. Storytelling did not cost anything, and it helped people who were underfed, sometimes starving, to remember who they were, and that their heritage mattered.

"Tell me a story," I would beg my mother. "Tell me a story about when you were a little girl."

I was a solitary only child growing up on the asphalt island of Manhattan. My mother grew up in a vast family of cousins in a small southern city. From my bedroom window I looked out over a courtyard to other apartment buildings. My mother, as a child, looked out over azalea and gardenia bushes to the St. Johns River, the only other navigable river that flows the same direction as the Nile. Although we both grew up in the aftermath of a great war, our childhoods could not have been more different.

My mother and her cousins—there were dozens of them—accepted their poverty as most children are able to accept what is. My mother remembered one Christmas when her beloved grandmother took sand from the beach and, using food coloring, dyed it pretty colors so there would be something for the children under the tree.

A group of little girl cousins playing together didn't need toys. They had their imaginations and their imaginary worlds. They sometimes watched their brothers and their friends catch large grasshoppers, borrow their mother's sewing thread, and harness the hoppers and race them. "We thought that was unkind," my mother said, "but we watched anyhow, betting on the boy we fancied, hoping his grasshopper would win."

On rainy days they sat indoors and played the Bible game or told stories. The households were a mixture of wealth (beautiful silver, large portraits) and grim poverty. During the war, the portraits had been cut out of their frames and, along with the silver, buried under the live-oak trees. Because of this foresightedness, I still have much of the silver and several of the portraits, and all have stories. In my living room in New York City hangs a large portrait of two young women, one holding her flute, the other with her hands on her harp. It was painted by Samuel

Morse (who later invented the Morse code) in a day before photography.

"Tell me about them, please, Mother."

She would not answer directly. "When I die, you ought to put that portrait in a museum."

"But you don't have it in a museum, Mother," I would reply. "I plan to enjoy it, too."

The portrait is of my great-great-grandmother and my great-great-great-aunt, Margaret and Leonis. Their father, William Johnson, was Thomas Jefferson's first appointee to the Supreme Court, and the first dissenting justice. At that time the chief justice wanted all the justices to eat dinner together; my great-great-great-grandfather announced he preferred to eat dinner with his family, thus making secure a continuing family tradition that eating the evening meal together, by candlelight, is the focal point of the day.

Justice William Johnson also had a passion for education and literacy for everybody. After a slave uprising in Charleston, South Carolina, there was an edict prohibiting the teaching of reading and writing to any slave. Johnson hotfooted it back to the court, declaring, "This is unconstitutional. Every child born in this land, black or white, slave or free, has a right to learn to read and write." He was often not very popular in Charleston, but he did what he believed to be right, and his daughters followed in his footsteps.

To look at their portrait, as I do many times daily, is a challenge. Those are wonderful young women. I do not want to let them down. I want to be part of their story, to carry on their love of music and beauty, along with a concern for fairness in an unfair world, for education for all, for open-mindedness. They have given me good stories to be part of.

So, too, has another great-great-grandmother, Susan Fatio, who likewise knew what she believed and acted on it. I have a picture of her when she was in her seventies: a determined face with dark eyes and a mouth that could be called either stubborn or forceful. I suspect she was both.

Susan was a great storyteller, and sometimes when she was a very old woman, she would tell the same tale so many times that her little great-grandchildren (my mother included) would get bored and wander off. They already knew the stories by heart; the stories were by then part of their own story.

When she was a young woman, Susan wrote her memoirs for her descendants, so that we would know something of what pioneering life was like in north Florida, where she was born. Susan had seven houses burned out from under her, because the Floridas, as that part of the country was then called, were constantly being fought over—by the British, the French, the Spanish, and, occasionally, the Indians. Susan wrote that one day she was talking with a servant who was polishing a handful of knives when another servant rushed up, saying that the Indians were going to attack. "No, no," Susan's father protested, "the Indians are our friends." "Right now," he was told, "they aren't friends with any white man. Get in the rowboat. Quick!" Just as the Indians appeared with guns, shooting, Susan and her father and both servants rowed across the river, somehow managing to avoid the shots. The Indians then burned the house and all that was in it. The only possessions saved were the knives.

When Susan was around seventeen, the family took in a young Frenchman for the winter. He had, quite obviously, an assumed name, but in the Floridas there were many causes for people to use false names, so no questions were asked. He was a charming guest, courteous, helpful, and very musical. Susan was musical, too, and she and the Frenchman spent many hours playing duets together. When he left in the spring, he gave her some of his music and on one of the sheets was his real name: Jean Laffite, the famous pirate.

A woman with joie de vivre and fortitude to match Susan

Fatio's was Madeleine L'Engle, after whom I am named. This first Madeleine, my mother's grandmother, grew up in Charleston, South Carolina, and lived abroad when her father, Romulus Saunders, served as ambassador to Spain. Madeleine was often his hostess. I still have the heavy silver tray that was brought into the drawing room with the after-dinner coffee, and the huge silver pitcher that was filled with hot milk. Madeleine's closest friend during those years in Spain was the princess Eugénie, who later became Empress Eugénie of France.

One day Madeleine and Eugénie were out riding, and the princess's brothers, riding along with them, announced that males were braver than females. "Nonsense!" the young women retorted. The men then got out knives and plunged them into their forearms. The young women followed suit. Foolhardy, perhaps, but they weren't going to let anybody be braver than they were.

Madeleine needed all her courage later on, when she returned to the United States and married a young surgeon with whom she trekked all over the continent as he battled yellow-fever epidemics. They crossed the Isthmus of Panama long before the canal was envisioned. Her first child was born in an adobe hut in Texas. When the War Between the States broke out, William L'Engle returned to the South and was killed. Madeleine, despite her grief, managed a large army hospital, where she nursed those who wore blue and those who wore gray with equal devotion. Asked later to be president of the Daughters of the Confederacy, she refused, saying that this organization would only prolong bitterness, and what was needed was healing.

I am proud to have women like Madeleine in my family and proud to tell their stories. They remind me that many things I value—music, justice, laughter—are not entirely particular to me; they are my richest inheritance.

We all have that inheritance, but sometimes we have to go looking for it. Some of my friends have found family pictures in their attics, and that has been a great source of stories for them. They discover a wedding picture and begin to wonder: *Who are these people who are so in love?* We may have to do some research before we can find their part in our own life patterns. But once we find their stories, we are impelled to tell them.

And, in my case, to write them down. But we're all able to write our stories for our own pleasure and for our friends and family. The writing needn't be fancy. The characters will provide the structure, their adventures, the plot, the lessons learned, the poignancy. What makes the stories special isn't high drama but glimpses of personalities that echo ours, clues to what life was like before we were born.

Now my children and grandchildren and I all tell stories, of my mother, my husband, the next generations.

"Tell us a story, Gran," I am commanded, and, like my mother, I launch in with delight. "Once, when I was a little girl, I had a pair of two-wheel roller skates. . . ."

MESSENGERS

OF THE HEART

Susan Minot

When my grandmother died, she left behind a household of possessions, things that had been in the family for generations. There were canopy beds with twisting carved posts, highboys with brass knobs, a grandfather clock, platters of Canton china, Persian rugs worn in the center. They were to be divided up among her children.

The item I found most interesting was not listed in the appraiser's report. It had been saved in the bottom drawer of a marble-topped bureau among unhung picture frames and Florentine block-printed envelopes: a cube of old letters tied with a string. My grandmother had written these letters in the late twenties during the time of her engagement. The letters covered a period of four months during which she wrote my grandfather from a tour of Europe with her parents and from her usual summering place in Maine. My grandfather, for his part, was working in Boston and would visit Maine on the weekends.

I first read the letters, curious to know my grandmother's character, particularly since they show her in love in her twenties. She seems far more grown up than I. She complains about her social duties and wishes her fiancé were there to hold her hand the way he'd done on the piazza. She writes that she gazed at his coat hanging in the closet, that she's learning how to order steak for him, she teases him for waking up talking to her. In one letter she explains how she will take my grandfather's letters and tie them with a yellow ribbon, as she understands that's the correct form, but will wait till they cease with their marriage. The letters she refers to did not survive. Only a few remain, addressed to his parents or involving business. Had there been more of his letters, I might have gotten to know him better, too.

The post arrived twice a day in 1926 and letters were both messengers of affection as well as practical agents—requests for lunch, notes of thanks, times of weekend arrival by train were all set down and sent off. Telephones did exist but were not yet used the way they are today. My grandmother's letters were written on small folded stationery, some ivory colored, some with pale blue pinstripes, some with the name of an ocean liner for a masthead. She wrote with a fountain pen of blue-black ink. Her handwriting was small script with garlands and peaks. The prose was grammatically correct, the observations amusing and clever. I could not imagine receiving a similar letter today.

The look of the paper, browning now at the edges, the phrases used—"tea dances," "I thought him swell," "We've been to dine"—all made the past vivid and personal. When my grandparents had spoken of the olden days, their reminiscences had pulled back a curtain; the letters filled in the scene. I saw now far more than I glimpsed in their conversation or could gather from the note cards in my grandmother's hand taped beneath the mahogany sideboard, stating it once belonged to a Stuart M. Moore of Garden Street in Cambridge.

The letters stayed with me and years later when I was writing *Folly,* I used them as a touchstone for evoking that time. *Folly* is the story of a young woman growing up in Boston in what would have been my grandmother's era, as I imagined it.

Letters stop time.

Today we use them differently than we once did. The telephone has immediacy, while letters preserve, and steep with time.

One can go over a phone conversation in one's head but how much more satisfying to read and reread a good letter. There are few thrills equal to getting one's first letter from a lover. One pores over the details—the paper he chose, the physical object to hold, still warm, one imagines, from his hand.

A rich life can exist in letters, separate and untouched by life's usual demands. I have a number of correspondences with people with whom I do not share my day-to-day life: in letters we share a great deal. I often feel more inclined to write a letter than to pick up the phone. One feels safer in a letter, time cannot catch you there.

After graduation from college I began to trade letters with a girl from New Orleans I'd known vaguely from writing class. She suggested a North-South correspondence. I had liked her for a line in one of her stories: "You know you're in the North when you're wearing a black dress, and in the South when you're wearing a yellow one." I was at the time living in some isolation, trying to write fiction. She was writing a novel. She turned out to be a most prolific letter writer, far more chatty in print than in person, and I was given a lively account of a somewhat debauched and colorful life in New Orleans. In this way we got to know one another through the mail. I decided to dedicate *Folly* to her.

Great letters can be as powerful as great literature. Gustave Flaubert's letters to his lover, the poet and novelist Louise Colet, while he was writing *Madame Bovary* are famous for their depiction of a writer's agony of composition. For days he searches for the right word. He misses her terribly, she must stay away; it is necessary that he preserve his solitude.

Vincent van Gogh's letters to his brother Theo are powerful for showing an artist's intentions and beliefs as he paints on with enthusiasm in the face of poverty. And Madame de Sévigné's *Letters to Her Daughter* provides us with one of the most eloquent documents of maternal love for a daughter in the early eighteenth century who has married and moved away.

Letters litter my past; I find it hard to throw them away. I still have the fluorescent-pink letters decorated with flower stickers from my summer friend when I was eleven. There are letters stored in a papier-mâché Chinese trunk from boys I pined over when I was fourteen, from ones who let me down, from ones I missed, from ones I chose to ignore (but still saved their letters). I have kept letters from my sister on her first trip away from home, from my brother depressed in college, from my mother telling me to buy a winter coat. There are letters from people who are dead now. I have the letter from the literary magazine accepting my first story, and the watercolored invitation to an old friend's wedding. The letters keep me in mind of those dear to me, of other times, of people's kindnesses. They are kinds of fossils, they endure, unchanged.

A few months after each of the seven children in our family was born, my mother wrote each of us a letter on her sea blue stationery in which she described the circumstances of our births. In my case, she had to leave a matinee of *Tea and Sympathy.* She wrote about how long we slept, what sort of faces we made, and other fascinating habits of newborns interesting to no one but those involved. We all have these letters now and it's hard to articulate why they are so important. It has more to do with my mother's having recorded her care for us—the fact that twenty years of child rearing is rarely recorded—than with discovering that at three months old we liked to grab our toes. It is consoling to have it set down in ink.

My friend has a story about letters in which remembrance plays a part.

Around the time she was in college she had a boyfriend very happily for a few years. After their graduation when they were both deciding what to do with their lives, they realized they were too unformed and broke up. His name was George.

Every Valentine's Day since they went their separate ways, my friend would receive a card signed with George's name. She recognized the hand of George's mother who had always liked her, and having no hard feelings, my friend thought it sweet. George, however, was also receiving these valentines and did think they were from my friend, and over the years her name kept appearing. He might never have found out the truth if not for the toast at the bridal dinner on the eve of his wedding some ten years later. My friend raised a glass to her future mother-in-law, thanking her for making it so difficult to forget George.

PANSIES FOR

REMEMBRANCE

Judith Thurman

*I*t is an understatement to say that my parents were not lovers of nature. They had once considered buying a farmhouse, my mother said, but halfway to the country, a wasp flew into the car, and they headed back home. She didn't like sunlight or fresh air. The only vegetable she could stand to eat was coleslaw. My father didn't golf or fish, and he couldn't swim. We lived in Queens, New York, and our garden, such as it was, was a sour little plot we shared with our downstairs neighbors.

Once a year, both families drove out to a suburban greenhouse and split the cost of a flat of marigolds, a new azalea to replace the one that had died, a bag of topsoil, and a bottle of weed killer. The children were then allowed to choose some seed packets from the display rack. I looked for the names of those flowers that grew in the cottage gardens of my storybooks. No one advised me that hollyhocks, bluebells, honeysuckle, tiger lilies, foxglove, violets, mulberries, poppies, morning glories, eglantine, or primroses might need sun, drainage, mulching, or fertile soil.

Neither my city-born parents nor my immigrant neighbors knew the first thing about horticulture, except that it was educational, and somehow noble. The garden, I think, was a metaphor for their parental ambitions. They wanted their offspring to reap those tastes, pleasures, and privileges, which they had, with much privation, sown for us.

It seems incongruous that my mother, Alice, not only had a favorite flower but also a covetous, lifelong passion for one—the pansy. She particularly loved those velvety black and rather funereal pansies with a yellow eye, which are called *fausts*. We tried to grow them in our Queens garden, but of course they never took, so my mother cultivated pansies in other forms. They were her folly, the one exception she made to her principle of wanting nothing, the only form of tribute her love exacted from us. Her drawers were filled with pansy handkerchiefs and her cupboards with pansy china. She had a watercolor, a set of prints, and bookmarks and pillows done in petit point, a papier-mâché hatbox in which she kept her antique pansy valentines, and a pressed pansy in a glass paperweight. When my fortunes improved, I bought her a Victorian needlepoint rug with a pansy motif, and for her seventieth birthday, an enamel-and-gold pansy pin.

It was mysterious to me that someone who mistrusted her senses and lived so resolutely in her head, among her books and daydreams, should identify so intimately with a flower. I never asked my mother to explain the paradox, but not long ago, reading Colette, I was reminded that "the common pansy, which thrives in the little gardens of the nuns" is called, in French, *la pensée.*

The most extraordinary pansies I ever saw grew in two giant urns of weathered stone in a terraced Tuscan garden. I think they must have been those *cornuta* Colette describes—"rivals of the violet and Sido's favorites above all others, as full-bodied as Henry VIII, with bearded chins, all staring up at you at once."

The garden belonged to the mother of my college roommate, Beatrice, who had invited me to spend a summer in Italy. She thought it was hilarious that I had never gathered a bouquet of wildflowers or a mushroom, had never seen an olive tree, a fig, grapes on a vine, nasturtiums in a salad, a lavender bush, a cypress grove, potted lemons, the poisonous bougainvillea, or wisteria cascading down an ancient wall. "Judith is a virgin," she told her Italian friends. "She's never tasted a ripe tomato."

Beatrice's English mother was an Elizabethan scholar who practiced homeopathy and raised medicinals in addition to her prize flowers. Whenever you had a bite, a cold, a stomach ailment, a rash, an earache, or a feminine complaint, she administered an herbal poultice or a tisane that cured it. I had never met anyone her age who was still so adventurous and beautiful, and it's hard to remember that Beatrice and I are nearly her age now. She took an interest in my poetry, but she warned me about a poet's life. "It's a great struggle," she said, "especially for a woman who wants a child. No one should write unless she has to. But I think that perhaps you have to."

It was an unusually dry summer, and we watered the garden twice a day—just after sunrise and once again at dusk. I took the late shift, and Beatrice's mother would watch me from the millstone table, under the rose arbor, where she'd brought a book or her sewing. When I was done, she would pour me a little glass of her homemade red wine, still cool from the cantina. It was strong but very pure, and it never made you drunk, although the scents of the garden did, steaming up from the drenched soil. On one of those evenings, Beatrice's mother told me about a Danish writer whom she loved, and whom she had met in Rome. "She was very helpful to me when I was your age, and like you, grandiose and lonely. I'll lend you her memoir. It's called *Out of Africa*."

Fifteen years later, I had the singular honor of staying at Rungstedlund, the country house where Isak Dinesen had spent her childhood and written her books. My biography had just appeared in Danish, and the invitation was a publication gift from the Dinesen family. It was a dark November afternoon when I arrived, and I was received by the young couple who live in the gardener's cottage and care for the estate. Morten Keller is Dinesen's grandnephew. His wife, Martha, does the spectacular bouquets for the house, now that it has become the Karen Blixen Museum.

Morten had laid a fire in the salon, and we shared a bottle of champagne I had bought at the airport. Then he carried my bag into the guest room. But before he set it down, he said: "You don't want to sleep here." "I don't?" "No," he said, "you want to sleep in her bedroom." "I do?" "Yes," he said. "It's only fitting. Follow me." And so we climbed up to a paneled garret with a low ceiling and a bare pine floor that smelled of beeswax. The window looked out onto the sound, which the moon had silvered. Here was Dinesen's monkish bed with its white coverlet. Morton put my bag down. "Pleasant dreams," he said.

I woke to the scent of the chrysanthemums, which Martha had arranged with foamflowers, bittersweet, and some gnarled branches in an old Chinese bowl. That morning she gave me the house tour and asked if I would like to see the gardens. She brought a basket and secateurs, and as she cut the flowers for a centerpiece she told me that a bouquet wasn't satisfactory until it met Dinesen's prime directive. "What is that?" I asked her. "To make the beholder mysteriously happy," she answered.

Isak Dinesen had a genius for arranging flowers. In her old-fashioned view, of course, any well-bred girl should be able to arrange flowers. Yet she was not an amateur—there was something more driven and inspired about her bouquets. She had studied painting in Paris as a young woman, and her earliest ambition was to become an artist. Instead, she had sailed to Africa to marry her cousin, Baron Bror von Blixen-Finecke, manage a coffee plantation, and lose her heart. Once she returned to Denmark, bereft, to begin writing, she never painted again. But back at Rungstedlund, she did recover a sumptuous box of colors. And that was her garden.

Even when Dinesen was so frail she could barely walk, she insisted on scouting each branch or blossom by herself. She knew what she wanted, and if her own grounds lacked some essential element, she was not above poaching from her neighbors. She was a virtuoso who sought unlikely harmonies of form and color, and her bouquets were, like her tales, fantastical. She composed them, I think, the way she did the placements for her imaginary dinner parties—her symposia, as she called them—taking an impious glee in matching unlikely partners. So Ibsen might find himself sitting next to Sappho, Don Juan beside Saint Teresa, while in a vase behind them, on the buffet, a branch of copper beech leaves consorted with arum lilies, bulrushes, milkweed, and parrot tulips.

The privations of your childhood always come to have a special prestige, and I can't live without cut flowers. I do my bouquets once every two weeks, and in between, I'm conscious of the void and the avidity you feel when you've been fasting. I've also noticed lately that I'm particularly hungry for blue, as if that color were a vitamin that had been missing from my diet. "The Creator of all things," notes Colette, "proved himself rather tightfisted when he was handing out blue flowers here below," and they are especially hard to come by in New York City. If you want delphiniums, aconites, lupines, violets, wild iris, or convolvuluses, you have to get up at dawn and go down to the wholesale flower district, which is the closest thing this city has to a meadow.

On Dinesen's birthday, April 17, I always try to do something special in her honor, which is to say, I indulge myself in her name. Unlike Colette—an Aquarian—Dinesen was born auspiciously for floral tribute. The cherries and the magnolia have just bloomed; you can sometimes find lilies of the valley; the first white lilacs and peonies are out. It's the moment for black pansies.

Wrapping Up a Memory

Catherine Calvert

Christmas 1957, and all is steeped in darkness. But then, that's natural, since it is only half past five in the morning. The children, who had lain awake whispering bed to bed, listening to the clock tick till the unheard of hour of eleven, have been up for an hour, little engines of excitement, ears cocked for the faintest sound of stirring in the parents' bedroom.

I, the oldest, stretched my legs in my pajamas-with-feet, and hatched a plot with my sister. We padded down the hallway, our plastic soles going whisper-whisper, and crept into our little brother's room, where he lay in his crib, a yellow-haired, pink-cheeked heap. It took only a little pinch before he was bolt upright and screaming for Mother, and the lights flipped on, and we scurried to the door of the living room. "Can we go in now, can we go in now, everybody's up, can we go in?"

We were, like all children, flexible moralists. We weren't allowed in the room with the tree, and we weren't to wake our parents. We honored the first prohibition and played havoc with the last. For who, impaled on anticipation like a medieval martyr, could stay in bed till the sun rose?

We had been good. We had patiently performed every step of December's rituals: sung in the pageant, worn scratchy petticoats to the officer's club party, and watched the candle gutter in our hands as we left the Christmas Eve service. But now we were down to the very heart of Christmas.

Presents.

In the days when home movies required the lighting of a Hollywood set, we had to stay frozen in place until the lighting system was operating. It made the living room a magic place with shadowy edges and floodlit center that caused our sleepy eyes to squint as we began burrowing in the present heap. Some families arrange their gifts in piles, some choose an official distributor, and the Queen of England has the servants set up tasteful little tables of presents for each member of the family. We, however, tore into the mound and ferreted out our own until our pile tottered.

There was the unwrapped Big Present, perhaps a bike shining behind the tree branches. There were all those aunt-and-uncle presents—promising, but you can never tell with aunts and uncles. And grandparent presents, though we had one set who were mitten-givers, and consequently not to be looked to for real excitement. And there were those from Santa Claus, who visited well into our teens, a man of uncanny sense and nonsense.

If all was a flurry till we were settled, Mother on the sofa with the writing pad for thank-you-note reminders, Father fiddling with the framing of the shots (and managing to get endless pictures of children just as they turned their backs to the camera), we were nearly silent as we approached the gifts, selecting each one to be opened slowly, with concentration. There were the practical presents to be held up to the camera, and—if the predictable hat or scarf—to be donned and modeled. There were the intuitive presents from those who knew us—just the book series I was reading, just the kind of toy ponies I was collecting. And then the heart-stopping gifts of imagination that those who loved us managed to produce, such as a dollhouse complete down to the fireplace implements, with handmade curtains and a tiny sewing machine with a real treadle.

And of course there were the gifts that weren't there, the secret longing unsatisfied, as much a part of the morning as the sharp shatter of candy cane in the mouth. For we did, and do, expect a lot out of our presents. As early as October we'd begun to haunt the toy department, with its intoxicating smell of new dolls, and the beginnings of Barbie's lifestyle on parade. We'd pored over the Sears catalog, counting up the items that came in one doll's trousseau versus another's. Then the delicious terror of putting together a list. Ask for one big thing? Spread the goodwill into several lesser ones? (And there were secret desires kept close, like that amazing ballerina doll whose feet could really swivel *en pointe*. "I'll see if there really is a Santa Claus. He'll know.")

For what we wanted of gifts, then and now, was a dose of delight, and even more: something that expressed recognition of ourselves. Quite a freight for a box. It could go very wrong. I remember the gruesome Christmas when I, known to be book-ish, received from well-meaning relatives three copies of *Winnie the Pooh* in Latin and a shirt embroidered with a bespectacled owl, while my little blond sister squealed as she unwrapped a white fluffy kitten and a bottle of bubble bath. Or the times on the cusp of adolescence when I didn't know quite what I was, and turned my nose up at new ski jackets, secretly longing for one more doll.

You know you've grown up when you remember what you've given for Christmas, rather than what you've gotten. Perhaps one of the burdens of adulthood is losing the sense that all dreams can be contained in a tantalizing square box, gaudy with wrapping paper. For those of us nurtured on Christmases that were bacchanals of present-mongering, sitting down in one's robe to a discreet pile of gifts, nice as they may be, bought by a loving husband who had asked for a list of wants and patiently filled it, leaves me with a tiny, childish wisp of regret. Where, says that nasty little voice in the back of my head, is the ballerina doll? Where's my *surprise?*

But then, we come from different traditions, my Scottish husband and I. My first visit to Scotland with him was at Christmastime, and I'd jettisoned outfits from my suitcase to make room for the splendors I'd carefully chosen for each member of his family, as yet unknown to me. As I put my bundles down under their tree, I felt my usual Christmas Eve bubble of excitement, sure they'd love my gifts.

Up early, I waited through the day—through the oatmeal, the church, the Christmas lunch, the port and cigars, the brisk walk with the labrador, the steaming teakettle and Christmas cake—before I drew Alasdair aside and hissed, "The presents, what about the presents?" And he, bemused, summoned the family, who looked at my brightly wrapped boxes and opened them carefully, thanked me, then exchanged woolen socks with one another and poured more champagne. And I knew the culture gap was wider than it seemed.

The solution, of course, was to have children, on whom I could work my Christmas magic. "Don't they have enough?" asks Alasdair. "What's 'enough' mean?" say I, and start next year's Christmas shopping at the January sales, and listen hard all year for the "I wants" that aren't fad-driven. I'm thrifty and foresighted, but I still end the week before Christmas in the stores, searching for just the right dream-in-a-box, threading my way through the crowds, the bustle as much a part of my holiday joys as trimming the tree.

And if down the hall the children toss and turn on Christmas Eve, I'm almost equally excited. Did I guess right? Was this really the year Zara would like that book I picked out, and will

Kate's love of kittens find reflection in this gray stuffed marvel that meows? And, the next morning, I take my place on the sofa with the thank-you-note list. I watch their eyes kindle and their breath catch as Kate snuggles her kitten, unwilling to lift a hand to open another box, and her sister sits amid the wrapping paper, turning the pages of her book, and my husband fiddles with the camera, wrapping up a memory.

PLAYING SANTA

Judith Thurman

*T*wo Christmases ago, my five-year old still wanted to be a policeman. He had all the gear a boy could want: hats, badges, a nightstick, sunglasses, sirens, and a large stable of vehicles. But early that December I found a surprise for him in a shop that specialized in novelty candy and tucked it into his stocking. At six-thirty on Christmas morning he woke me, and with a huge grin (and a sticky brown mustache) exclaimed, "Look, Mommy! There really must be a Santa. Who else would have thought of—who else could have come up with—chocolate handcuffs!"

William received other, much fancier presents, but he still talks about the chocolate handcuffs. They represent one of my greater, if more selfless, moments of triumph as a gift shopper. It's a role I take pride in and for which Santa is my model. Every year he proves again that, when a gift is well chosen, it intuits a heart's desire.

Giving is a form of dialogue and, at its most refined, of

telepathy. The most memorable gifts seem to answer a question, settle a doubt, or anticipate a want the recipient perhaps hasn't yet thought of or been able to express. It's also a little mirror in which we see ourselves through the loving eyes of the giver. Once, at a particularly drab and melancholy moment of my life, a male friend gave me an unusual and lovely Spanish shawl, sumptuously embroidered with black flowers on fringed ivory silk. "This looks like you. It feels like you," he wrote simply. His perception was as precious as the shawl itself, and I recover my original emotion—the surprise grace of his recognition— every time I wear it.

We have all received gifts which, on the contrary, make us wonder what the sender's message was, if any. I have at different times puzzled over a plastic elf that dispensed toothpicks, a barbecue cover (I was living in an apartment), and a box of staples. Were they a joke? A metaphor? A reproach for frivolity? Did the stapler get lost in the mail? Had the giver simply run out of ideas, or, more likely, of money? It's the thought that counts, of course, and not its cost, but a gift that falls short of its mark, failing to delight and enlighten the recipient, resembles an incomplete and therefore incoherent sentence, one lacking a subject. Giving has its own grammar and syntax. It takes a certain rigor to translate a thought into an expressive gift. My own ideals as a giver are therefore the same as my ideals as a writer: eloquence and precision. (At least that's how I rationalize the hours I spend shopping!)

Unlike writing, however, shopping is pure pleasure for me. It comes naturally, with no anxiety, and with a kind of easy access to inspiration my workaday self can only envy. It is related to another very ancient feminine art (and another of my amateur sidelines), which, I have been told, was practiced by my female ancestors in the villages of Hungary: matchmaking. One cannot always hope, though, in the frenzy of the last weeks before the holidays, to make the perfect match—the kind of love match between a gift and a recipient—that is so satisfying to both parties. That is why, by the time the decorations go up in department stores, most of my presents are already wrapped in the embossed paper and lamé ribbon I bought on sale the year before. I have been Christmas and Hanukkah shopping ever since I threw out my old tree.

I prefer to do most of my shopping, holiday and other, at flea markets, state fairs, thrift emporiums, resale stores, tag sales, country auctions, secondhand bookshops, and in the little ethnic souks of New York City. It's not that I'm particularly cheap—I'm a would-be Pygmalion who prides herself on cultivating potential in unlikely places. I feel an almost religious mission to redeem lost treasure. And I love the adventure of thrifting, the thrill and challenge of the hunt. It engages my senses and challenges my prowess. Going to a mall or browsing through a mail-order catalog is as dull for me as shooting goldfish in a barrel is to a true sportsman.

The end of summer is my favorite shopping season. The sales are on, and I can stock up on secondhand Charvet, Hermès, and Armani ties from the thrift stores, on vintage handbags, costume jewelry from the fifties, and antique bric-a-brac that, with a little repair and polish, becomes utterly charming. In a single reconnaissance mission last August I found a challis foulard from Liberty for three dollars, a pair of silver candelabra for the price of a pair of candles, a twenty-dollar alligator purse with a silver clasp, and a set of eight Limoges dessert plates for less than a single new teacup. It's a simple matter, come December, to match these treasures with the right recipients. What's harder is parting with them.

I have used many different principles to vary and to organize my shopping forays. One year my theme was art. Everyone on my list received a framed print, map, watercolor, photograph, or drawing. Another year it was pain relief. I dispatched bottles of champagne, CDs of sacred music, antique caddies filled with linden tea, visits to an astrologer, cashmere mufflers, homemade chocolate truffles, massage gift certificates, feather pillows, decanters of port, pomanders, velvet slippers, herbal oils and incense, and books of philosophy.

This year in reviewing my list, I realized there were a number of naturally recurring organic categories: new mothers, for example. Each of them will receive a museum membership, which is to say the gift of some solitary and contemplative adult time. Then there are the intellectuals: I will give each of them a first edition. (It was a great summer for library sales in the small towns of Connecticut.) Those who have worked on a book or a thesis for more than five years, however, will qualify for a jigsaw puzzle, a fly rod, a satin boudoir pillow, or an ice-cream maker— something to distract from the ticking of the clock and the blankness of the next page. People who love gear—golfers, fishermen, hackers, teenagers, cooks, and gardeners—are relatively easy to make happy. So are boys between seven and ten. Each one on my list will receive a basketball jersey with his lucky number and a book of horror stories. As for the new brides and my women friends married more than twenty years, they (and their husbands) are destined for a piece of lace-trimmed lingerie.

This still leaves me with a long list of loved ones who are unaccounted for. But all year long, I review and update the mental dossiers that I keep for them. I know, for example, that Joan needs soup plates, that the Phillipses want a dog bed for their schnauzer, that Connie and Joe have begun to collect copper molds, that Max has been yearning for a vintage tuxedo jacket, that cousin Emma craves a Victorian sewing basket, that Catherine broke her last two Venetian glasses, that my aunt's rheumatologist has suggested she buy a feather bed, that my hairdresser would like a subscription to *Car and Driver,* and that my neighbors, who have three of the little boys on my list, would love a week in Hawaii, but would probably be thrilled with an ice bucket.

I don't think of myself as hard to please, but my husband tells me that my exacting standards as a giver make me a daunting person to shop for. (You can just back up my hard drive, darling, and leave something in a tiny velvet box under my pillow.) My dear Aunt Charlotte, however, has an inspired solution to "Judith's gift problem." She has observed that in the course of twelve months I inevitably wear out my wallet. Every Christmas, she gives me a new one.

Thank-You Notes:
Acts of Grace

Jane Howard

"Women," as Oscar Wilde observed a hundred years ago in "The Importance of Being Earnest," "become like their mothers. That is their tragedy." Now "tragedy" is Wilde's poetic overstatement, but the older I grow the more persuaded I am how right he was in the first half of this proposition. Though my own late mother was blessed with several traits I conspicuously lack, among them tidiness, punctuality, and the ability to sew, the older I grow the more I remind myself of her in certain ways, reassuring and otherwise. It is not so much that I look like her, though to some degree there's that. What strikes me more is the speed and constancy with which her ideas, her inflections, and her very syntax tend to find their way into mine, especially when it comes to thank-you notes.

Several times in the last few years I have heard myself uttering sentences with italicized phrases that sounded exactly like hers: "Well, I *hope* they got the andirons, though of course I have no way of knowing" or "I *assume* their car didn't break down on the way home from their weekend here, which they seemed to like" or "I wonder if the twins *are* enjoying the receiving blankets."

My mother, who was born in 1904, lived nearly all her sixty-six years in the Midwest, one of the world's premier centers of niceness. One thing I'm sure of is that nobody in all the twelve states of that region could ever have written prompter, more heartfelt thank-you notes, or bread-and-butter letters, than she did. She was a champion. No sooner did anyone send her a gift, wave her off after a visit, or accord her any other kindness, than she would hasten to her stationery box and pick up her fountain pen to express her indebtedness.

In so doing, though she may not have known this, she wasn't just crossing a chore off a list, but helping to ward off mental distress. A thank-you note, she knew instinctively, is a small but sure remedy for anxiety, insecurity, and imagined slights. It can help prevent downward spiraling moods that lead toward trains of thought like, "Don't mind me, you run along and have fun: I'll just have a tray in my room." It can prevent its recipient from wondering "Have I done something to offend her? Or can it be—worse yet—that she doesn't care? Ah, that must be it."

Hurt feelings, to my mother, were anathema. Soothing others, to her, was second nature. She bequeathed the wishful, wistful notion that everyone, at all times, should be not only in touch with but on good terms with everyone else. On the regrettable occasions when this was not the case, it was the task of her daughters somehow to make it so. And one of the ways we could help to do this, she instructed us (though probably not in so many words), was with well-timed thank-you notes.

As soon as we had learned to scrawl such phrases as "Dear Uncle Fred," and "Love, Jane," we got busy. We weren't really expected to produce these notes before we had even opened our packages at Christmas and on our birthdays, but that's how it felt. Our notes, with their three-cent stamps, went into the mails promptly, and so did the bread-and-butter letters that were required after an overnight sojourn under anybody else's roof. In these we not only said what a nice time we'd had, but decided and described what the visit's "highlight" had been. And if anyone sent us a check for five or ten dollars, which in those days were no trivial sums, we had to go into some detail about what plans we had for spending the money. None of this was optional.

Though I produced these notes as quickly as I was trained to, I rolled my eyes while I did so, privately thinking there was something silly about the whole enterprise. But now, though I don't literally have children of my own, I find myself a keeper of this same flame, an arbiter of the manners of—how can it be that so curmudgeonly a phrase has actually crossed my mind— "today's young people." It pains me to think that thank-you notes may be an endangered art form. Unless some of us take the trouble to be vigilant about this, they may go the way of stained-glass windows like those at Notre Dame and Chartres cathedrals, stonemasonry like that of Giotto's bell tower, and lattice-topped pies.

It isn't entirely accurate to say I'm nobody's parent. I cherish close ties with several relatives and friends who were born during the sixties, the period when I came nearest to having kids of my own, and I have a very firm idea of what sort of children mine would now be. As I did for Tommy, the brother I alone could see and hear when I was three or so, I've given them names: Kate, Sam, Dan, and Elizabeth.

I realize that Kate and Sam and Dan and Elizabeth, who now would be in or near their thirties, would surely be flawed and complex people. Much as I'd love them, they and I would have had our share of differences and stormy scenes over the decades. But I know one thing they'd do: They would write great thank-you notes. I'm not talking about store-bought greeting cards. The sentiments these children of mine would express (and sometimes charmingly illustrate) would be original and handwritten, in penmanship quirky but legible. Born when they were, of course, they would have been witness to the dawn of the information superhighway, which, thanks to genes from their father, they would understand. They would know how to program VCRs, and they would be unfazed by computers and Internet and E-mail. Still, in their hearts would be a soft spot for the feel and look of pen on page, preferably black ink on white paper. They would know that no new form of communication makes any old one entirely obsolete.

Sometimes Kate and Dan and Sam and Elizabeth would have too much to do to write formal thank-you notes. On these occasions they would at least compose postcards, which they would post at once instead of carrying them around for a week. Or they would make a phone call. One couple I have known since college made sure their sons sent handwritten thanks to donors of every single Bar Mitzvah gift but now excuse the sons from writing notes to their only living grandparent because they phone him frequently, not just after he has sent them a check.

Different households have different traditions to make sure that givers and recipients keep in touch. A young woman I've met recently says in her family the usual situation is reversed: It is she who reminds her parents, not they her, to write thank-you notes. In another reversal, I have found that the task of writing thank-you notes is no longer solely the female's. When I gave a pair of South Dakota Hutterite pillows to one set of newlyweds, it was he instead of she who wrote to thank me. Since I'd never met the bride until the wedding and had known her husband since before his voice changed, this seemed appropriate.

My imaginary children would write thank-you notes not only for birthday and holiday gifts but after any gathering that had caused its host or hostess special pains, and always when they've been the guest of honor. Some of their best notes would catch the recipients by surprise, arriving when least expected, and prompted not by presents wrapped in paper to mark official holidays, but in gratitude for gifts more diffuse and abstract. They would often send notes after job interviews, and to people who had gone out of their way to help them professionally.

Never for a moment would my imaginary children allow anyone to wonder whether a gift had reached them at all. In this respect they would be unlike a nonimaginary tall young man who is dear to me for many reasons having nothing to do with his habits as a correspondent. This tall young man, word has it, did receive the article of clothing I bought for him last November, gift wrapped, and mailed to him in time for Christmas. The postal system, outrageous though it often can be, was not at fault this time. The collar and sleeves of the shirt, word has it, are not too small: The young man is even rumored to like it, as I had pictured him doing.

Why then do I let it nag me that he hasn't told me so himself? Why can't I be more like the ancient philosopher king Marcus Aurelius? In his *Meditations,* published in the second century A.D., he asks why anybody who has performed a kindness should be so foolish as to look for gratitude, any more than a vine should expect acknowledgment for bearing a bunch of grapes. Do horses and greyhounds race in anticipation of praise? Do bees make honey in order to be thanked?

Moses Maimonides, ten centuries later, asserted that the noblest gifts are anonymous. Delineating what he called the "eight degrees or steps in the duty of charity," he drew a spectrum whose first step was giving "with reluctance and regret." His eighth step, the "most meritorious of all," was to prevent poverty and need by allowing people to "earn an honest livelihood and not be forced to the dreadful alternative" of holding out their hands. In other words, if you give somebody something, that should be that. You shouldn't even think about having a building named after you or receiving a note of gratitude. True generosity, like virtue, should be its own reward. The sages through the ages, in other words, have not gone in for the nit-picking scorecard mentality I struggle to keep at bay.

What's important, what I should focus on, is how the recipient of that same Christmas shirt, a few months earlier, came up with a last-minute third-row-center ticket admitting me to a fabulous sold-out concert at Carnegie Hall. I should also keep in mind how generous is one of his contemporaries, equally tall and equally disinclined to write letters, who never fails, whenever he comes to see me, to fix every broken thing in sight. Am I not lucky to have bighearted, nonfawning young men like these for kinfolk?

It's not as if I were a moral giant myself. A week or so after I had gathered the unanswered Christmas cards of 1993 into a manila folder, I came across a similar (and to this day still unacknowledged) folder of cards from 1992. I could spend a full week tending to overdue library books, unpaid bills, unreturned messages, and many other things I have promised to send and do and, for that matter, be.

But the message is this: Do what I say, not what I do. Because I know. A thank-you note is an act of grace. It completes a circle. The circle may have been set in motion when you interrupted your routine to welcome me under your roof and allowed me to put my feet under your table. Or when you went to the trouble of choosing a present for me, wrapping it, schlepping to the post office, and standing in line to mail it. Or when you did me some less seasonal other favor, like puncturing a fit of pomposity or cheering me out of a funk.

If I take the trouble to tell you, on paper, what a difference you thus have made to me, then it makes your gift, or your kindness, an act of mutuality. It is something between us, something we share. It connects us, and makes us both feel not only better, but possibly even saner. This is a lesson I learned originally from my mother and, more recently, from Kate and Dan and Sam and Elizabeth. Pass it on.

A Crosswicks Kind of Christmas

Madeleine L'Engle

Christmas, that time of light coming in the midst of the darkest nights of the year, has always been important to me. When I was a little girl, I lived in New York City and one of my loveliest memories is of searching for all the trees in the city that were decorated with colored lights, something that once more captures my imagination now that I am back in the city. But when my children were growing up, we lived in a dairy village in Connecticut where the nights were usually illumed with nothing but stars. The traditions of my girlhood—I was an only child and Christmases were often spent with just my parents—didn't quite work in an old farm-house like Crosswicks, filled with three children and lots of hustle and bustle. So my husband, Hugh, and I set about inventing our own ways of celebrating both Christmas and the other special times that knit a family together.

My birthday comes as Advent begins, so those weeks before Christmas are the first weeks in my personal New Year, as well as the church's. In my small book, *The 24 Days Before Christmas,* I write about some of the little things we did as the days of Advent moved through December. One year I found a cardboard cutout of about twenty small elves dancing, and I hung it in the kitchen windows. That quickly became a tradition. So did taking an old coat hanger and some fishing thread and a dozen decorations to make a mobile that swung from the ceiling and dangled over the kitchen counter as we rolled cookie dough. When I found brightly colored cutouts of Santa Claus with his sleigh and reindeer, they went up the front staircase, so that we had to be careful not to knock them off as we held on to the banister. Everything new that we did quickly became a holiday fixture. We added and added and only subtracted when something fell apart.

One of the greatest of all the great days of Advent was driving five miles to the house of a retired Congregational minister and his wife to cut down our yuletide tree and have high tea, a real experience for my children. In our village, there wasn't much chance for a plain cup of tea in the afternoon, much less one spiced with cinnamon and cloves and accompanied by soft-boiled egg, sandwiches, and pound cake. Tea, however, was only a prelude to the main event. Warmed to our toes, we were given a saw and rope and we headed to the woods to choose just the right tree. Row after row of pines had been planted many years ago by this wonderful couple in anticipation of Christmas visits from children just like my three. We all took a turn sawing, and then we tied the tree's branches together and dragged it back to the car.

When I was a child my parents decorated the tree together on Christmas Eve, and I never saw it until the next morning. I'm not sure how my husband and I started Christmas-tree Sunday, with the children helping with the decorating, but that became our tradition. We sang carols and had eggnog round the piano. The unbreakable decorations were given to the little ones to put on the bottom branches, a tradition that evolved not only for the sake of eager little fingers, but for the cats (who in my memory are always kittens) and for the dogs, who were always overinterested in what was going on.

For several years we included the celebration of Hanukkah, another feast of light at the darkest time of the year. What I loved most about Hanukkah was that the rejoicing was not so much for the victorious battle, but for the lamp in the temple that had oil enough for only a day, yet burned brightly for seven days and nights.

Since I was the choir director of our little church, the Christmas Eve service was a big part of our lives, as well as decorating the church with greens and many candles. It seemed to me that we all sang better by candlelight than by electric light, and I don't think this was only my imagination.

Reading aloud at bedtime was an every-night tradition, but on Christmas Eve after church my husband would read "The Night Before Christmas" and the Christmas story from St. Luke, while we all sipped hot cocoa. Then the children went up to bed, being warned about not waking us up too early in the morning.

We gave each of them a present to open in their rooms so that Hugh and I had a fighting chance of getting some sleep. We needed it. Christmas was a very busy time at the country store we ran—we usually had a number of people's turkeys thawing, countless orders only just filled—and the wee hours of Christmas Eve were traditionally spent putting together a bicycle, or a doll's house, or a train set. Neither of us was born with carpentry skills. We read the directions, but they were usually wrong. Oh, for a magic wand to make all those little pieces go together!

In the early days we had Christmas dinner at noon, but no one liked it. The idea of sleeping with the newspaper over one's face all afternoon wasn't appealing. So we settled on brunch and then dinner, which, as a concession, was planned to be an hour and a half early. But somehow we always ended up eating at the regular time anyway. Over the years we had innovations— one Christmas it was a goose, another a suckling pig—but finally we settled on the more traditional turkey. Actually two turkeys, twenty-five pounds each, one with bread-and-herb stuffing, the other dressed more experimentally with cornbread or oysters or chestnuts or apricots. Because my mother was a Southerner, we always had rice and gravy. We gave up the candied sweet potatoes a good many years ago. Delicious though they were, I finally realized nobody ate them. But the creamed onions, the leeks and carrots, cut lengthwise and braised, persist to this day. Dessert? I am not a dessert cook! Sometimes there's a plum pudding to flame, sometimes a pie someone has baked and brought. After our regular meal, we really aren't interested in desserts.

Families grow up, change. Traditions change. We can't hold on to them too tightly or they become rigid. Wait. New traditions will happen.

Today Christmas comes to Crosswicks with an influx of family and friends, old and new. Breakfast is cooked by my son, who keeps an eye on the modern concerns of cholesterol. The unbreakable ornaments are still hung on the bottom branches. Are the children old enough for us to assemble the train set? Not quite. Let's wait. Next year, perhaps, that will be yet another Christmas tradition.

By the Tuileries,
the World in a Teacup

Angeline Goreau

here are certain places I can trace to the last detail with my eyes closed: places with so many memories gathered to them that, no matter how far away I may be, they remain palpable. I have been going back to Angelina, an old tea salon in Paris, for twenty years, memorizing its particulars so that in the dark moments of a New York winter I can call forth the way the afternoon light filters through the tall windows overlooking the Tuileries.

I was twenty, a student in Paris, when I fell in love with Angelina. I was already, of course, under the spell of France. I had never been in a country before where people spoke a foreign language, and French sounded like music to me—the exotic rolls of the "r" (still far beyond my own capacity to reproduce); the silky rhythm of the talk I listened to with the special intensity that only someone discovering the world at twenty knows.

Paris itself was a revelation to me: I loved its cafés, with their animated air of conversation no matter what time of day; I loved watching the women whose instinct for color and line showed in the last detail of the way they dressed; I loved the tall windows that one could throw open to the scent of chestnut blooming, to the view of the courtyards, the narrow streets of the Left Bank and the grand boulevards of the Right; I loved seeing people strolling along the Seine holding hands. I loved feeling that where I walked so many people had been before.

I had walked the streets until I thought I knew every stone, but I did not come upon Angelina on my own. A rather romantic young man named François (who, like so many other young Frenchmen then, dressed like an English gentleman) invited me to tea at an address on the rue de Rivoli, across from the Tuileries Garden. Wishing to surprise me, he neglected to mention the name of the place we were to meet.

Angelina and I, you see, share the same name—with the small exception of a vowel. My name has been in my mother's family for at least seven generations—that is, seven I know of. It used to be a common name in the time of Queen Victoria, both in England and in France, but has since become so rare that I have only twice in my life come across someone else who shares it. I've met many more people who have a grandmother or a great-great-aunt named Angeline, as mine were.

It wasn't just the name that made me feel, though, the first time I saw Angelina, that I had arrived home; it was the atmosphere of time recaptured, the feeling I had of walking into a Paris of elegance and ceremony that carried on unchanged while the world outside speeded up. The waitresses wore black with proper blouses and neat white aprons, as I suspected they always had. Tea arrived on a large tray with an array of little pots, served on diminutive round mottled-green marble tables; we sat in comfortable old bergères. There were mirrors and arches, gold-and-cream columns, elaborately carved moldings, and, best of all, time-softened paintings of landscapes from the Côte d'Azur, the Baie des Anges (Bay of Nice) in blues and yellows and greens—an unspoiled, unhurried Riviera that exists now only in the imagination.

Angelina, I learned, also has interesting ghosts. When it first opened, in 1903, Angelina was called Rumpelmeyer's, after the Rumpelmeyer's on the Côte d'Azur, which had been for several years a watering hole for fashionable Europe: Russian princes, French counts and countesses, and English lords and ladies wintering in the South of France. Before long, *le tout Paris* was arriving at the doors of Rumpelmeyer's on the rue de Rivoli.

I was thrilled to find that Proust took tea here, and so did England's George V, who kept his own engraved glasses on the premises. During *les années folles,* Coco Chanel lunched with friends at Rumpelmeyer's. The Aga Khan came for a special confection called a Mont Blanc—a mountain of chestnut cream, with a crisp meringue center. It was Madame Rumpelmeyer who gave the old *salon de thé* its new name.

Angelina became my post of observation in Paris. At afternoon tea one could see ancient Parisian ladies with hats and veils and gloves—one of them carried with her a little white dog who ate dainty bits of pastry. There were fashion models and diplomats, students and intellectuals, and a sprinkling of what Paris called *jeunesse dorée* (privileged youth) having croissants and champagne for breakfast in the late afternoon. It was at Angelina, not surprisingly, that I developed the ability to follow three different conversations at the same time—for there was always something to listen to.

I have never had one of Angelina's famous Mont Blancs because the very first time I went there, I ordered a pastry called Victoria—a small tart filled with what can only be described as essence of chocolate. In the center of a Victoria is a candied violet. The exquisite texture of the chocolate alone would have been sufficient to assure my undying loyalty, but the addition of a candied violet—which since childhood I had always thought of as the most exotic treat one could have—fixed it indisputably.

Every time I come to Paris, Angelina is, after dropping off my luggage, the first place I go. I do not insist on sitting at any particular table, but I always have the same pastry—a Victoria. I have dreamed about Victorias. Angelina epitomizes Paris for me now: So many other things have changed, but it remains very much the same—some of the waitresses who were there when I first came, I recognize—and they still wear white and black, with proper blouses. The dreamy mural of the Baie des Anges still graces the wall, and one still has tea or hot chocolate or champagne at the familiar green marble tables.

But I am looking for something else, too, when I come back to Angelina. I am looking for my earlier selves, remembering what it was like to be twenty and falling in love with Paris. Angelina for me brings back friends and rendezvous, learning to speak French, the first time I read Proust. I can, at Angelina, almost remember what it was like to have time and world enough to do as one pleased.

A PLACE

AT THE TABLE

Jane Howard

hanksgiving, at our house on Willow Road in Win-
netka, Illinois, meant the arrival of a happy swarm of guests—
typically my father's parents from their farm in Iowa, some cousins from Wisconsin, a war widow from around the corner—
enough company, in any case, to set our table for ten or twelve.
Then, one year in the mid-1940s, something unthinkable happened: At the last minute, everyone had to cancel.

My resourceful mother saved us from a lonely Thanksgiving
by rounding up two households of neighbors for "a darned good
turkey," as she noted in her diary. But I've never forgotten that
moment of panic. How could we celebrate properly if "we" were
just the same old four of us—my parents and younger sister and
I—who always ate together? Gathering was something my family felt a historic hunger to do. Descended on both sides from
large, outgoing midwestern clans, we were bred to expect a feast,
a wide range of voices, however off-key, to join in that sturdy
old hymn of the season, "We Gather Together," and, not at all

incidentally, place cards. These, we had been taught, would help our guest feel "framed and central," to borrow a phrase from Margaret Mead.

Figuring out who was to sit where, and why, was a lesson in the subtle and important arts of diplomacy and social choreography. Our object, on Willow Road, was to make sure everyone had a good time. So we drew a diagram of our table (with all its extra leaves inserted), wrote the name of each guest on a separate slip of paper, and experimented with different designs for the cheeriest seating arrangement.

Which two guests were the most honored, for reasons of seniority or some other distinction, and should therefore sit to the right of Daddy and Mommy? Who was the shyest? Whoever won that title, along with whoever was the newest among us, should be seated next to whichever guests were the likeliest to put other people at their ease. The wittiest should sit where everyone else has the best chance of hearing the jokes.

And was anyone likely to make trouble? Might a feud be brewing among our guests? In our family, as in many, this could happen. Grudge-holding, like wacky humor and bibliophilism, was a trait that persisted throughout the generations. You might think that holders of grudges would give each other a wide berth, but they didn't always. Place cards enabled us to position Uncle Francis and Cousin Winifred as far apart as possible if this was one of the years they weren't speaking. (We always kept in mind that the person you sit across from can have just as much effect on your digestive system as the person to your right or left.)

From one Thanksgiving or Christmas to the next, our place cards were rarely the same. We never bought them at fancy stores like Tiffany's, though some families do, or had them engraved with coats of arms, or hired calligraphers. When we could, we relied upon the work of my mother's elegant Auntie Grace, our family's itinerant eccentric and designated artist.

Never traveling without her sketchbook, she was easily persuaded to make place card–sized watercolors evoking her travels: Mexicans under sombreros, Scots wearing kilts, old houses in the Berkshire Mountains, sunsets from Pacific beach shacks, and portraits of Santa calling to mind the line, "and the smoke, it encircled his head like a wreath."

In Auntie Grace's absence, we kids were appointed to design and make the place cards, which not only kept us out of the way but allowed an outlet for our developing artistic talents. From our first crude place cards cut from construction paper and labeled with crayons, we progressed to more elaborate models, displaying our skill as caricaturists. And we weren't allowed to misspell names. Names, my newspaper-reporter father often reminded us, are something people take very seriously.

Some years when enough cousins joined us, we'd either cluster the kids' place cards at one end of the extended table or set up a separate "children's table." In theory (my theory, anyway) generations should intermingle, with people born before 1920, for example, seated next to those born after 1985. But in reality, kids tend to prefer the company of kids. They don't necessarily want to join in discussions of tax reform or recite one by one "what we have to be thankful for since last November."

If the dinner's going to last a good while, as festive dinners tend to, it's smart for the host and hostess to agree that at some point they'll trade places, or arrange for certain guests—every other person, maybe, or all the men—to take new seats before dessert. On the back of their place cards might be written instructions like: "After the salad course, please change places with Johnny O'B."

Now, childhood long gone, I look back over many holiday rituals, some years as a hostess and some as a guest. My happiest Thanksgivings (and Christmases and Easters and Passovers) have involved place cards. We even used them the year when twelve or so of us roasted our turkey over an open fire in a cabin in New Hampshire. By each place that year, at rustic picnic tables, was a card propped next to a tiny pumpkin. Another year, at a dinner within the sound of the surf, place cards were set between small cairns of special stones and shells gathered from the beach. Christmas tree ornaments also make useful props, as do tiny bottles filled with sprigs of bittersweet or holly.

One holiday dinner, when the state lottery stakes zoomed up to the multimillions, each guest found a ticket by his place card. Other years I've seen place cards with messages from Chinese fortune cookies or with snapshots of each guest from the archives of a host who was a photographer. At a party of writers the hostess made anagrams of all her guests' bylines: Thomas Harris came out "Shorti Marash;" my three given names (the middle of which is Temple) became "Althea Jompen Drew." At a much larger holiday party than any I can remember from childhood, the theme was "Great Couples From History." As guests entered the dining room, they reached into a bowl to pick out slips of paper telling who they "were" and which table to head for. When Héloïse got to table three she'd discover her Abélard, just as Narcissus found his Echo, and Victoria her Albert.

Place cards, I've realized, can be playful or sentimental or both. Sometimes guests are allowed to take them home as souvenirs, sometimes not. In downtown Manhattan I have friends whose loft has been the site for seasonal festivities over many years. On Easter Sunday their place cards are eggs dyed long ago in onion juice and decorated with guests' names. As we search for our eggs at that long table (actually several tables joined together), many of us feel related to these hosts, though technically we aren't, because of their genius for making us feel like family.

We gather there, in custom and ceremony, for the same reason friends and relatives gathered for holidays at our house on Willow Road, and our ancestors assembled on the farm in Iowa: to hear grace said or to pause for a silent moment, to be distracted from the uneasy feeling we all have now and then that we're rattling around in a random, uncaring universe. For a while, at tables like these, our place cards show us where we belong. And that's not a small thing.

PARTIES REAL

AND OTHERWISE

―――――――――――――――――

Carol Shields

Who doesn't love a party? All my life, it seems, I've been drawn to the idea of parties, of people gathering together in order to observe an occasion, to celebrate or simply rub up against each other.

Nevertheless it came as a surprise to me to discover that all of my novels contain party scenes. It was a book reviewer who pointed out all these parties in my pages; I hadn't noticed, probably because parties seem so tightly woven into the fabric of the lives I write about—and my own life, too—that it would be unthinkable to leave them out.

Even my first novel, *Small Ceremonies,* contains a party. Judith Gill, the main character, invites her friends and her husband's colleagues for a Saturday night gathering in the suburbs. I couldn't resist providing the invitation.

BUFFET SUPPER
Where — 62 *Beaver Place*

When—*April 30, 8:00*
Judith and Martin Gill

The time is 1975. Judith serves lasagna and a tossed salad, knowing full well that her party menu is ten years out of date—as are her decor, her hairstyle, and her skirt length. But she is a woman who understands the essence of hospitality, who refuses even to confess to the notion of datedness. The party hums along beautifully, just as we all hope our parties will. Judith's guests have a terrific time. Her simple supper for old friends is what I've come to think of as the "good-enough party," where the buzz of human interaction matters more than the quality of the flowers or the food. People, it seems, love any kind of party, and who can imagine a guest so churlish as to refuse an invitation because the occasion promises to be less than chic.

Judith Gill's party occurs about three quarters of the way through the novel, and I suppose I felt it was time to show my heroine in her hostess role—a role almost all of us take on from time to time, planning parties and then seeing them through, even though we sometimes panic at the last minute and wish we'd never thought of the idea.

My own mother put on her entertainment hat four or five times a year, hosting a tea, a luncheon, a few tables of bridge on a Friday night or, occasionally, as Christmas drew near, an "open house." But for all her skill at "entertaining," she remained a nervous hostess.

And so is Janey Carpenter, in my 1980 novel *Happenstance,* who exhausts herself in her quest for the perfect party. Janey is careful to invite only those guests able to advertise themselves with a modicum of celebrity, and she introduces them to one another with their labels attached: "This is Jack Bowman, our local expert on Great Lakes Indians," or "Meet Hy Saltzer, he does bricks." The wine that is served is both expensive and rare, as Janey's husband, Larry, carefully points out to the assembled friends. An up-to-the-minute buffet is served: curried crab rolls, lobster salad with pecans and a ghastly dip made of grated turnips, my own fictional invention. Sadly, the evening is one of those occasions that tries too hard, forcing the celebrants into various modes of false posturing. This chillingly artificial event dies of its own self-consciousness and leads, in the small hours of the morning, to a near-tragic conclusion.

This party, like Judith Gill's more successful party, gave me a chance to bring my characters together on stage, as it were, and draw the story to a dramatic turning point. But I also felt compelled to write about the ceremonial aspect of getting ready for a party, a set of rituals we can all recognize even when they differ from one household to the next.

I remember being baffled as a child by what adults actually did when they got together. It seemed they did nothing but talk. No pin-the-tail-on-the-donkey, no musical chairs, no competitive edge or excitement or wrapped prizes for the victor, only talk, talk, talk. It was worrying. Was this what the future held? Was this what a party was for?

Our human need to come together is primitive, and I suppose you could look all the way back to prehistoric feasts and ceremonies and see them as the world's earliest parties. If you set aside those parties that are merely obligatory and exist for the sake of reciprocating the hospitality of others, then there is something biblical and compelling about raining down a lot of food and drink on a group of people who have come together under a single roof at an appointed hour. Parties can be cathartic, too, signaling a release of withheld generosity. The doors and windows are temporarily opened. Merriment is invited in, and we sometimes find that a different self emerges: our party self.

All this is useful material for a novelist who wants to show a book's characters from as many angles as possible. Judith Gill is a serene and competent hostess at her own buffet supper, but when she is invited to a friend's lunch party she slips into another role and becomes an exuberant storyteller, a vivacious and slightly out-of-control guest.

I can remember the mystery of seeing my mother and father transformed from dull parenthood into their other, and perhaps truer, party selves. I recall on bridge evenings—ribbon sandwiches or asparagus rolls would be served afterward, along with coffee—my astonishment at hearing their voices rise with social urgency, even breaking into unaccustomed laughter. They seemed younger on these occasions, stronger, lighter of heart, almost like someone else's parents. In the morning we children would find the living room splendidly disordered, the card tables still in place, and, if we were lucky, there would be a few delectable salted cashews at the bottom of the glass candy dishes.

Our need for parties may be constant, but most of us can look back and see how different a sixties party was from a seventies party, how our expectations were subtly changed in the eighties and nineties, how our own chronological age and family conditions create new ways for us to come together. And new party menus! When my parents were newly married, they served their friends Welsh rarebit or scalloped oysters. Later, in the forties, came chicken à la king with perhaps a Waldorf salad at the side. A company meal in my childhood was a good roast beef with browned potatoes and a lime gelatin pie for dessert or, if it was summer, my mother's homemade pineapple ice. In the fifties, my teenage years, we were served sloppy joes at parties, and a curious new snack food called nuts 'n' bolts. Along the way someone invented chips and dip, that revolution in casual party food, followed by such period offerings as minipizzas, wine and cheese, seafood crepes, beef fondues, and pasta salads in their various flavors and hues.

These shifting menus—familiar to all of us—make for fascinating social history and allow a novelist to set a scene in a precise period in history.

I love to read old newspapers, especially those from the early part of our century. We sometimes think of the old-fashioned society page as being rigidly formulaic, but it was also alive with sentiment and a warm effusiveness. Society editors knew what their readers hungered after: details, details, and more details. Readers of that time demanded the full gush and glow of other people's wedding parties, what exactly the bride wore, the style and material of her dress, the cut of her veil, a precise flower-by-flower description of her bridal bouquet. They wanted to know what was served at the prewedding shower, how the tables were decorated and especially who was there.

Here is such a journalistic account from 1927 as it appears in my most recent novel, *The Stone Diaries*. My description is pure fiction, of course, but it follows very closely the format I found when doing my library research on the period, and I confess that I stole the name Grace Healy and her musical contribution—with its perfect twenties feel—from a real newspaper's society page.

Mrs. Alfred Wylie entertained at a kitchen shower Thursday afternoon in honor of Daisy Goodwell, a June Bride-to-be. The rooms were prettily decorated with wisteria, bells, and streamers. Guests included Mrs. Hoad, Mrs. Stanton Merrill, Mrs. A. Caputo, Mrs. B. Grindle, Mrs. Fred Anthony, Miss Labina Anthony, Miss Elfreda Hoyt, and the Misses Merry Anne and Susan Colchester. During the afternoon, Miss Grace Healy contributed several delightful vocal and piano selections.

I also found, while reading my reel of microfilmed newspapers from the twenties, a number of mysterious references to something called a White Dinner, an event hosted by parents of the bride in the week or so before the wedding. What on earth was a White Dinner? My first thought was that the guests would be expected to come to dinner wearing white, but a friend of mine set me straight: A White Dinner is a meal in which all the food is white, or at least off-white.

This type of meal may not strike us today as being particularly attractive, but in the interest of authenticity I decided to give my heroine Daisy Goodwell a White Dinner before her marriage. The menu included bay scallops, fillet of Dover sole, supreme chicken served with an accompaniment of creamed onions and a dessert of vanilla chantilly ice, molded in the form of twin doves. I set the table with a profusion of white flowers and lit it with ivory tapers.

Finishing my White Dinner description I felt suddenly sated. It was almost as if I had actually attended or even hosted such a celebration. And herein, of course, lies one of the unlooked-for pleasures of writing fiction. Picking up our pens or sitting before a word processor, we writers can happily attend the kind of parties to which I for one will never be invited. As a novelist I have the freedom to dream up eccentric parties-on-paper, elaborate formal parties, crazy impromptu parties, parties that sing or else go slightly out of whack. Just moving a pen down a page I can do the planning, the shopping, the cooking, the greeting at the door. I can set the table any way I like, I can decide on background music, define the mood, introduce a charming invention or two and, most important, I can create my own guest list.

In my 1992 novel, *The Republic of Love,* I hosted (that is, I wrote about) a house party celebrating a fortieth wedding anniversary. Being fond of round numbers, I invited one hundred people exactly, and the invitations were extraordinarily beautiful, tiny handmade leather folders—one of the daughters of the family is a cobbler by profession—holding two photographs, one of the couple as they looked on their wedding day forty years earlier, and another, more recent likeness. The hundred guests are specifically instructed not to bring a gift, but only a single long-stemmed flower, and these flowers are placed in an immense pottery gift vase, the centerpiece of the party. There is recorded music, dancing, generous pourings of wine and then— because this is a novel with a story to tell—an intimation of trouble ahead for the celebrating husband and wife. This, in fact, is why the party is planted in the novel, though I like to think it's there for its own pleasures as well.

An entirely different party—my favorite fictional party for some reason—takes place in my novel *Swann,* set in 1987. It is Christmas Day in a small Ontario town. Rose, the town's unmarried librarian, has invited her friends in for eggnog and a snack as she does every Christmas Day, and as her mother had done before her. Rose is too modest to call the occasion a party; instead she calls it, "asking people in." She makes better eggnog than her mother did, adding more rum, for one thing. And invariably she serves something called a cheese log. This offering from the fifties, or perhaps earlier, was made by combining cubed processed cheese, crumbled soda crackers, pieces of green pepper and a dash of Worcestershire sauce. The mixture was shaped into a log (or a Christmas tree if you wanted to go fancy), decorated with strips of pimiento and sliced stuffed olives, then placed on a platter and surrounded by crackers.

Every writer has a favorite fictional character, and mine is Rose. I wanted her to have a successful Christmas party because she is at a point in her life when she is deeply frightened by the thought of the future. I wanted her friends to appreciate the effort she's gone to, and they do. There is ease in the little room, merriment, a stirring of hope. The eggnog goes down, the cheese log is nibbled away, time slips by. Rose is seized with optimism, and from nowhere comes the sudden shine of happiness and faith in the future.

I am an invisible presence at this gathering, an authorly mouse under a fictional chair, watching as Rose's friends come together to share holiday warmth and hospitality, saying to one another as they at last put on their coats and scarves and head for home: "Thanks so much. It was a wonderful party."

In the Company
of the Past

THE DANCE OF LIFE

Doris Bryden Randall

e named her Melissa Eve, the Eve after her paternal grandmother, deceased long before I married her son. In Eve's pictures I saw a beautiful woman with high cheekbones, proud in bearing. Her family, originally from France, had settled in Lewiston, Maine.

Melissa weighed a mere six and a half pounds at birth, much too tiny to bear the weight of her full given name. We would softly coo to her, "Missy Boo, Missy Boo." Her hair was thick and black, so profuse that it extended to her forehead, and tufts grew along her ears. Her eyes, a deep purple, gave her an enigmatic look, and the high cheekbones were a copy of Grandmother Eve's.

And now, shortly before her thirty-fifth birthday, Melissa Eve is nine months pregnant with her first child. No longer a Missy, but an alive, vibrant woman—a Melissa. These last days before the birthing, I am staying with my daughter and son-in-law. She and I take morning walks along the tree-lined streets of her

Sacramento neighborhood. It's May, and the air is intoxicatingly perfumed with the scent of orange blossoms. Our talks are light—soft as the spring air.

At home, Melissa sinks back into a recliner—tired and uncomfortably warm. I massage her swollen feet with cool lotion. The touch of her is heady—a long journey from the baby she was to the one awaited. I put my ear to her distended belly. She and I and the baby within. At Melissa's feet I am witnessing the humility of a universal rite—I am mortal, and this mortal daughter, whom I conceived, is repeating the season with the birth of a "he." Now in the autumn of my declining, I am witness to new life beginning. We are a dance of life, a change of places—a daughter, now a mother; a mother, now a grandmother. And so the dance of life—do-si-dos in our oneness and aloneness—a Möbius, at once one-sided and intertwining.

The father, so close and perceptive of his wife's needs, now is an intimate, compelling part of the birthing. He watches over his wife, my daughter, sees to her comfort. (I smile, delighting in his tenderness.) His ears are like a cat's—sharp, attentive, alert for any sign of her discomfort, or the knit of Melissa's brow. As if on toe, he is ready to anticipate each silent need of his love. In deference to him, I glide away in silence, content that I have been invited into this magic circle.

Just a few weeks before Melissa's birthday, Taylor is born— a healthy, beautiful baby with the same cheekbones as his mother and grandmother. Joy unparalleled for mother and father.

The arrival of a new generation gives birth to the past, to the cycle of life, the coming of each new season. To this grandparent, it brings a clarity, sharp, bittersweet, the panorama of childhood memories—of the generations that came before me, grandparents, great-grandparents, and all the tales of lives that preceded them. I remember the parlor bedroom where I was born, where my dad and my grandmother were born—that very bedroom where my great-grandfather died. My mother, carrying a tray of food, shut me out of the chamber. I was two years old then and can still feel the eeriness of that forbidden place.

I walk to our brook, and my granddad holds my hand—and I'm carrying this new, wonderful grandson of mine. A log spans the brook, a place for me to play Tarzan and Jane. Its waters are safe and inviting. Beneath the roots of an oak, just under the water, swim harmless minnows. There are no generation gaps in our generations—no distinction between those living and those no longer with us. The time that is of the births and deaths does not play by the rules of linear time. Granddad and I, and little Taylor—we walk the same path, the time that winds, the time of the seasons; we all walk together—interwoven, the Adams and Eves of us. Taylor, in my musings, is playing on our sap-bush hill. I sense the urgency of crocuses pushing through the snow, fresh sap and the compelling fragrance from the sap house, where a vat of the precious liquid is becoming maple syrup. The rich, honeyed essence wafts its way up through the chimney, bringing that hot, tantalizing aroma to the child in all of us—to Granddad, to me, and to Taylor. The baby-to-be now is!

IT ALL STARTED WITH

THE SAMPLER

Susan Crandell

y great-grandmother Agnes made it when she was ten, and my mother gave it to me when I turned sixteen. It was my first important gift. We bought a handsome cherry-wood frame, and I hung the sampler in my room. "A. Hutchinson, 10, Kendal, April 12, 1875," the needlepoint read, below a carefully stitched alphabet in browns and reds.

Struggling through my own adolescence, I'd flop onto the bed, stare at the sampler, and try to imagine the girlhood of someone who, at ten, had such reservoirs of patience and skill. Growing up in a city in the north of England, Agnes lived without cars or telephones, on a street lit by gas lamps. She fascinated me in a way no other ancestor did. Probably it was her reputation as tough-minded matriarch, a woman of independent emotional means.

In time, I grew up and had a daughter myself. Brook, too, was captivated by the Kendal sampler, but even more so by a gold brooch that held a lock of Agnes's hair. Agnes and Brook were the only blondes in the family, their own special bond across the years.

So maybe it was inevitable that Mom and Brook and I, three generations of women and Agnes's only living descendants, would journey to England to see her hometown. We didn't really know what we were looking for; it just felt like something we had to do.

Brook, then thirteen, dragged boxes from the attic, sorting through dusty piles of photographs and mementos no one had looked at for years, assembling every clue we had to Agnes's English past. Each time she unearthed a new find, she'd phone my mother: "Grandma, I've just found Agnes's wedding certificate. The original. It's handwritten!" But it wasn't until we met for the overseas flight that the three of us had a chance to sort through our clues together. Mom filled us in on the Agnes she remembered. "She came to America because she married a millworker; her parents, who had their own wood-joinery business in Kendal, had opposed the marriage. She left England for love, but I wonder if she knew she was leaving part of her heart in Kendal. Because every time she saved enough money, she'd go back." A deliciously sentimental story; we couldn't wait to see the place she had loved so much.

What we found was a small working-class city with tidy streets of limestone houses, where Agnes's family had lived near a pretty park called Kendal Green. We spent an afternoon in the town archive, looking up birth dates and weddings. We stood in the church where Agnes was married and took pictures of one another in front of five houses in which various members of her family had once lived. We located the shop of Agnes's father, now a chain appliance store. We phoned the four Hutchinsons still listed in the Kendal directory. Not a relative in the bunch.

As a genealogical expedition, I guess it was a bust. Yet we all considered the trip a success. Traveling around England's

Lake District, its pastureland jigsawed by miles of stone walls, triggered the sort of conversations we rarely got around to at home. Every evening after dinner, Brook would steal away to her grandmother's room. I imagine there are oodles of things they talked about that Brook doesn't bring up with me. Over dinner one night, Mom talked about how strong-willed Agnes had been, marrying against her parents' wishes, the only one among her six siblings to leave England, who then dragged her husband back whenever she could, spending all their savings on steamship tickets. And she told us what her father remembered best about his own boyhood trip to Kendal: the joy of tossing another boy's cap into the ship's broad wake, the dismay of being made to replace it with his own.

In the end, our memories of Kendal aren't any more consequential than that small cap bobbing on the Atlantic. For the trip really wasn't about the girlhood Agnes, who remains a shadowy figure in a small English mill town we can now fix in our mind's eye. It was about Brook's coming-of-age, being old enough to hear the complicated stories of struggles and rewards, feeling the tenderness and strength of the family bonds that run from her grandmother to her through me. And understanding that she could be the latest in a century-long line of strong women.

Since then, when people ask me about finding their roots, I say: Pay attention to those you go with as much as to the ancestor you seek. If there's a tough-minded matriarch lurking in the upper branches of your family tree, by all means search her out. And think about leaving the menfolk behind.

PIANO FOR FOUR HANDS

Marjorie Sandor

y mother, who is the musician in our family, has waited years for a miracle: for one of us to get serious about the piano. I am her youngest and only daughter, and her tactical shift was so quiet I never guessed what was afoot.

"Just tell me when you're settled down, and I'll send the piano," she said, long distance, a little breathless, as if the migratory patterns of my generation left her slightly winded. This was the way her domestic magic worked: She waited until I married and set up housekeeping in a small Boston apartment and let me discover for myself that something was wrong, missing from our living room. "Of course," she said casually. "You need the piano."

How far back had she planted the seeds of my adult longing? There was always a piano in our house when I was growing up, as much a part of daily life as any bed or kitchen table. While it was an obstacle in our games of tag, its bench a place to hide things, it was being secretly rooted in our memories, in our vision of what belongs in a home.

My mother herself is an organist, and when we were growing up, she kept her Hammond organ safely out of the way of domestic traffic, in our best room, one forbidden to us. This was her private domain. The noises of kitchen and family room were distant, muffled against the ever-complicating Toccata and Fugue in D Minor. In the evenings, she dabbled in Bach, Franck, and Duruflé. Then, like a good wife of her generation, she came down to earth and played tunes from *South Pacific* to keep my father happy.

Once in a while she let me sit up on the bench with her and improvise dramatic scenes: "Storm at Sea," I remember, and something called "Graveyard at Midnight," in which I tolled heavy low notes on full vibrato, bringing myself to rapturous tears of invented grief. But mostly I lay on the fancy pale-gold carpet, watching her feet cross and speed over the pedals, listening to the deep trembling notes of the organ accompanied by the music of evening insects in our backyard.

Each of us began piano lessons promptly at the age of seven; none of us blossomed. At fourteen, one of my brothers switched to guitar and got as far as "Norwegian Wood"; another one switched, too, and memorized the opening bars of "Classical Gas." I was next. After a year of lessons, I suffered through a monumental one-page minuet, then strode to my mother. "Listen. I can play it good," I said. "*Well*," she said quietly. "You can play it *well*."

That night, with the pencil kept at the piano for notes during lessons, I carved, in small, distinct letters, the word "well" into the soft wood. I was sent to my room, but for years after, I noted the little blemish with triumph and amazement at my own nerve, pressing my fingers over the grooves of my careful childhood script as if it were a battle scar, my first serious mark on the world.

The upright was eventually delivered to my oldest brother's house, after his first child was born—my mother was thinking ahead, as usual. Back at our house, perhaps figuring me safely past the age of impromptu wood carving, she ordered the Yamaha, an ebony baby grand. With a sigh, she directed the movers to put it deep in the belly of our house, in the carpeted basement room where we kept photo albums and relics of family outings. She did not suggest lessons; she simply shrugged and gave me the same resigned smile she'd fixed on the movers. She knew I would subject the beautiful instrument to the same three or four chords of folk rock. While I played, she waited patiently. Sometimes she sat behind me, quietly tapping out the tempo on her knee. "You have a good ear," she'd say. "Someday you'll see you don't have to bang so hard."

When the baby grand arrived in Boston, it fit with uncanny ease into our living room's bay window. It shone. It appeared to be waiting for something. I tried out a mournful Jackson Browne tune from the early seventies and was mortified by the monotony of the progressions that had gripped me as an adolescent. I was acutely aware that at any minute my mother might call and ask about my playing. I contacted a local music school and said shakily, "Beginning intermediate."

My teacher was a dark-haired Russian named Ludmilla, who prescribed violent medicine: Czerny's "School of Velocity." The first exercise in this book has no flats or sharps but is daunting nonetheless, with its command, *presto!*, and its strenuous arpeggios and cadenzas. It was penance for a lifetime of musical and filial neglect, and I took it up with a sinner's compulsive certainty.

My mother was pleased, in a careful, reserved sort of way. "You're actually reading music," she said as if this were one of the miracles in the desert—like manna or the burning bush. There was a little catch in her voice that surprised me. "What are you working on these days?" I asked. "Oh," she said lightly, "my fingers are a little stiff. I stopped a while ago."

I was too stunned to answer, and, in her unfailing sense of domestic grace, she quickly added that she was of course keeping the organ for her grandchildren. "They love to bang on it so," she said.

We aren't in Boston any more. A single, indecent year after she sent the baby grand, we moved again, this time to the South and university teaching jobs. I was nearly afraid to tell her, as if after claiming to "settle down" I'd broken some unspoken pact.

In our new house, the piano was destined to fit only in one place, a low-ceilinged "rumpus room" lined with books and family pictures. This is not the best place for a piano, with its broad Florida windows and a steamy private jungle of vines and sable palm all around. But we feel protected back there, comfortable; it is where, as a family, we spend our evening time. But for months that time passed with no Czerny, no Jackson Browne. The Yamaha itself was cluttered with little soft baby toys and pale laundry in heaps. My mother, who had come to see the baby, sighed when she saw where we had put the piano. "I guess there really isn't anywhere else," she said. It was a day or two before she tactfully, almost shyly, mentioned the dust on the lid. "You should play," she said quietly. "I always played when you slept."

It would be a long time before I managed to make good on this suggestion. But miraculously, one late afternoon, while my two-year-old slept, I found myself sitting at the piano with a book of Mozart sonatas, its pages gummed together from the humidity. Just beyond the big Florida windows, in the sable palm, in the oaks of our yard, the cicadas made a fierce, metallic racket, and suddenly it sounded like home, like the evenings of my childhood, when I lay on my belly watching my mother play.

I was hunched over the keys, hair in my face, with the slumped posture of my teenage self, when I noticed that I was reading. Breathing. Thinking. Start pianissimo, begin the crescendo here. A phrase repeated in a minor key resolved and came back major—depicting Mozart's love of parody in the midst of the sublime. Here were the forms, earthly and celestial, my mother had loved all her life and once made with her fingers. I wanted to call her and say, "Mother, listen," but I made a little deal with myself: Get through the rondo first.

That's where I was, laboring along at half speed, when I heard my daughter waking up from her nap. A minute later she appeared at the door to the family room and scrambled up onto the piano bench with a single hoist, her feet flipping up behind her in the air like a seal flinging itself onto a warm rock. She pushed my hands off the keys. "Hannah play," she said.

What she wanted to play, it turned out, was the bass, the low, tolling bells and gloom of my old "Graveyard at Midnight." I pressed my foot on the sustain pedal. And with a straight back and fat, greedy, beautiful hands, she banged away at the deepest notes in the world.

In the Company
of the Past

Susan J. Gordon

n the photograph that hung on my bedroom wall
when I was a child, it is 1912. My grandmother is wearing a
honey-toned satin dress edged in fine lace and a strand of seed
pearls around her neck. She is a slim young woman with lustrous
brown hair piled on top of her head. In her arms is her beautiful
baby daughter, who is dressed in a long, white cotton gown and
wrapped in a soft fur throw.

I don't remember when I first noticed the photo. It had always
been there beside my bed. I saw it when I went to sleep at night
and played beneath it during the day. When I look at it now,
it's me I'm remembering, as a little girl.

My mother, brother, and I lived with my grandmother ever
since I was two years old, when my parents separated. My
mother went to work and my grandmother took care of us.
Weekday mornings, she gave us our breakfasts, packed our
lunches, and sent us off. When she kissed me good-bye, I

smelled a sweet mixture of shampoo, soap, and her morning cup of coffee.

On rainy and lazy winter afternoons, when I was home from school and particularly bored or restless, she'd take a break from housework and sit with me. As we sifted through the piles of family photographs, she would tell me stories. "This is your Aunt Sel, before she was married. She was going to art school. That's one of her paintings in the background." Or, "These are your parents, when they first met. They got married so quickly. . . . And they were so young."

Some photographs were of my grandmother's parents, taken soon after they emigrated to America. My sweet-faced great-grandfather sits on an ornate chair, and his solemn wife and young children stand right beside him. Everyone stares straight ahead at the camera. Taking pictures had once been serious business; you put on your best clothes and went to the photographer. Years later, my brother and I still put on "dress-up" clothing, but everything took place outside. "Look toward the sun!" my mother would say, and consequently, in all my childhood pictures, I am squinting.

There are no photographs of the interior of our home. There is no picture of my grandmother cooking, ironing, or reading the newspaper, or making dresses for me on her Singer sewing machine. Nor is there a picture of my mother's dressing table where she sat and transformed herself, before my eyes, from a pretty woman to a most beautiful one. And yet, I can see these people, and see the rooms they occupied, as clearly as if they were pictures in an album. I see every piece of furniture, where everything stood, and how the sunlight shifted from our living room in the morning to the kitchen in the late afternoon. Photographs really aren't necessary when I think about home. Still, there are days when I am drawn to look at them.

Click! I am four years old, standing in front of a restaurant with my family. Since eating out was a treat, we probably were celebrating something, but I don't remember what. I do remember the green wool coat I am wearing, and its deliciously soft velvet collar that I loved to press against my cheeks.

Click! My brother and I are shaking hands in front of the apartment house. We squabble all the time, but my mother has asked us to assume a conciliatory pose. "You were happy together sometimes," she tells us. "One day, you'll want to remember this."

Click! I am dancing with a boy at a high school party. Since I'm the "new girl" in the neighborhood, for a short while I'm popular. Other teenage boys and girls dance much closer, with their hands around each other's necks. My partner and I smile and wave toward a friend, who catches our expressions with her new Polaroid camera. Caught in the photo is another boy, who is laughing in reaction to someone else's story. One day, this picture will become especially dear to me, for it has unintentionally included the young man I will marry.

Click! I am holding Edward, my firstborn baby, in exactly the same way that my grandmother held hers. I think about how much she loved me and know I love my son as passionately and completely. My husband takes our picture, then hangs the antique photo above the baby's crib; eventually it will hang by his brother Peter's, too. It will be a part of their childhood years, as it once was a part of mine.

Today, my house is filled with photographs. It's my nature to save things—hold the moment and try to freeze it in a frame. Photos cover the kitchen wall; my sons win prizes, hit baseballs, wear costumes, sing camp songs, graduate from kindergarten, graduate from high school. Edward's eyes sparkle like my mother's when she was a girl. Peter's smile resembles that on his great-great-grandfather's face. Who will look at all these pictures in future years? Will a young child take them out of boxes some day and study them with fresh curiosity? Will our photographs explain what we were really like or simply acknowledge that, for a time, we were here?

Not long ago, I saw Edward in his room looking through piles of family pictures. I started to approach but silently backed away. It had been a long time since he had shown any interest in the pictures, but now he was ready to leave for college. He handled everything with a gentle reverence and smiled to himself again and again.

I didn't need to take a photo of Edward that day, because the picture in my heart will last forever.

THE STITCHES
THAT BIND

Linda Sunshine

My grandmother believed that you could tell a lot about a woman from her needlework, especially if you looked on the wrong side. "You can't hide anything from the back," she would say. In many ways, the story of the women in my family can be told through our needlework.

Grandmother crocheted lace—tiny, white snowflake shapes—spun from fine cotton thread and sewn together into huge cloths. Each one took several years to complete. She was a stern, disciplined woman whose ramrod straight spine never quite touched the back of her chair. She believed in correct posture and high standards for herself and everyone else. There are no right or wrong sides to my grandmother's cloths. They are perfect, any way you look at them.

I have the lace cloth Grandmother made for my aunt, and, even after almost thirty years, her work has held firm. It was stitched together with such precision that it never needs mending. Like my grandmother, it refuses to unravel.

My mother, on the other hand, is much less stringent about her work. She enjoys the challenge of taking on seemingly impossible projects—wall-size needlepoint pictures (copied from the cover of the first book I ever published as a young editor) or huge sweater-coats knit on the smallest needles. She is now knitting a sweater so intricate that each row of stitches is different, and suede strips are woven into the wool. It will be a showcase piece, but, like all my mother's work, after a few wearings threads will hang out and holes will form where the pieces are not carefully woven together. The backs of my mother's sweaters are a creative jungle, I think, because my mother swallows time in huge gulps. She works furiously to complete a project and then get started on the next one. In her haste, she will not stop to tuck in loose threads.

My sister, certainly the most talented among us, creates her own designs and executes them in painstaking detail. She knows how to follow directions, and she does not believe in shortcuts. My mother and I defer to her whenever we're confused by a knitting pattern. She alone has the patience to reason out any instructions whatsoever, no matter how complicated they seem to us.

You will never find a flaw in a pillow or sweater my sister has completed. She is the only one in the family who will rip out an entire sleeve if she discovers so much as one slipped stitch in the cuff, even if you can see it only when the sweater is inside out. My mother and I tease her, but, at the same time, we know it is this very perfectionism that gives her work the kind of quality lacking in ours. It is no surprise my sister's crocheted pocketbooks have sold for hundreds of dollars in retail stores.

As for myself, I get impatient with directions. Being told what to do brings out a rebellious streak—I always think I can come up with an easier way to make something. Usually I'm wrong. I make lots of mistakes, and I tend to ignore them (assuming they will go unnoticed or, if not, most people will be too polite to say anything).

But, for all the sleeves that are not exactly the same length, the insides of my sweaters are nearly as meticulous as my sister's. Perhaps because of my grandmother, I value perfection; perhaps because of my mother, I have a weakness for believing in my own creativity. I work hard at finishing touches. Consequently the insides of my sweaters often look far better than the outsides.

When my nephew Adam was born, my mother, my sister, and I went into a frenzy of sweater making. Cardigans, pullovers, vests, jackets—if it could be made with knitting needles, the child had it. By the time he was five years old, Adam's hand-knit wardrobe could easily clothe his entire kindergarten class.

Stack those sweaters up and you'll have a barometer of the women in my family. They are tributes of our devotion, our love, and our mutual compulsion. Yes, those sweaters will tell you a lot about us, especially if they're turned inside out.

GINGHAM —

FOREVER FRESH

M. J. Andersen

The fabric stores of my childhood were entirely women's places. They shared the serious hush of the town library, as women and girls leafed slowly through the pattern books, then moved with steady concentration up and down among the bolts of fabric, which stood shoulder to shoulder in colorful, fresh-smelling rows. Here, the world brimmed with possibility. Here, time stopped, and a girl despairing over herself could privately dare to picture being beautiful.

It only took choosing just right—cloth, matching thread, the perfect buttons, or lace trim.

Because I had seen once or twice the great cloth emporiums of Minneapolis, I knew that the fabric stores in our small South Dakota town had only modest offerings. But all of these stores could be depended on to have one material in abundance: gingham. Gingham and more gingham, perfect checks—from nearly microscopic to big and bold, suggesting picnic tablecloths. You could use gingham for anything: pajamas, curtains, a smart but simple sheath dress.

I loved the bolts of gingham for their crisp orderliness and, especially when I was little, for the fairy tale they seemed to tell about life. Here were all the colors I knew; here were the ascending check sizes, like the stages of life we would pass through: child, bobby-soxer, college student, woman, grandmother. Gingham suggested a sunny world where no one could lose her way. It told of a life simple and pleasurable, in which you needed but little. And everything you needed could, conceivably, be fashioned from gingham.

My gingham outlook was reinforced in high-school home-economics class, where our first official sewing project was a gingham apron—a flounce of fabric tied at the waist and featuring a cross-stitched border design of our choice. Most of the girls picked cheerful spring garden colors and floral designs, but I struck a saturnine note, strewing cross-stitched autumn leaves across dark cocoa-colored cloth (in gingham, about as sophisticated as you can get). It was a triumph.

Hooked by our apron successes, my friend Colleen and I were eager to do more. We looked at fabric often and inspected every bolt—floral prints, velveteen, corduroy. But we shared a cultlike enthusiasm for gingham. We conquered yards of it, tackling one sewing project after another. Our output tripled in summer, on long, warm days when there was nothing to do.

We found that you could decorate gingham with braid, eyelet lace, or rickrack (in fact, no other fabric serves rickrack so faithfully). You could make just your sleeves gingham, or an inset in your dress, you could put gingham patches on old jeans, or make shoulder bags out of quilted gingham.

Colleen replied to the caftan craze by running up her own version, full-length, in tiny baby-blue checks. She spread her arms and whirled. She looked like a kite. She wore her gingham caftan on summer evenings, barefoot, or with Dr. Scholl's san-

dals, and looked fresh as a breeze. It felt as though we were
going to be in high school forever, as though we would never
stop sewing.

One winter, my friends Jackie, Judy, Lesley, and I formed a
singing group to compete in the Snow Queen talent contest.
We were the Girls for All Seasons, we decided, and we needed
a costume fast. We settled quickly on an easy-to-sew pattern for
a long dress with puffed sleeves. But the fabric debate was a
protracted agony of warring preferences. At last, because it was
inexpensive, and the only thing acceptable to all, we bought
gingham—brown for two of us, vivid, Easter-egg blue for the
other pair, suggesting a kind of earth and sky idea, though the
colors owed their selection less to a deliberate concept than to
the matter of which bolts had enough cloth on them. The night
of the Snow Queen pageant, we filed onto the high-school stage,
resplendent in our gingham gowns. We sang "One Tin Soldier"
and "I'd Like to Teach the World to Sing" and won the contest.

Because we had the costumes, we sang elsewhere; our voices
were lyrical, a sweet butterscotch blend that half amazed us. It
came so easily. A lot of our songs were soft-core war-protest
songs, but we scarcely heard our own words. We were testing
what we could do, figuring out who we would become. Vietnam
seemed far away and barely able to touch us. We were isolated
among tall corn crops in summer, high snow drifts in winter.
We kept at our projects of growing up, always stitching our
way toward the next milestone—a prom gown, a dress for graduation day. Still dreaming that we would advance in orderly
fashion through the stages of life, we laid out the wardrobes we
had made for college in upstairs bedrooms and studied what to
wear with what. We could not wait to move to the next square.

Inevitably, most of us spun away from our gingham roots.
Life turned out to be a messy, disorderly affair, and if in our
small-town girlhood we eluded history, it found us in adulthood.
Judy became a professional nightclub singer in Texas. I know

this because we ran into each other in an airport once, and she missed a plane while we were catching up. Neither of us seemed capable of getting married, but we could not have said why.

Lesley, divorced and with a daughter to support, pluckily talked her way into a position as a music teacher at a school for well-to-do West Coast teenagers and was astonished at how little natural grasp of harmony they turned out to have. Colleen gave up meat and dairy products and teaches a kind of New Age gospel of self-care in our hometown. Jackie stitched the neatest path: She married and had children. She is a nurse in North Dakota.

I thought of these friends recently when I opened a catalog and saw that, among a new collection of bedroom furnishings, a fashionable designer was offering a gingham sheet. It was a small check, in something like a grape-jelly shade, summery and fresh, all-American, and nostalgic. The price brought back to me the rallying cry of all the women I knew who had ever turned the wheel on a sewing machine: "You could make that for less." I could only think of Colleen and me toiling over our projects in July and August as the fans droned away and we waited for school to start again, for the next stage of life to come our way.

It is not that gingham has faded from use—it is, of course, a classic, and will always be around. But we wore it without irony, and with an innocence that even then was dying all around us.

MY GRANDMOTHER'S SHELL

Faith Andrews Bedford

*A*bove my mantel is a painting of a little girl with a conch shell. As she holds it up to the light, the sun streams through, turning the smooth, inner surface into glowing pink satin. No matter what the season, the painting's sunlight fills my study with summer's brightness.

Looking at the painting, I remember the story of its creation. The little girl is posing for her father, a painter. Her arms grow heavy, her neck aches, she longs to rest a bit. "El, El, look into the shell," her father murmurs, and she remembers what a privilege it is to pose for him, how sought-after his paintings are. "Just a bit longer," he promises, "and then we'll stop for tea."

Eleanor was my grandmother, and the painting—one that her father could not bear to part with—has been handed down through the generations. For as long as I can remember, the shell in the painting sat on my grandmother's desk. In the winter, when cold fog rolled in off the sea, she would hold it up to the lamp and its rosy sheen would fill her with summer's warmth once again.

Grandmother found it washed up on the rocky shore of the little island in Maine that was her family's summer home. She used to tell me how, when the morning's silvery mists had lifted, she and her sisters and brother would run across the open meadows with their kites or pick bouquets of wildflowers or gather the wool left behind on the bushes by the wild island sheep. The children would hunt for blackberries and watch birds with their father, who taught them the birds' names and all their many songs. After tea, they often explored the wide beaches looking for pirate treasure. It was on one of these adventures that Grandmother found the shell, scoured smooth by the waves, bleached clean by the summer sun. As generations before her had done, she placed the shell to her ear and heard the sound of the sea.

By the time my mother was born, Grandmother had left that island home and created a new summer place for her own children. They spent hours sailing in little dinghies, galloping their ponies across the marshes, and gathering shells on the broad white beach that bordered Cape Cod Bay. In this new home Grandmother re-created many of her childhood loves: She seeded meadows with wildflowers, designed perennial borders, and planted blackberries. And from the porch she could look out across the tidal river and see ospreys nesting in a tall pine tree.

When we grandchildren began arriving, she set aside a part of her garden so we could know the joy of planting vegetables and flowers. How proud we were to place a plate of our radish harvest—ruby globes scrubbed shiny and clean—on a dinner table made brighter still by vases filled with our flowers. She taught us the birds' calls and told us how they returned each summer to her woods and meadows, just as we did. And she let us listen to the ocean in her shell.

Each autumn, as my family and I returned to our Midwestern

home, I ached for the sounds of the shore: the cry of the gulls wheeling overhead, the low mournful song of the foghorn, so deep I seemed to feel more than hear it. The tangy smell of the salt air was replaced by the smoke of burning leaves. But I missed the tides and the wildness. Grandmother knew my yearning.

One year, shortly after Thanksgiving, the postman brought a large box mailed from Massachusetts. Mother hid it in that secret place she kept all boxes that arrived in December. On Christmas morning I opened my grandmother's present and saw, nestled in tissue paper, the delicate pink and white of her shell. I picked it up and held it to my ear, and there was the ocean, murmuring. Outside, snow was falling softly past the window, but in the shell, cupped in my hand, waves lapped on a summer shore.

This year I have a granddaughter of my own. Her birth heralds the beginning of a new generation. When she comes to visit, I shall hold the shell up to her ear and she will hear the sound that has always drawn the women of our family to the ocean. It is the sound of her own heart.

On Writing and Writers

The Narrated Life

Perri Klass

*I*n my mind is an image of the perfect diarist. Pensive, ruminative, leisurely, she sits in a cozy bookish room and fills the pages of a leather-bound notebook with even, clear writing. She chronicles her days, sketches fond but keen and pointed portraits of her acquaintances, muses without self-consciousness about her own relationships and about the important issues of the day. Her diaries are everything mine are not.

I flip through the blue loose-leaf binder that served as my diary from the three years of my pediatric residency. Ratty sheets of hospital paper, scored at the top where they were pinned to my clipboard. To Do lists, endless To Do lists. And squeezed in at the top in my not particularly pretty and ridiculously tiny handwriting, the crabbed and self-pitying sentences of my innermost thoughts. "I'm too tired and I have too much to do and I don't like John. And if Carrasquillo doesn't get better? Will it ever be the weekend?" And now, of course, I don't remember who John was or what was wrong with Carrasquillo, and though

I suppose it always did eventually get to be the weekend, I can't remember any individual week. Those self-pitying notes do conjure up for me those overtired, overcrowded days—but the patients and the incidents I wanted to remember are lost in a haze.

Going further back, I look at those notebooks I kept on my year-off-from-college hitchhiking trip in Europe. I chose those individual notebooks with such ceremony: the bound French book with the graph-paper-squared pages, the Finnish softcover notebook. I was traveling on very little money, of course, but a new diary, a new notebook, was an important purchase. But when I read through the accounts of what I saw and did, I am faced with an eighteen-year-old girl who knew very little beyond what her guidebook told her and had very little talent for description or evocation. "It was built in . . ." "Has a very interesting facade . . ." "Supposed to be a good example of the Romanesque style . . ." "My favorite painting was . . ." You would be better off reading the guidebook.

I carried tape and scissors along in my backpack and painstakingly cut out pictures of the things I saw, taped them in, and wrote around them. Those diaries are stuffed with the illustrations from a thousand travel brochures and pieces of glossy tourist literature, with entrance tickets and even money-change receipts.

Increased age, and increased experience as a writer, has not made me into the diarist of my fantasies. There are pictures of my children taped into the diary I've kept over the past few years. Surely a loving mother who is also a writer should be able to conjure her children in words, describe their stages and their changes so that she will read back over her journals some day and find her long-grown babies waiting there. Well, not me. "He's really growing up," I write and put in a picture. "She's unbelievably adorable," I write. "See figure 1."

I have been keeping a diary almost since I could write. I started out with those one-year diaries that are given to little girls on their birthdays, and I unfailingly lost the keys, though usually not before I had fallen hopelessly behind with my page-a-day routine. But I was fascinated by the idea of a diary, of the diary completed, of every day described on its page. By second grade or so, I was already writing diary entries in my head during the school day, thinking of sentences that sounded gloriously real and adult ringing in my head, sentences I would invariably forget or mess up when it came time to write them down.

I graduated to real notebooks, always selected with ritual and deliberation. I gave up on the page-a-day discipline. But the impulse to record, the tendency to narrate the events of the day to myself, rehearsing the diary entry—those got stronger all through high school. I read, and reread, *The Diary of Anne Frank.* It was for me, as I suspect it often is for Jewish girls growing up in the safety of postwar America, the book that brought home the message: this really happened to real people, it would have happened to you if you had been there. And it was also intriguing as a diary: Anne Frank actually set out to describe the people with whom she lived in her secret hiding place. She explained their complex relationships to one another, detailed their physical appearances, analyzed their characters, and quoted them when they spoke. When she wrote to her imaginary friend, she explained her life as you would explain yours to someone you cared about, someone who did not already live inside your head. She created a real narrative, and because she did that, you can read her diary, decades after her death, and feel you know her.

I imitated her, of course. I wrote letters to an imaginary friend all through high school. Anne's letters were written to Kitty; if I cannot bring myself to reveal the name of my own correspondent, it is probably for the same reason that I cannot actually bring myself to reread my diaries from high school. Someday, no doubt, I will achieve a state of adult security and bemused distance from my own adolescent agonies and posturings, and I will read the outpourings of my high school heart with gentle self-indulgence, but not yet. I'm only in my middle thirties. It hasn't been long enough.

And what am I afraid of? Not of rediscovering that I once thought David Somebody was cute (all the boys my age were named David), or even remembering the day I found out the hard way that he thought somebody else was cute. I have enough maturity to handle the actual events of adolescence, I think, but I'm nowhere near grown up enough to face my teenage affectations. The depressions and despairs that I tried to make grandiose cries at an unfair world. The precious sense of my own misunderstood uniqueness. The (oh, yes) political consciousness. The self-admiring honest chronicling of my developing sexuality. I'm just not ready for it all.

The most recent diaries are easier to read. College—the first year I ever tried typing my journal, keeping it in a loose-leaf binder. Much easier to read, of course, but I missed the ritual of buying the notebook, filling the lined pages. Europe—some of the tape they sold over there wasn't up to standard, and there are pages where the dried and yellowing tape needs to be replaced. And though I am not the diarist I long to be, I suppose I can say with some pride that I am someone who keeps a diary, has always kept a diary, will always keep a diary.

But why say it with pride? What is the point, where is the virtue, in recording your own life as you go along? My diaries are clearly not great literature, or even little literature, and I would hardly qualify either as someone who has experienced extraordinary times, as Anne Frank did, or as an extraordinary chronicler of more ordinary times. Open at random a volume of Virginia Woolf's remarkable diary, and you might find the following, from November 1928: "And there was the meeting in Mr. Williams Ellises' studio—a vast hall in Ebury Street, with ostentatiously ragged chair covers. Our raggedness, as a profession, was not ostentatious alas; it is part of our souls; a dowdiness that is not ragged, however; a meticulous respectability which is not my working state; for then I am, I think, almost picturesque." Yes, she lived an extraordinary life, and knew extraordinary people, but the fact is that everything she touched turned to evocative and interesting prose, and that is why the diary makes wonderful reading. And as for being picturesque, I wonder whether in fact my mental diarist now has Virginia Woolf's cheekbones.

But what is this impulse to write it all down and record it? It is not, in fact, that same proactive nostalgia that drives people to fill in baby books, that strong sense of someday I will want to remember these details. Diaries, proper diaries, are not really written for posterity, however much some of us may yearn to leave behind a brilliant chronicle. Diaries are written for ourselves, and the desire to write is a need to shadow our own lives with a narrative voice, however faint, however inarticulate. When I write in my diary, I am telling what is happening, in my life, in my mind, in my body, rather than simply experiencing it, and that telling is itself a gesture toward consciousness and control. If you keep a diary, you live a narrated life, and a narrated life is intrinsically different; it has an extra layer.

Yes, it has value as therapy. It's still what I do late at night when I can't sleep, when some anxious worry repeats over and over in my brain; I write it down. I may not remember who Carrasquillo was, but I understand the kind of anxiety that keeps one patient appearing and reappearing in your mind; there are plenty of other children I have cared for whose medical conundrums I have scribbled out at odd hours of the very early morning. Will he be okay, Am I doing the right thing, I can't get her out of my mind. Here's what I did, Here's what I was thinking, Here's how the baby looked; and once the anxiety is written down, I inevitably feel calmer.

And yes, keeping a diary remains, in any busy life, a piece of hard evidence that every now and then you take a moment to discuss things only with yourself. It is, I suppose, a gesture of faith in the importance of your own voice, your own opinion: This is worth considering, worth recording, worth cherishing. It is a celebration of privacy and of keeping things private, therapy without the therapist, solitary conversation.

And the truth is that when I look through that loose-leaf binder, that residency diary, those tiny desperate notes amid the lists of things to do recall accurately my state of mind, my sense of self, during those interesting years. I recognize that dogged and unimaginative chronicler of the historical sites of Europe as well; she is not the eighteen-year-old I would have liked to be, nor even the one I would like to have been, but I recognize her. And I wonder whether, in fact, when I sit down to write in my diary, when I take those bits of time, as I have taken them all my life, and put them to that one particular use, whether what I am actually doing, what I have always been doing, is recognizing myself.

Edna St. Vincent Millay:

Afternoon on a Hill

Catherine Calvert

She was only twenty, still a slip of a girl, when she stood among the crowd of summer people at the inn and began to speak her poem in her low, musical voice. Her sister Norma, a waitress there for the season, had chivied her into going along to the waitresses' ball, where several of the young girls had been asked to recite or play the piano. No one was surprised that Vincent, as she was called, had a poem to recite, for she had long been known locally as a writer, her verses and songs and stories printed in the Camden paper and the mainstay of the school literary magazine. Now she stood in this simple, wide-porched inn overlooking Camden Harbor, and the crowd must have rustled, then quieted, as they listened to the powerful verses that winged their way among them.

"All I could see from where I stood,/ Was three long mountains and a wood," she began, with lines from the poem we now know as "Renascence." These were simple words that gathered force as she explored her themes of suffocation and boundaries and renewal; a later reader called it "part birdsong, part essay in philosophy." And the poem, recited to a roomful of sunburnt summer people and townspeople who'd known her life long, was to be the catapult that launched Vincent Millay into the world beyond—and a permanent place in American letters.

Yet far as she traveled, she remained bound to her Maine origins; she was among those writers whose sense of place was bedrock in their work, a theme to be returned to again and again. A childhood spent clambering along the rock-edged sea-splashed coast of Maine endowed her with strong memories and strong feelings for its natural beauty. "The earth passion! I have always had that," she later wrote. She learned names of flowers, trees, and constellations, the names and habits of birds—knowledge that would fill her life and her art forever.

The Camden years provided her with something else, too. She was one of those rare writers who would say, as she did in later years, that her childhood had been "extraordinarily happy."

Certainly its beginnings were unpromising. Cora Millay brought Vincent and her younger sisters, Norma and Kathleen, to Camden after divorcing their father; arriving as a divorcée in a small town in 1900 could not have been pleasant. She trained as a nurse and worked nights to support them, despite well-meaning friends who advised her to take the girls out of school and put them to work in the mills. "I want them to have their chance," she countered. Well read and gifted musically, Cora had her own aspirations, which she put aside for these years of round-the-clock labor.

She believed in the genius of each of her children and in her own ability to encourage them. Later, a magazine article described Cora's as "the story of all women who sit at night in clean-swept kitchens near the stove and read with wonder in their hearts and an unnameable longing." Each child was given music lessons and access to bookshelves filled with classics, and, most of all, the gift of her fierce belief in their potential. Their futures were left to them to determine (though she said later she thought they might each learn an instrument and form a little orchestra).

It seemed a household less bound by the era's strictures than many. According to the magazine article, the Millay girls enjoyed, for instance, a rainy-day game called Ribbons. "Ribbons floating in uplifted hands, they ran out into the lovely soft rain, playing tag in the long, high grass, in which they were almost lost; catching, releasing, giggling, screaming with fun and laughter, the rain showering them, until, exhausted, they came in and mother stripped off the wet clothes." Such uninhibited fun must have stood out in this small Maine village, and as the girls grew, the Millay household, unusual as it was, became a favorite place for schoolmates to gather. The girls and their friends glided around the harbor in sailboats, picnicked in the woods, and, always, climbed Mount Battie—the town's backdrop. "Such friendly mountains," wrote Norma later, "high enough to make one glad of a pause in which to look out over the bay, but possible to climb and get back in time for dinner."

Cora began to leave the girls to themselves while she went away on nursing jobs for weeks at a time. Ten-year-old Vincent was in charge and drew up schedules to regulate her sisters' day, with fifteen-minute portions of time strictly allotted. The girls were self-reliant and interdependent and full of wit and chaff. "They were good, but not goody-goody," said their mother. They hated tidying up and enlivened household tasks with games and songs and carryings-on; once Mrs. Millay came home to find them all skating on the kitchen floor, which had been flooded by a broken pipe, then the water frozen in the winter cold. The burden of household chores fell on the girls, but there was always time made for reading and practicing and "scribbling."

Mrs. Millay treasured Vincent's first little poem, written when she was five—"One bird on a tree,/ One bird come to me. . . ." In a few years Vincent began to submit poems that were accepted by the national children's magazine *St. Nicholas,* wrote and composed for her school, and took part in amateur dramatics. In a time that valued poetry and encouraged children to memorize and recite in school, Vincent's talent was readily appreciated, especially by her mother, who would interrupt any task to listen to a newly finished work. In 1910 Vincent compiled her own handwritten anthology, titling it *Poetical Works of E. Vincent Millay,* and dedicating it to her mother "whose interest and understanding have been the life of many of These Works." In the view of Vincent's biographer, Nancy Milford, "Lyric poets, like mathematicians and musicians, often show their talent early."

Vincent graduated from high school, showered with academic glory—but then what was she to do? There was no money in the Millay household for college, nor a good job in town for a young girl, and she'd outgrown the *St. Nicholas* competitions. So she kept house for her sisters and wrote for herself. She still took long walks and spent hours contemplating the sweep of sea and sky, though the horizon that once seemed limitless must have now appeared as a close-pressing border to her world. At nineteen, in the midst of these frustrating and lonely years she began to work on "Renascence," which explored her sense of "the things that bounded me" and the underlying faith in the delights of the living world. A year later, her mother, on duty in a sickroom while her patient drowsed, fished out of the rubbish bin a magazine announcing a poetry contest. Cora wrote immediately to Vincent, who was away visiting her ill father, urging her to enter. Vincent finished her poem and sent it off to join the pile of ten thousand manuscripts sent to *The Lyric Year;* weeks later she came in from blueberrying to find the poem had been accepted for publication.

Even before its appearance, however, "Renascence" opened another pathway for Vincent. Among the summer visitors listening that evening at the inn was Caroline Dow, a YWCA executive from New York, who drew the girl aside and listened to her talk for hours about her hopes. Miss Dow left Camden resolved to send Vincent on to college, and by autumn of 1913, Vincent was both a published poet and a freshman at Vassar. She had, by strength of will and pen, fulfilled the vow she'd made in a poem at fifteen, to "pierce a way into the world's great heart."

Passport to

the Universe

Patricia O'Toole

he town where I grew up was so small and safe that
from a very early age children were allowed to rove by themselves from one end to the other. They couldn't get lost: Everyone knew which child belonged to which parents and whose
family lived where. Free to explore, I would go to the lumber-
yard in search of scraps for basement carpentry projects, to the
telephone company to watch the operators at work, and to the
office supply store, where, in the summer before second grade,
I had my eye on a fake alligator book bag (green with red trim).
It was so fine it made me ache. But I seemed to be the only one
in the family who thought it was worth the $3.98 on the price
tag. Desperate to raise the money, I regularly dropped into the
post office to study the faces in the "Most Wanted" posters. If
I nabbed one of these scoundrels, I would collect a reward from
the F.B.I.

That summer was a lonesome one. Most of my friends had
learned to ride bicycles, an art that still eluded me. While they

pedaled around town together, I spent a lot of time on my own. One hot, quiet afternoon, as I walked along the main street hoping to find someone to play with, I stopped in front of a store I had never noticed before. Through the plate-glass windows I saw people sitting in knotty pine armchairs with big cushions. Everyone was reading. I supposed the place was a store, like every other establishment on the block, and I guessed that the people who were reading were waiting to be waited on, like diners in a restaurant. I went inside to look around. I had never seen so many books—shelf after shelf rising higher than I could reach. Were there hundreds? Thousands?

From the back of the room a lady at a desk asked if I would like some help. I asked what kind of store this was. She said it wasn't a store, it was a library. Nothing was for sale, but everything could be borrowed. To become a borrower, all I needed was a library card. Would I like one?

Would I like one? Who wouldn't like one?

On a small orange card with rounded corners she inscribed my name and a number, 1221. She wrote with a fountain pen, and in the eternity it took for the ink to dry, my feelings zigzagged between amazement and fear. The very idea of a library seemed too wonderful to be true—like free candy. There must be a hitch. Maybe you could borrow books without money but had to pay when you brought them back. I didn't dare ask.

The librarian pointed out the children's section. I browsed for less time than it had taken the ink to dry, checked out a book, and left before she could change her mind about granting me this astonishing privilege.

There were more astonishments to come. The first was that nobody seemed to mind if I too sat in one of the knotty pine armchairs and looked at magazines. The most intriguing, something called *The New Yorker,* let me glimpse a world of wit and sophistication that was as far over my head as the books on the library's top shelves. But when I did understand a cartoon, the pleasure was as intense as the first lick of an ice cream cone. I could hardly wait to grow up and see this shimmering city of theaters and museums and gentlemen with walrus mustaches. I would be there in pearls and one of the elegant evening dresses I saw in *New Yorker* ads, which often ended with a line I found mysteriously beautiful: "Prices slightly higher west of the Rockies."

Next I discovered that children could borrow books from the adult section. Imagine! The librarian showed me how to find my way around: Fiction was arranged alphabetically by author, nonfiction by an ingenious numerical code, the Dewey decimal system. Years later, when I first encountered the regular decimal system, it seemed a colossal bore compared to the magic of Mr. Dewey, who had invested every number with meaning.

In the first weeks after discovering the library, I went twice a day, always checking out a single book, until the librarian thought to mention that a person could borrow several at once. Think of it.

At home I began to talk about how handy it would be to have a book bag and how lucky it was that we didn't live west of the Rockies, where the price would probably be higher than $3.98. By the end of the summer my parents caved in. There was another conquest, too—the bicycle. It happened shortly after I figured out that a pile of books could easily be carried in the basket.

Over the next few years I read voraciously and indiscriminately. Dr. Seuss, Nancy Drew, biographies of everyone from Amelia Earhart to Herbert Hoover, history, social science, and junk of every description, including a memorably torrid novel set in a prison camp during World War II. I also read, over and over, certain fairytales that offered reassurance I did not consciously understand I needed. In "The Ugly Duckling" was the comforting hope that someday I too might be graceful as a swan. "The Emperor's New Clothes" confirmed my hunch that adults were not all-knowing and all-powerful, despite what some of them said.

The little orange card was my passport to the universe. With it I was introduced to uncountable people and ideas I could not otherwise have known in the isolated, homogeneous little town where I lived. Louis Armstrong was the first black I ever met, in a biography that also made me aware of the horrible fact of prejudice. There was no art museum for two hundred miles in any direction, so until I went to college, the only paintings I saw were in the library's art books. Through the marvel of the interlibrary loan, I was furnished with stacks of books on Judaism, cellular biology, and whatever else sank a hook into my curiosity.

Along the way I acquired a large if idiosyncratic vocabulary. Many of the words I learned from books were words I had never heard pronounced, which meant there was a high risk of humiliation whenever I showed off one of my gems. "My appetite is *insashable*," I informed the mother of a friend who had invited me to stay for supper. "Do you mean *insayshable?*" her father asked. My friend, a maddeningly gifted athlete who had no patience for a pastime that required sitting still, flashed me a hideous grin. I wanted to murder her, but I had already died of embarrassment. The day the librarian explained how to decode pronunciations in a dictionary was one of the happiest of my life.

At college, where everyone seemed to have read more of the "right" books than I had, and read them with more intelligence, I began to feel that my thousands of hours of reading were wasted.

English classes were full of directions on how to read, what to read, and the true meaning of the words on the page. I was mortified to hear a professor say that Polonius's instructions to Laertes in *Hamlet* ("To thine own self be true . . .") were the words of a tiresome old windbag. Reading them on my own a few years before, I had thought they were profound. My mortification about this lasted for years, until it finally occurred to me that just because Polonius is customarily played as a windbag doesn't mean that Shakespeare saw him that way or that his advice is inane.

I began to dislike reading, and I loathed the idea that I did it as gawkily as I had once ridden a bicycle. But my reading problem was easily solved. I stopped taking English classes.

I never stopped going to libraries. Every time I opened one of the heavy glass doors of the main college library and went inside, I was suffused with awe. This was a sacred place. Here under one roof were millions of books—an infinity of wisdom and humanity and beauty. Even the most "insashable" of humans could not exhaust it.

I now travel with several passports—community library cards, permission to use various collections of rare books and manuscripts, and, for a fee, privileges at one of the largest university libraries in the world. The idea that libraries exist for anyone who wants to use them still fills me with wonder, and I seize every chance to spread this joy. If, as often happens, children stop to watch while I'm using a library microfilm reader, I ask their birthdays and fish out the appropriate reels of *The New York Times.* Once they start reading a birthday issue, they don't want to stop. I tell them about Dewey and his decimals. I ask about their favorite books and point them to others by the same author. I encourage them to load up their book bags. And I hope—oh, how I hope—that their first passports carry them to as many worlds as mine did.

JANE AUSTEN'S HEROINES

Jane Smiley

nce, in Greece, I took the overnight ferry between Pi-
raeus and Iráklion, Crete. Our sleeping accommodations in the
bowels of the boat were five-foot-long cubbies stacked three
high, like boxes, in a long hall with bathrooms at either end.
Our fellow passengers were mostly dressed in Cretan black—
boots and breeches for the men, dresses and shawls for the
women. There may have been chickens, or that might be the
product of fevered memory. But what I remember best about
that voyage is a heated argument out on the deck, just at dawn,
with another, slightly older and more authoritative American
passenger (I was twenty-two, he was thirty) about whether Jane
Austen was a great novelist. My conviction that she was was
unquestioning. He was ready to throw her neat little works overboard in favor of Henry Miller and every other sexy romantic
who had done what we were then doing—enter exotic climes,
go among strange peoples, experience new sights and sounds,
tastes and smells. I didn't feel I was prevailing in the argument,

but I did feel that in throwing Jane Austen overboard, my new acquaintance was discarding most of female experience as valueless and trivial. I probably fell silent without conceding, but I never embraced Henry Miller, either.

Jane Austen has always had loyal devotees—known as Janeites—who have admired her skills and her wit. Since the rise of feminism in literary studies, they have also learned to admire her subject matter—the moral lives of women who, though dependent and circumscribed in many ways, are autonomous, thinking beings of intelligence and sparkling personality. Literary studies have also shown us that she was not so alone in her craft as we once thought—the rediscovery and renewed appreciation of such writers as Anna Laetitia Barbauld and Maria Edgeworth have put Jane into fuller context.

Janeites have always relished arguing among themselves the relative merits of favorite heroines. The leaders are Elizabeth Bennet, of *Pride and Prejudice,* Emma, and Anne Elliot, of *Persuasion.* Each, depicted with the sort of insight, wisdom, and wit usually reserved in traditional literature for heroes, has a full range of alluring qualities. Elizabeth is straightforward, affectionate, skeptical, and good humored. She has a full measure of self-esteem and is an excellent judge of character, even in the teeth of the snobbery and foolishness of the class system into which she has been born. Emma has more faults—she is arrogant and manipulative, blind and sometimes petty, but she is also intelligent, forbearing with her extremely tiresome father and sister, loyal, and eager to mend her ways. Of the three, it is Emma who most thoughtfully embraces the social system of her world. Anne is more subdued—although no less intelligent or thoughtful than the others, she is more in the habit of being used by others and submitting to their demands. The wit of *Persuasion,* some of it deliciously cruel, is clearly located in the narrator's voice, not in Anne Elliot. It is hard not to read into each fully depicted heroine a mood belonging to Jane Austen herself—sparkling and hopeful to begin with, realistic and clear-sighted after that, then, at last, rueful, recognizing life's costs. But, of course, we know very little of Jane Austen herself, and we must turn back from the few pictures and documents of her life and look into her novels for hints of how she thought of herself and her world.

One thing I have noticed about *Pride and Prejudice, Emma,* and *Persuasion* is that one is an eighteenth-century novel, one is a nineteenth-century novel, and one even has affinities with the twentieth-century novel. Jane Austen was a bolder artist than she has often been given credit for being, and she could mold her form to suit her material. In *Pride and Prejudice,* Austen, like her eighteenth-century contemporaries, gives the narrator considerable space and opportunity to tell the story. Large, important scenes, like Darcy's first proposal, are set pieces. But in general, exchanges of dialogue are brief; long letters are given in full; and while Elizabeth is the heroine, we remain outside of her head. *Emma* is decidedly different, developed entirely through dramatic scenes in which everyone, even Mr. Woodhouse, gets to have his or her entire say. The technique makes *Emma* longer and richer in some ways, but not as exciting. The intricate plot that brings Elizabeth and Darcy together is exhilarating. The careful setting right of Emma's misapprehensions and her final reward in marriage to a man she has always known hasn't quite the same energy. In *Persuasion,* Austen is impatient with her usual bag of tricks, and elects not to lampoon characters, like Mrs. Clay and Anne's sister Elizabeth, that she would have depicted more fully in an earlier novel. What she is interested in is the evolution, not of Anne's behavior, but of her feelings, her inner life. Unlike Emma, and to a certain extent, Elizabeth, Anne has already learned to behave properly. What she needs to learn in the novel is what love is and how to express it. This focus on Anne's mostly unexpressed feelings seems quite modern to me, anticipatory more of Virginia Woolf than, let's say, Charles Dickens, though of course Austen had no modern theories of consciousness to shape her art.

When I first read through my thick Modern Library edition of all six of Jane Austen's novels, I was younger than Elizabeth Bennet. When I reread the novels in graduate school, this time in standard editions plumped out by scholarly matter, I was nearly as old as Anne Elliot. Now I am older than Mrs. Bennet, and my daughters are nearly Elizabeth and Lydia Bennet's contemporaries. (I am almost as old as Sir Walter Elliot.) I no longer read for the love story, or even, in some ways, for the comedy. I read Austen in order to contemplate her views on the proper behavior of women, and her views are complex. They evolve from novel to novel. They cover a lot of ground, too—small things like the rudeness of not answering letters quickly fully express larger problems of selfishness. A quick joke at the expense of a well-meaning but foolish woman who is getting by on a pittance reveals much about the responsibilities of life in a stable, hierarchical community, where social relationships may last entire lives. Finally, in the character of Anne Elliot, Austen contemplates how one may live among those who place little value on one's virtues and none on one's desires. The resulting portrait, in *Persuasion,* of English society is one no less insightful or disquieting for all its dignity.

I recently ran into the man I argued with in Greece. He still reads Henry Miller, but now he reads Jane Austen, too, and was amused to be reminded that he once found her work trivial (read: feminine). Now he likes her a great deal. With a somewhat Janeian sense of moral authority, I decided he'd matured quite a bit.

LOOKING FOR EDITH

Susan Minot

dith Wharton is one of my literary heroes, and I have long traveled many places with her through her books. One summer day I decided to visit the Mount, her hilltop residence in Lenox, Massachusetts. She had been actively involved in creating both the house and the grounds. I came to see her stamp on the place, hoping to find a glimpse of Wharton the writer.

The first book Edith Wharton wrote—before *The Age of Innocence* and *Ethan Frome,* before *The Custom of the Country* and *The House of Mirth*—was *The Decoration of Houses,* co-written with the architect Ogden Codman. It might have been titled *The Declaration of Houses* so forcefully does it put forward classical principles of design. There are practical statements: "Doors should always swing *into* a room," or "Pale tints should be avoided in the selection of carpets." And more philosophical ones in which I hear Wharton's ring: "Proportion is the good breeding of architecture," and "The boudoir is the room in which small objects of art . . . show to the best advantage." Wharton traveled widely to the great houses of Europe and in the Mount incorporated those elements of French, English, and Italian design she so admired. Raised in affluence and surrounded by what she felt was uniform materialism, Wharton brought a higher sensibility to architectural concerns, a kind of nobility. In her fiction one often encounters rooms and landscapes used as metaphors for her characters' feelings and psyches.

It was a clear warm day when I arrived. The Mount, recently opened for the season, houses a theater group, Shakespeare & Company. When I pulled into the driveway, a young man told me to park by the stables. I walked down the driveway at the pace of a horse and buggy, taking the bends and dips, the house coming in and out of sight as I approached. Along the road were ferns, new and green; I knew Wharton had brought them from nearby Stockbridge. Inside the entryway, a couple of employees lingered by the cash register near the small bookshop. At one o'clock I was given a private tour (I was the only one there) by a young man in his twenties wearing a crisp shirt. We stood outside in the middle of the gravel courtyard surrounded by a high brick wall. Standing in the sun, my guide related some familiar facts of Wharton's life: She was born in 1862 into the moneyed social world of New York, entered into a loveless marriage, and found literary success at age forty. Just before she and her husband divorced in 1913, Wharton sold the house and moved to Europe, a continent she felt was more sympathetic to her interests and where she lived until her death in 1937. A couple from New Orleans lived in the house for twenty-three years, and eventually it was sold to the Foxhollow School for Girls in 1942. Though the general structure of the building was never changed, fire escapes were put up, damaging the facade. Inside, original decorative objects such as vases and tapestries had long since disappeared. By the mid-seventies the house had been abandoned, its gutters rusted and pipes burst. In 1978

Shakespeare & Company rented it, and in 1980 the Edith Wharton Restoration project was created in a full-scale attempt to restore the Mount. So far, that effort has produced a new slate roof and a rebuilt cupola.

The facade, with the flat white elegance of European houses, was inspired by Belton House in England, a 1684 design thought to have been by Christopher Wren after an Italian villa. My guide pointed out that one of the arched shuttered windows was false, placed there for symmetry. I thought of the parallels between the false window and her writing—the balance of plots in her fiction and the illusion of art. Above the doorway, flanked by pillars, was a central arching window on the second floor where one could see through another window to trees and sky. But this, too, was a trick of the eye: A mirror inside reflected the window.

The front entrance had a low vaulted ceiling with cool terracotta floors and a niche where a scalloped fountain once held a statue of Pan playing his flute. The plaster panel inlays resembled water dripping down stones. "Like a grotto," my guide explained. Here her guests would arrive—Henry James, Walter Berry, Beatrix Jones Farrand, her niece who'd helped with garden designs—sweeping up the stone staircase with the wrought-iron rail. Wharton had a great gift for friendship, and in her autobiography, *A Backward Glance,* she speaks more about others than about herself.

My guide assured me the color of the entry's walls, a pistachio-blue trimmed with white molding, was the original, but I spotted a chipped area where the underlying hue was more subtle, faded with age perhaps. I pictured Wharton choosing this color; seeing her as a decorator added another dimension.

The upper gallery seemed least altered by the changes of ninety years, and I could easily visualize Wharton by the windows. She was not beautiful, but slight and graceful, and the reserve of her manners may have given her a brittle air, yet she had a good sense of humor and great sensitivity—a fact amply proven by the emotional complexity of her characters.

Privacy, Wharton believed, was "one of the first requisites of a civilized life," and every room in the house, even the large drawing room, could be closed off. Privacy was particularly important to her. Without it, she could not write. The room she loved most was the library. We stood there surrounded by its built-in oak shelves. The carved panels were designed by her coauthor Codman, whom she could not afford to hire as an architect—Francis L. V. Hoppin took the job. One imagines Wharton an exacting and probably exasperating client. Henry James called the Mount "a monument to the almost too impeccable taste of its so accomplished mistress." In the fireplace was an original cast-iron fireback portraying Hercules slaying the lion. Wharton, who had an opinion about everything, found scenes of violence most appropriate seen through flames.

A picture of Wharton I've often seen shows her sitting at a desk in the library, wearing a dress with lacy sleeves, bending forward from her narrow waist. But she did not write here. She wrote in bed, in the early morning, dropping sheets of paper to the floor as she finished them, to be gathered up by her secretary. She would finish by ten or eleven and then was free to take part in what she called "country cares and joys." My guide pointed upward; above us was the bedroom. That was what I especially wanted to see.

Next door in the wide drawing room, I felt the first real intrusion of the present on the past. The theater company performed here now, and rows of folding chairs were set up. I glimpsed the ghosts of the fringed silk sofa, the circle of curving French armchairs, and the Aubusson rug.

I drifted out onto the terrace. The large green awning was gone, and in the sun I could see the terrace floor was chipped. Here Wharton had stood watching "the glowing summer weeks, and the woodland pageantry of our matchless New England autumn." Amid the beautiful surroundings, she wrote her first novel, *House of Mirth*. An immediate best-seller, it allowed her to pay off the Mount's loans. Looking out, I could see where the Lime Walk—rows of linden trees that made a pathway connecting the two main gardens—used to be. Now there was a lawn. Beyond, the grass was taller, blowing in the wind, and becoming wilder and wilder as it rolled off to Laurel Pond in the distance. The original view included Laurel Lake, even farther off, but woods had grown over the space.

Bringing culture and good company, Wharton's visitors would go for motorcar rides and sit by the fire on winter afternoons. When I saw the dining room, I was reminded of her great appreciation for good conversation. She would seat her guests at a rather small table, with candles under little lampshades. At her feet would be the striped pillows where her Pekingese slept—among them Miza, Mimi, and Toto—as beloved as children. They were buried on a shady hillock above the flower gardens.

A most important visitor was journalist Morton Fullerton, a friend of Henry James. Wharton was quite taken with him during a snowy ride in the country; later in Paris they began a love affair—the great one of her life. She was forty-seven years old and she was finally introduced to, as she put it, "what happy women feel."

Visits were usually substantial, and guests brought a lot of luggage. A hydraulic elevator, a wire cage of sorts, ran parallel to the stairs in the servants' quarters. My guide explained I was not allowed to look at the servants' quarters. They were, I was told, now administrative offices.

Upstairs the tour came to a near halt. The doors were shut, and we stood looking down a dark hallway. My guide pointed to a door. It was where Henry James stayed. Could I see? No one was supposed to, my guide said; it was a dressing room for the theater company. A quick look? He seemed distressed. He put his ear reluctantly to the door and let me dart in. There were sheetrock dividers and the kind of long tables used for bake sales. A few costumes and props were lying about. A narrow passageway led down steps to another door—my guide watched anxiously as I moved off. In this passageway Henry James had perhaps hung something on this hook. I felt that odd sense of being where a great person has been—what I'd been searching for. But I'd yet to find it with Wharton.

We were back in the hall. "Can I go down?" At the end of the hall, closed off, was her suite: bathroom, boudoir, and most particularly the bedroom where she wrote.

"No." His tone was firm.

"Not just run down?"

He shook his head. Clearly this was more serious. I pestered him further and was told he'd have to check with his boss. When he returned he said to follow him—I would get to see the servants' quarters!

The offices where we went to see his boss were little cubicles, rumpled and friendly. I was shown into a small room where a woman sat behind a desk talking on the phone. She indicated I should sit. I gazed at an enlarged picture of Wharton, appearing casual, her hair blurred-looking. She was a daunting figure, Edith Wharton. Besides being the greatest American woman writer at the beginning of the century, she was accomplished in language, travel, and knowledge of architecture. She managed to create this house, dress with elegance, and still see to the smallest detail, such as making sure her houseguests got the morning papers.

Eventually, the woman put down the phone. I explained my business and asked if there was some way I could see the bedroom. The woman shook her head.

"Really?"

"I'm sorry, no."

"But—" I think I laughed.

She had very pale blue eyes, and they looked at me matter of factly. "Those rooms are used by the theater company."

"I couldn't look in?"

"They would be very upset."

"I wouldn't—make any noise. . . ."

She sat immobile. I suggested the magazine piece might help the restoration project. She seemed to stir. I pressed on.

Finally she stood up, not happy. "I'll see if anyone's there. I can't promise you—" I leapt after her.

Down the dim hall we went. She knocked on a door to the right. Silence. The door opened, and I was allowed into Edith Wharton's bedroom. It was empty, except for a table or two, and full of light. Those were the corner windows through which Wharton looked out on her flower gardens and through which she had observed "the glory of their coloring actually vibrates in the sunlight." I felt a thrill. I thought of the characters who had been born here "seemingly from nowhere." She'd written of the process, "the character draws nearer, and seems to become aware of me, and feel the shy but desperate need to unfold his or her tale." Sconces on the wall showed where her bed would have been, and my impression was so vivid I am not altogether sure now a bed wasn't there.

After the tour I walked around the grounds. I'd felt a charge in her bedroom, but perhaps it had more to do with the triumph of getting inside. I knew her gardens were important to her. In them she became "lost in the mazes of an inarticulate happiness." News of phlox made her "mouth water," and while living in Lenox she won many prizes in local flower shows. So involved had she become with her plants that she wrote a friend, "I am a better landscape gardener than novelist." At one end of the lawn is where the principal flower garden had been, with a square fountain in the center surrounded by a tangle of white petunias. The eight gumdrop-shaped bushes long ago grew into trees, and now the garden is all leveled. I could see its outline.

I crossed the lawn below the split staircase through a stand of cedar trees, past the smell of orange blossoms, to the walled Italian garden. A gravel path and shallow stairs led down to the *giardino segreto*. Classically, this is a garden with no flowers and with more gravel than lawn, giving it "a charm independent of the seasons." A pair of curled dolphins sat in the center of a dry fountain, and on one side stone pergola posts were bare of vines.

Walking back I passed under a lilac bush, really more of a tree with a twisting trunk and arching branches. I stood beneath its fat blossoms, which looked white from a distance but up close were a subtle shade of lilac. Suddenly it seemed as if this bush had been there in Wharton's time. She may have walked under it. I held a flower and felt the stirring sensation. Edith Wharton was there.

THE GROWN-UP CHARMS OF

CLASSIC CHILDREN'S BOOKS

Michele Slung

From Oz's winding yellow brick road to the rabbit hole into Wonderland, from the prairie where the little house stands to the barnyard where Charlotte is forever spinning her web, the sights and sounds of the books we loved when young still tenaciously inhabit some corner of our memory long after we're supposed to have put away childish pages. Many parents settle down to read favorite books to their children not simply for the warmth of the shared experience but for the secret pleasure of finding themselves transported once again to those well-remembered places where enchantment reigns.

I count myself lucky to own a complete collection of the first three series of Oz books. And whenever I decide to curl up with one of the hefty, brightly colored volumes, I am quickly lost again, savoring the adventures of the eccentric inhabitants of that magical land. When I look up from the page, it's hard to remember where I am, for in my mind I am nestled again in a corner of my aunt's cellar, where a forgotten cache of my grown cousins' books was stored away.

Other still-loved literary survivors from my childhood tucked into my shelves include Kate Douglas Wiggin's *Rebecca of Sunnybrook Farm,* T. H. White's *Mistress Masham's Repose,* Rachel Field's *Hepatica Hawks,* James Otis's *Toby Tyler,* Jean Webster's *Daddy-Long-Legs,* Margaret Sidney's *The Five Little Peppers,* Charles Kingsley's *The Water Babies,* Noel Streatfield's *Ballet Shoes*—the list could go on and on, with each person who reads it indignantly wondering why I've lacked the good sense to cite Hugh Lofting, P. L. Travers, Kenneth Grahame, or Mary Norton, C. S. Lewis, Walter Farley, or Arthur Ransome. One finds, truly, that a discussion of beloved children's books can be passionately personal.

But adults who cherish old-fashioned, romantic storytelling need not confine themselves to familiar scenes. They can widen their reading horizons by starting anew, discovering from a grown-up perspective what many of us already know: Children's books are fun.

Three novels I've read recently illustrate this perfectly. The first, *The Little White Horse* (Dell Yearling) by Elizabeth Goudge (author of such splendid adult titles as *Green Dolphin Street* and *Pilgrim's Inn*), was initially published half a century ago and was awarded the prestigious Carnegie Medal for 1947. Yet in the way of all great works of art, it is completely timeless, as fresh as its young heroine's excitement when she wakens for the first time in her never-before-seen ancestral home, Moonacre Manor. Maria Merryweather has come here, accompanied only by her governess and her haughty spaniel, Wiggins, because, as a just-minted orphan, she is now the ward of her uncle, Sir Benjamin, the master of Moonacre and its charmingly hidden village, Silverydew.

As she explores her new residence, every discovery that Maria makes—about who it is that so silently delivers her breakfast to her tower room every morning or about the true nature of the small white horse she's glimpsed in the midnight forest—is thrilling. Not only a beautifully domestic fairy tale (with tantalizing descriptions of cozy repasts and snug interiors), the book also embodies the classic theme of goodness triumphing over evil. With its emphasis on cycles of spiritual growth and on ancient symbols of purity and rebirth, *The Little White Horse* will have special appeal for those already devoted to the Narnia books and the works of Madeleine L'Engle.

L. M. Boston's *The Children of Green Knowe* (Harcourt Brace) is the first of a five-book series. Originally published forty-one years ago, it also begins with the arrival of an orphan—this time a small boy, Tolly—at a magical house that holds both his past and his future. His grandmother, the enigmatic Mrs. Oldknow, is mistress of the estate Green Knowe (referred to as Green Noah), and it is under her loving guidance that Tolly slowly begins to understand the seamlessness of time in places blessed by the continuity of family and tradition.

Lucy M. Boston set her Green Knowe books in a likeness of the 850-year-old house she herself had restored—The Manor, Hemingford Grey, Cambridgeshire, England. The stories follow the history of the property as revealed by affectionately mischievous spirit children, who move as easily through the centuries as they do through the rooms and grounds and who often allow themselves to be seen by their descendants, such as Tolly. Lucy Boston died in 1990, aged 98, after having dedicated her energies to The Manor since 1935; but her son and daughter-in-law remain there, working to preserve the captivating aura of the real-life "Green Noah."

Another adventure that will come as no surprise to admirers of *Five Children & It* is E. Nesbit's *The Enchanted Castle* (Puffin). The young protagonists are two brothers and a sister possessed of impulsive tendencies. Humor is abundant as they lose control over a magic wishing ring, which brings shattered nerves and just plain havoc to their west-of-England countryside. The trouble begins when Jerry, Jimmy, and Kathleen abandon their picnic lunch in quest of a rumored enchanted castle. What they discover is a maze that winds its way to a sleeping princess at its center. Unfortunately, the princess is only a girl with a flair for self-dramatization called Mabel. However, the wishing ring she's unearthed turns out to be all too genuine, and the four irrepressible children somehow manage to keep unleashing its power when they least wish to.

Go ahead, try these books. I know I'm inclined to reach for anything with orphans and princesses, and it wouldn't astonish me at all if others felt exactly the same way.

So I Knew
Rachel Carson

Tovah Martin

On rainy mornings when scampering outside was not permitted, my mother perched me on her lap, donned her reading glasses, cleared her throat, and opened a well-worn copy of Rachel Carson's *The Sea Around Us.* At the time, I was much too young to fathom ebb tides and flood tides or to concentrate on continental drift. So my mother patiently paraphrased each section, weaving stories of the seas.

As she turned page after page, she pointed to the pictures and spoke of translucent fish, of volcanoes that gave birth to islands, of barnacles and buried fossils, of global warming. Caught in the stories, dreaming of summers at the beach, remembering the crash of mighty waves and the whine of gulls, I would sit rapt until her voice trailed off and it was time for lunch. Then, while she was busy elsewhere, I would pull *The Sea Around Us* down from the bookshelf, shuffle through the pages, and tell the stories for myself.

So I knew Rachel Carson—the poetic marine biologist who

made the ocean come to life. She opened my eyes to all the sights and sounds of the shore, turning summer at the beach into more than merely sand castles and skipping over the swell. She gave each bird, every fish and seaweed a personality and a purpose; she explained that I was simply a grain of sand among all the rest—singular and small but related to a vast ocean of life.

I continued to read Carson throughout my formative years. Although she wrote about the ocean and I loved the land, she taught me to know the earth and its creatures intimately, just as she knew every aspect of the waters. Then, when I was still little more than a child, *Silent Spring* was published, and suddenly I had another reason to read Carson. While other teenagers worshiped Marilyn Monroe and Jacqueline Kennedy, my role model was Rachel Carson, the shy scientist with the wary smile. Somehow, the gentle lady who slept with a copy of Thoreau's *Journals* by her bedside found the courage to stroll out of her tidal pools, pick up her cogent pen, and wage war for what she knew was right. She had scant history of defiance, and her life was already overflowing with pressing personal responsibilities and concerns. She was single-handedly raising a young orphaned nephew while simultaneously fighting a losing battle against cancer. And yet, as she put it, "everything which meant most to me as a naturalist was being threatened." She had no choice: "There would be no peace for me if I kept silent."

So she wrote *Silent Spring,* a plea for caution in a world that had adopted the wanton spraying of dangerous chemicals fully capable of haunting the environment decades after they were applied. As she explained, "They sprayed truck gardens and dairy farms, fish ponds and salt marshes. They sprayed the quarter-acre lots of suburbia . . . and showered insecticides over children at play." In writing those words, Carson went where no one had dared tread before. *Silent Spring* was the first book to protest the unrestricted use of chemicals, and Carson was the first author to describe how poisons trickled into the waters, the earthworms, and the robins.

A few months before *Silent Spring* was published, it was serialized in *The New Yorker,* and critics immediately lit into her, calling Rachel Carson "unscientific," a "hysterical woman," a "sensationalist" and "propagandist." And yet, she scarcely blinked and certainly never withdrew. Even as her own health deteriorated, *Silent Spring* triumphed. Like so many other men, women, and children of the time, I added my voice to her environmental crusade.

Carson, the meek heroine, died in April 1964. She lived only two years after *Silent Spring* was published, and yet she saw the book win a bevy of honors. Among other awards, she received National Audubon Society and American Geographical Society medals and was elected to the Academy of Arts and Letters. President Kennedy's Science Advisory Committee supported her findings. But, most important, her words had a lasting impact: Some would say her book, so skillfully and simply written, saved the world from witnessing a silent spring.

Carson's footsteps continue to echo through my life. They resound in the words of *The Sense of Wonder,* her posthumously published book about kindling a child's inborn fascination with nature. Now I often take that book down from the bookshelf, sit a young niece or nephew on my lap, and weave stories about the sea. Whenever I go to the woods, I watch the chipmunk's antics and the red fox's exploits with eyes trained by that naturalist. Rachel Carson showed me when to sit quiet, and when to rush forth. She gave me a sense of wonder; she keeps it strong.

THROUGH THE WINDOW

OF A BOOK

Susan Schneider

"Read!" she commands, and unceremoniously hands me a pile of books. It's the end of a long, busy day, my voice is hoarse from a cold, and part of me would dearly love to tuck in this bossy four-year-old and sneak out of her room. Instead, I bargain with her about the books—two short ones or one long one.

I help her arrange her dolls and pillows and quilt around her and then she reminds me to turn on my answering machine so that we are not rudely interrupted. Finally, I sit next to her and she cuddles up to me, resting her chin on her hand and leaning on my knee. I open the first book—a different version of Cinderella in which the heroine is "clever as well as beautiful"— and we're instantly immersed.

According to my daughter, India, the best thing about reading aloud is that she gets to stay up longer. I'd add that it's the best thing we do together because it nourishes both of us. It isn't that I don't get bored and annoyed at times—such as tonight, when I stop to clear my aching throat and sip my hot tea and she says, "Momme-e-e-e, read!"

"Okay, okay," I grumble. It isn't exactly fair that once I start, I'm not allowed to stop until I have uttered, "The End." Nor is it quite fair that she follows every word and makes me backtrack if I dare to skip a line. Or stops me and fills in what I've left out.

India assumes that I can spin stories out of air just the way the miller's daughter spun straw into gold in "Rumpelstiltskin." Sometimes when we're out—in the supermarket, the car, the park—she asks me to read. "I don't have a book handy at the moment," I'll say impatiently, throwing her breakfast cereal into the shopping cart or making a tricky left turn. "Then read without the book, Mommy," she'll say very patiently, implying that, as usual, I've missed the obvious.

No, it isn't exactly fair. But I wouldn't have it any other way. I'm afraid that television and movies are often substituted for reading aloud these days, and I'm sad and distressed at the thought of kids growing up without this special kind of communication. There is no substitute for reading aloud to your child. It is a tangible way to connect and express love, and it is private and exclusive; together, you create a safe, magical circle of two. For India and me, reading aloud is the cornerstone of our closeness.

Before having a child, whenever I imagined what it would be like, I envisioned that special intimacy: myself and a little girl bent over a book, utterly absorbed in our own world. When I told a friend of mine, a mother of two, she chuckled tolerantly and said, "Oh, it's a nice dream. But believe me, you won't have much time for it!"

I sensed she was right, but I dreamed on. Partly, I wanted to re-create the best of my own childhood: the hours spent reading *Little Women, Five Little Peppers, Rose in Bloom, Anne of Green Gables, Alice in Wonderland.* And partly because I know what happens when a child's imagination is fired early. I know a ten-year-old who is writing a novel on her parents' word processor about a small heroine similar to Meg and Jo and Anne and Alice in pluckiness and intelligence but with the sophisticated sensibility of a New York City schoolgirl. Like the authoress, this first fiction is amazingly funny and smart.

The fact is, the child who has been read to will delight you in the most unexpected ways. As India and I read a Babar book from the 1930s, she will repeat archaic phrasing naturally: "Oh, Mommy, look—'Turtle joined the chase!'" Or, "Look at the baby elephants in their perambulator—what is a perambulator?"

And after we'd repeatedly read an African folktale about why mosquitoes buzz in people's ears every night, she startled a friend and me by reciting several paragraphs, complete with dialogue: "'What's a mosquito compared to a yam?' said the iguana grumpily." My friend and I burst out laughing as India barreled on with more snappy dialogue between the iguana and the mosquito. By now, we've already started writing books, cobbled together with dialogue we've read and dialogue she's making up.

I know I was like her when I was a child. In my family, my father was the storyteller and I was the listener. I can still hear him reading me "Snow White," in rapid-fire dialogue, acting out the wicked witch's role with amazing gusto. Every Saturday he and I would go to the public library. I'd take out seven books, one to vanish into for every day of the week. But before any child can have access to this absolutely delicious form of solitary entertainment, she has to be read to. It starts there.

India and I started reading aloud early—when she was about five months old to be exact. One winter evening, when she'd been very fussy, I took a volume of Gerard Manley Hopkins off my shelf and, feeling slightly ridiculous to be reading some of the most difficult and subtle poetry in the English language to an infant, read it to her anyway. I don't remember if it soothed her tiny, savage breast or not, but maybe it did. Maybe she liked the rhythm of the verse and the sounds of language— maybe it even helped her digestion. It calmed me down.

From Hopkins, we moved on to those fat little cardboard books that babies like to chew. But we were quickly bored— we like the kind of books you can really sink your teeth into: a story about two African princesses, one "good," the other selfish; another about an Eskimo child who travels to the sun for warmth; yet another about a little Chinese girl who outwits a wolf. India loves stories about girls, and I've noticed that even in this day and age, there are far more stories with little boys as protagonists. We've discussed the fact that this doesn't seem fair. Also, in many stories little boys tend to do more than the girls—I always mention these biases to her because I want her to understand that not everything she reads in books is the "truth."

Recently, I found an illustrated 1920s children's edition of the Greek myths, and we started on them. We've read the tale of Romulus and Remus, and of Proserpina and Demeter—the story of a mother so determined to rescue her daughter from harm that she makes the earth go barren until her daughter is returned to her. There is no more powerful story of the love between a mother and daughter—can India really understand how much it touches my heart to read this to her? The act of reading aloud is an expression of love, but this particular myth gives voice to my feelings as a mother better than almost anything I can think of.

Writers such as Dante and Rousseau have created fictional characters for whom reading aloud is a way of connecting and loving. Nowadays, I've heard that fiction and poetry readings in bookstores have become a way for people to meet kindred spirits and even fall in love. Being a typical mother, I couldn't help thinking, "What a great way that would be for India to meet a really intelligent, interesting man someday!" Drawn together by the intimacy of a reading—second nature to India from her earliest childhood experiences—she and this wonderful young man first connect on a literary level and then allow a real-life love story to develop.

But before we get to India's wedding day, we first have to negotiate childhood. Since her father and I are divorced, we may have some stressful times. For now, I'm aware that one of the first things we do when she returns from weekend visits with him is sit down on the couch and read. It is our way of reconnecting, of finding our center. As she gets older, we won't have this special kind of glue. I know that we are forming a base of intimacy, but still, it won't be the same. So I have a wish. More than a wish—a determination to hold onto something that matters.

Our family of two has few traditions, but this is one I'd like to start with. I thought of it this past Christmas when she and I were strolling past a wonderful Victorian coach house in our neighborhood. In the large parlor window was an enormous tree covered with tiny lights. I had a vivid image of family and friends sitting in front of a fireplace, some in rocking chairs, others lying dreamily on the rug staring at the flames, as everyone took turns reading aloud. No television, no telephones, just people with their imaginations joined by the special, leisurely intimacy of the spoken language.

As India grows older, I want to clear a space in our lives for reading together. We don't own a huge Victorian house or even a modest fireplace, but we do have novels, biographies, poetry. A pile of books and a bowl of chips . . . a batch of chocolate chip cookies . . . a cup of tea, a glass of wine, "and thou beside me singing in the wilderness . . ." goes the rest. What else do we need? I can't wait to get back to my own favorites—the nineteenth-century triple deckers of Dickens, Eliot, Thackeray, and, of course, the Brontë sisters. To me, this is better than handing down heirloom jewelry. Even though you can't measure the worth of reading aloud the way you would diamonds and pearls, it's far more precious—an intangible heirloom of love, intimacy, and imagination that is the most priceless legacy I could ever dream of giving.

A Visit to "The Country of the Pointed Firs"

Susan Allen Toth

"The village was so still that I could hear the shy whip-poorwill singing that night as I lay awake in my downstairs bedroom, and the scent of Mrs. Todd's herb garden under the window blew in again and again with every single rising of the sea-breeze." When I first read about the village of Dunnet Landing in Sarah Orne Jewett's *The Country of the Pointed Firs* (1896), I instantly fell under its enchantment. I also wanted to go there immediately.

Of course I knew I couldn't. Although partly modeled after Martinsville, a hamlet on the Maine coast near Rockland, Dunnet Landing is fictional. Jewett created this late-nineteenth-century fading fishing port as the setting for a series of sketches and stories about the proud, dignified, often eccentric people who live there. She describes them, and Dunnet Landing, in a short book that is an enduring American masterpiece, yet surprisingly still relatively unknown a hundred years after its publication.

When I discovered Sarah Orne Jewett, I was a graduate student immersed in Hawthorne, Melville, Faulkner, Hemingway, among many male writers in the accepted grand tradition of American literature. Before an unorthodox professor put it on a reading list, I had never heard of *The Country of the Pointed Firs.* I read it as a revelation.

What struck me as so remarkable was the material Jewett chose to write about with such lucid elegance. I was used to stories and novels about war, violence, sexual passion, adventure, travel, and other male initiation rites. But Jewett cared instead about the seemingly ordinary, small events of women's lives— the pleasure of a long, news-filled visit from an old friend; the warmth of a welcoming cup of tea served in a treasured antique china cup; the delightful surprise of early mushrooms for supper.

In the towns Jewett grew to love, first on visits with her father, a well-connected country doctor, and later on her own, women held the social fabric together. Many of the men were gone, lost at sea, fallen in the Civil War, or lured to urban centers and richer Western lands. By the late nineteenth century, shipping had passed Maine by, and many of its villages were clearly dying. In the family burial ground near Dunnet Landing, Jewett writes, "most of the home graves were those of women."

In describing this world of women in *The Country of the Pointed Firs,* Jewett uses a structure that is deceptively simple. An unnamed narrator, a fictionalized version of the author, arrives to spend the summer with Almira Todd, an older, childless widow who earns a very modest living from occasional boarders and from her skills as an herbalist. A noble, somewhat mysterious figure, Mrs. Todd dominates the small society of Dunnet Landing with her wisdom, humor, and intuitive understanding of human nature. She is at the center of most of the subsequent stories the narrator tells about village life.

What the narrator notices—and records in New England vernacular—are the enduring customs and traditions that hold the community together. The women of Dunnet Landing know how to celebrate the moments of everyday life. When Mrs. Todd's elderly mother shows the narrator an old flowered-glass tea caddy and a pair of mugs, she explains a little shyly, "You'd laugh to see how we enjoy 'em Sunday nights in winter: We have a real company tea 'stead o' livin' right along just the same, an' I make somethin' good for a s'prise an' put on some o' my preserves, an' we get a-talkin' together an' have real pleasant times."

Visiting, in Dunnet Landing, is an art. Mrs. Todd eagerly awaits her turn for a sought-after houseguest who is known as "the best hand in the world to make a visit." To be the "best hand" implies expertise in a valued craft; "visiting" in an isolated community is just that. Guests bring with their bags and bundles all the excitement of the outside world. When the guest finally arrives, Mrs. Todd finds herself mildly chiding. "I come near giving of you up!" says Mrs. Todd. "I was afraid you'd gone an' 'portioned out my visit to somebody else."

But who could resist a visit when it meant being ushered into a "best room" and being served fish chowder and fresh dough-nuts? Of Mrs. Todd's mother, Jewett writes, "her hospitality was something exquisite," a gift that certain women have of "charming surrender for the moment of themselves and whatever belongs to them, so they make a part of one's own life that can never be forgotten."

In this gentle, slowly paced world, even the most humble task—digging a few potatoes for dinner—is deeply satisfying. Sent into the vegetable garden, the narrator reports: "I chose a fat-looking hill where the tops were well-withered. There is all the pleasure that one can have in gold-digging in finding one's hopes satisfied in the riches of a good hill of potatoes."

Although the dramatic incidents of *The Country of the Pointed Firs* are modest in scope, they have a haunting resonance. One such small drama is the story of Joanna, who, when she was jilted, became a recluse, living on an island until she died. Jewett eloquently suggests that any woman who has a hidden emotional life would reach out to the memory of Joanna: "In the life of each of us, I said to myself, there is a place remote and islanded, and given to endless regret or secret happiness."

When I finished *The Country of the Pointed Firs,* and then some of Jewett's other fine stories, I realized that her voice had sounded clearer and truer to me than that of any writer I had read for a long while. In an essay I had once read by Ralph Waldo Emerson, he had called for a new approach to American literature: "What would we know the meaning of? The meal in the firkin, the milk in the pan!" Only when I found Sarah Orne Jewett did I think I knew what he meant.

What her stories suggested to me was that perhaps I could look at my own life as she had examined the lives of women in Dunnet Landing. Mine had seemed commonplace from the outside, but I had experienced it intensely. By focusing carefully on the right details, Jewett had known how to re-create the dramas of daily life. Could I perhaps try that, too? I thought I might, and so in 1981 I began my first memoir *Blooming: A Small-Town Girlhood.*

The Country of the Pointed Firs closes with the narrator's regrets that "the days flew by like a handful of flowers flung to the sea wind." I love that line. With its light alliterative cadence and delicate imagery, it whispers—softly but clearly—something about the preciousness of each passing day. Sometimes when I am writing, especially when I am trying to convey that same feeling, I think of that line and repeat it to myself. As Mrs. Todd might say, it keeps my boat "trimmed proper."

Journeys with the Victorians:
Intrepid Women Travelers

Michele Slung

reparing to head off on a trip is simple enough today. Not only do we take for granted instant credit for booking tickets and hotel rooms (along with guide books addressing every imaginable special need), but once we arrive we demand that the plumbing be functional, all food digestible, and our routes free of brigands. Isn't it thrilling, then, to be reminded that it wasn't so very long ago that travel held the peril and excitement of the unexpected?

Such singular travels as those made by the indomitable likes of Mary Kingsley, Jane Digby, and Isabella Bird in the nineteenth century, or in the twentieth by Daisy Bates, Beryl Markham, and Freya Stark, were richly textured adventures that blended available time (there was, of course, much more of it) with the wit and daring to spend it far from home, in settings that, to say the least, were unpredictable. And yet, despite the hardships experienced—or perhaps because of them—the act of traveling for many of these women was inseparable from the desire to record the experience. In diaries and journals, as well as correspondence home, they offered their own sharply detailed and emotion-filled reactions to exotic worlds and outlandish peoples. And the realization, whether acknowledged or implicit, that every peculiar, foreign place is peculiar and foreign only to those who come upon it from somewhere else.

The writings of these "lady travelers," reflecting as they do the evolving process of discovery and change through which our planet became a more compact, more *connected* habitat, form a body of literature as irresistibly romantic as any fiction. For example, in the 1850s a paradigm of the breed was the intrepid (and immodest) Ida Pfeiffer, perhaps the earliest of her sex to make full-time journeying a way of life. Here, infused with zest for the undertaking, she describes her successful climb down the pyramids: "I never grow giddy; and so I advanced in the following manner, without the aid of the Arabs. . . . I accomplished my descent with so much grace and agility, that I reached the base of the pyramid long before my servant. Even the Arabs expressed their pleasure at my fearlessness on this dangerous passage."

Then there was the indefatigable Mrs. Alec Tweedie, also a prolific author, who in 1889 couldn't help boasting of her "boldness" in crossing Iceland by horse: "Riding man-fashion is less tiring than on a side-saddle, and I soon found it far more agreeable, especially when traversing rough ground. My success soon inspired Miss T. to summon up courage and follow my lead [since she] had been nearly shaken to pieces in her chair pannier."

Yet some of Mrs. Tweedie's equally peripatetic contemporaries traveled seemingly only to take exception to what they found. One of them, the querulous Frances Elliott, regularly gave voice to her dissatisfaction in such books as *Diary of an Idle Woman in Spain,* published in 1884; in 1893 she found Turkey an inferior sort of place: "But oh, how low these hills! How flat! How unimpressive! What a mess of walls, shapeless and void as was this earth before creation! Is this Constantinople of which I have heard so much?"

Two decades earlier, however, the Victorian governess Anna Leonowens, best known for inspiring Rodgers and Hammerstein's enchanting musical drama *The King and I,* had displayed her admirable flexibility. Upon arriving at the Siamese court and being informed by her autocratic new employer that her duties would include the teaching of sixty-seven royal offspring, she despaired inwardly for a second but refused to blink. "I simply bowed, however, and so dismissed myself for that evening."

Annie Taylor, finding herself unwelcome high in the Himalayas at the turn of the century, described her plight this way: "The chief was very insolent, but I kept my stand. . . . I told him that we had no food and no tent, and that the . . . road we had come was infested with robbers. He said that for eight days they would escort us, and then we might do the best we could . . . I said, 'I am English, and do not fear for my life.' "

If provisions were short on expeditions, travelers made do with what was at hand. Yet even a familiar and welcome staple takes on the air of the extraordinary when it is dished up, as it was to Miss Louisa Jebb, along the banks of the Tigris in 1908, to the accompaniment of a village's frenzied exultation. " 'The men have bought a piece of meat . . . and are singing to it' " was the explanation given her, and watching the revels, this gently reared English aristocrat was amazed to feel herself suddenly caught up by the madness of the moment. "The men seized me and on we went, on and on with the hopping and turning and stamping. And soon I too was a savage, a glorious, free savage under the white moon."

These and other colorful reports—of lives unvicariously lived, of spirits enriched by intimate yet far-off encounters—can all be sampled in Jane Robinson's appetite-whetting anthology of female travelers, *Unsuitable for Ladies* (Oxford). Rubbing shoulders

in one browsable volume are a group of women—Frances Trol-
lope, Fanny Kemble, Lady Lucie Duff Gordon, Karen Blixen,
Rose Macaulay, Harriet Martineau, among many others—who,
although obvious natural allies, might have made a less har-
monious whole if otherwise assembled. One thing is clear in
these selected readings: It was the individualism and self-
certainty of these women that both took them into and brought
them out of difficulties.

For us in our armchairs, it is difficult not to be enthralled by
what these persevering souls went through, whether it was pouring tea mid-jungle, hobnobbing with cannibals, or surviving
Bulgarian bombs. (This last experience was described by Flora
Sandes, a nurse who wound up a combatant, in her *Autobiography
of a Woman Soldier,* 1927. The man who carried her, wounded,
to safety, became her husband; she was awarded a medal and
achieved the rank of captain.)

Perhaps, however, it is Mary Wollstonecraft, author of the
Vindication of the Rights of Woman, who should have the last word.
During one of her sojourns, she penned a letter declaring that
"travelers who require that every nation should resemble their
native country had better stay home." Fortunately for literature,
not all her fellow female travelers followed her advice.

"I Feel the Same Way"

Judith Thurman

I can remember when I was young and words, like things, were alive. They were inhabited by spirits, with unpredictable personalities, not all benign, who woke up when I named them. Snout, viscous, boa, firebug, gristle, ice pick—I pronounce them now, and, of course, I can understand why they were terrifying. But why was I so affected by Chihuahua, tapioca, real estate, and suitcase? Why did I tremble at the expressions pancake makeup and a fine gent? And why was beeswax a magic good word, along with plume, doodle, buttercup, Pegasus, and baloney?

The work of Lewis Carroll helps transport me back to that state of being, where there is no fixed boundary between sense and nonsense, dream and waking. So does the myth of Orpheus. It alludes to the fact that all poetry is a descent to the place where the ghosts of the word dwell.

There is a magic window that opens, for most children, around the age of two. Suddenly language begins streaming through in awesome shafts, like those that pierce a cover of cloud to reveal the landscape, but also in lazy and capricious trickles, which illuminate the cobwebs, and in mischievous, spooky, or searching beams like those that gave me the metaphor for the title poem of my first book for children, *Flashlight and Other Poems.* For a while then, a child's life is a continuous revelation of shape, color, detail, and relation. It takes a Herculean effort to recall that age, to become that pure, to recover that intensity—but it is precisely the effort required to write a poem. To write poetry of any sort is to recapture that first light of language, and then to focus it. To write for children is to focus it on essential and familiar things.

I began to turn my attention to such things as soap, rain, kisses, scabs, balloons, lumps, a tunnel, an oil slick, a fire escape, feeding a pony, and hiding in a closet with the encouragement of the distinguished and prolific poet for children, Lilian Moore. Lilian, who in 1996 celebrated her eighty-seventh birthday, has never lost the ability "to see the world afresh," which was the title we gave to an anthology of poetry for children that we edited together. "Looking is not seeing," wrote Gertrude Stein. When Lilian looks, she sees. She is infuriatingly unjaded and insatiable. She has a poet's genius for selective forgetting, so that when she recovers an image lost or buried—the old bone, the locket, the fish thrown back into the pond—it is a new marvel. To see the world afresh means to regard it without prejudice—literally without prejudgment of any sort—esthetic, moral, even causal. "Johnny drew a monster," Lilian wrote, "the monster chased him. Just in time, Johnny erased him."

When Lilian was widowed two years ago, she sold her farm in upstate New York, packed up her books, her pictures, and her piano, and moved three thousand miles away to Seattle, where her son and grandson live. They found her an apartment with a view of the Pacific, and here she finished her most recent

book, which is called, not coincidentally, *I Never Did That Before*.
I am very proud to say that *I Never Did That Before* is dedicated
to my seven-year-old son, Will, who has been a fan of Lilian
Moore's since he was two. He would sit in his high chair squish-
ing peas, and I would read to him from her now-classic book
for very young readers, *I Feel the Same Way*. The wordplay, the
candor, the poems' combination of musicality, playfulness, and
bravado were irresistible to him. He learned the lines by heart.
Now it makes him feel very old, he says, to recall "Go Wind":

> Go wind, blow
> Push wind, swoosh.
> Shake things
> take things
> make things
> fly.
>
> Ring things
> swing things
> fling things
> high.
>
> Go wind, blow
> Push things—wheee.
> No, wind, no.
> Not me—
> not *me*.

A fortune-teller once told me that I would be romantically
susceptible to any man who could recite great poetry to me,
preferably in a language I didn't know. (Just for the record, she
was right.) I inordinately admire anyone to whose lips Shakespeare just comes naturally, or Rimbaud, Yeats, Auden, Brecht,
or the Bible. Reciting by heart was one of the gifts for which I

most envied and revered Isak Dinesen. She had a prodigious memory for poetry in three languages. The last of her mottos was *je responderai,* borrowed from the noble family of her friend, Denys Finch Hatton, and nothing charmed her more profoundly than a voice "answering" one line or stanza of a beloved verse with the next one.

My father's uncle, who belonged to the same generation and lived to be a hundred, used to keep up the courage and morale of his fellow patients in the nursing home by reciting to them the poetry that he had loved as a schoolboy: Christina Rossetti, Emily Dickinson, and Lord Tennyson. In extremis—in the face of death, in the grip of grief or fear or immense joy—there is no better companion than a poet. An infant, who lives permanently in extremis, first experiences the power of a poem to console—to keep the soul company—in the form of a lullaby.

Humankind's first memory palace was built of rhyme and rhythmic incantation, and it housed our collective wisdom. It seems like a great shame that teaching children to memorize poetry is now out of fashion. We were obviously designed to remember and to pass on the live flame of the word. The proof is that one never forgets the poetry one has, as a child, learned by heart. It is saturated with the scent and taste of the past— the archetype for Proust's madeleine.

Poets and children have much in common. They are both eloquent with very few and simple words. They are inspired scavengers. They have an utter disregard for what the world judges to be mundane. They can be sublimely silly. Parents, I think, sometimes spoil poetry for children by exalting it too highly—by presenting it as some indispensably wholesome nutrient, the taste of which has to be acquired—a kind of mental broccoli. No: Poetry is a subversive, delicious, and volatile substance, and one should treat it as such. I have floor-to-ceiling shelves in my library and an old-fashioned ladder on a sliding track, and I keep my poetry books for children on the very top shelf. If Will wants one of those books, he has to climb Everest for it. And, of course, he loves to.

What is on that top shelf? "Hiawatha" is up there, and "The Night Before Christmas," and "Wynken, Blynken and Nod," and "Jabberwocky." But there are also anthologies in which Philip Larkin rubs shoulders with Karla Kuskin, Gerard Manley Hopkins with Lee Bennett Hopkins, Myra Livingston with Emily Dickinson, Audre Lorde with Lord Tennyson, and the Hugheses—Ted and Langston. There are Lear and Milne, of course, but also Valerie Worth's exquisite and sensuous *Small Poems and More Small Poems,* and the limber, impious, and musical verse of my late friend, Eve Merriam. There is a fine, though torn and patched, 1944 edition of Stevenson's *A Child's Garden of Verses* with an introduction by William Rose Benét and pictures by Roger Duvoisin. Like all the older editions, it has "Judy's" bookplate—a faded Mickey Mouse flying through the air above an improbable Ali Baba landscape of pastel domes, on what looks like a striped bath mat, with the legend: "A Book Is a Magic Carpet."

I remember envying Stevenson's children many exotic things: their beautiful Victorian toys and clothes, their nannies with starched aprons, their idyllic meadows, haylofts, and gardens, their country villages with cobbled streets, and, perhaps most of all, the little candlesticks that they carried up the stairs to their wrought-iron beds. But there were also the poems that seemed to speak to and to have been written especially for me. One of these was "The Swing." Another was "Picture Books in Winter." And then my favorite, "The Land of Counterpane":

> When I was sick and lay a-bed
> I had two pillows at my head,
> And all my toys beside me lay
> To keep me happy all the day.

And sometimes for an hour or so
I watched my leaden soldiers go
With different uniforms and drills,
Among the bed-clothes, through the hills . . .

I was the giant great and still
That sits upon the pillow-hill,
And sees before him, dale and plain,
The pleasant land of counterpane.

At the time, I didn't wonder that a stranger had discovered and described one of my own greatest, most secret pleasures: a sovereign sick day in bed. Children may appreciate great poetry for its quality, but they have no scale by which to gauge its rareness. All marvels, from an anthill to a pyramid, are equal in their democratic sight. At the heart of every memorable poem, however, is the revelation that a stranger, and perhaps someone from another generation, culture, or country, has—against all probability—stood in your shoes, seen through your eyes, felt the same way.

"To Judith, who feels the same way," wrote my friend Lilian thirty years ago on the title page of what was then her latest book. But *I Feel the Same Way* turns out to be an apt title for all the best children's poetry. It suggests the power a poem has to breach that solitude that every one of us has felt, even—and perhaps all the more keenly—the best loved of children. It also suggests the nature of the unique complicity between a poet and a young reader, which is a bond composed of shared secrets, surprises, pleasures, guilts, triumphs, and fears. A poem, in fact, is a little foretaste of what it will be like to meet a soul mate.

WRITING TO THE
HUMAN HEART

Marian Seldes

*I*n the summer of 1995, Victoria *arranged a series of dra-matic readings by distinguished actors in New York City. The series began with Rosemary Harris as Elizabeth Bowen and continued with Marian Seldes as Willa Cather. Like Bowen, Cather is one of those artists who go in and out of fashion, but whose work endures because of its intelligence and humanity. Here, this renowned actress gives us her insight into Cather's lasting appeal.*

During summer vacations when I was in high school, I would sit in my father's cool study in a Victorian stone house in Croton Falls, New York, and read all day. I literally chose Willa Cather's books by their covers, intrigued by the bindings with their blue-greenish-yellow spines, her name at the top in dark blue letters and the drawing of a Borzoi dog (the symbol of her publisher, Alfred A. Knopf) near the bottom. The size of each book felt just right. I opened the first one. It was *Lucy Gayheart,* published in 1935. And then I read five more, working my way back to *O Pioneers!* (1913). I had no favorite, I loved them all.

But it was not until I began to work on a program of her words and her life that I felt I knew her as a living person.

Victoria had asked me to give a reading from Cather's works in June 1995. I arrived at Merkin Hall in New York City for a single brief rehearsal with a simple black evening dress in my satchel. Since I do not resemble Cather, I had not wanted to attempt a physical transformation, but I noticed the stage designer had placed a white linen coat and two straw hats on a coatrack, stage left. I took the coat and the sturdier of the two hats into the wings and put them on, pulling the hat straight down over my hair and buttoning the coat. Hearing the music cue, I walked on stage into Willa Cather's "study," carefully removed her hat and coat, opened her portfolio, and felt that we were going to be, for an hour or so, the same person. I would try to get inside her skin.

All I had, all I needed, were her words. And such words! Her poems, her stories, her reminiscences—everything was there, ready to be shared. The sights and sounds of Red Cloud, the prairie town in Nebraska where she grew up; the rhythms of her writer's voice so influenced by her early reading of the Bible and *Pilgrim's Progress;* her love of the land, of music and theater, of the pure prose found in other fine writers—Poe, Hawthorne, and Henry James, Pope in his translation of *The Iliad,* Shakespeare.

Cather once wrote: "Finding a new type of human being and getting inside a new skin is the finest sport I know. I can feel my characters stretching inside my skin."

But who was Willa Cather?

One reference book tells us that she was born in Virginia in 1873. Her formative years were spent in Nebraska among the immigrant farmers who became vivid characters in her novels. She graduated from the University of Nebraska in 1895. From

1908 to 1912, she was the managing editor of the popular *Mc-Clure's* magazine in New York. She died in New York in 1947. There is no mention of her nonfiction, her poetry, her Pulitzer Prize, or the indisputable fact that she is one of America's finest writers.

The editor Maxwell Perkins said in 1944 that he would put her "very high" in the company of Thomas Wolfe and Ernest Hemingway. In 1937 Alexander Woollcott reprinted Willa Cather's *Two Friends* (written in 1931) "as a signpost," he wrote, "hoping that reading it would make people rush to the nearest library for all her other works." He pointed out the contrast between the size of the printings of Margaret Mitchell's *Gone With the Wind* and Cather's *My Ántonia* and remarked how amazing it was that "so established and honored an author as Willa Cather remains after all these years an unknown quantity. Her novels are as nourishing and comely and unfailingly distinguished a contribution to American letters as has been made by anyone in my lifetime. Poetry or prose, one seldom catches Miss Cather in the act of fine writing. Not often can a passage of hers be taken out and held up to the light like a jewel. The serene and breathtaking beauty of many a scene in *Death Comes for the Archbishop* and *Shadows on the Rock* is as impalpable as a perfume. And as undebatable."

An older writer, Sarah Orne Jewett, advised the young Willa, "You must find your own quiet center of life, and write from that to the world that holds others, and all society, all Bohemia; the city, the country—in short you must write to the human heart." In all her works—including short stories ("The Troll Garden," 1905), poetry ("April Twilight," 1923), essays ("Not Under Forty," 1936), but most fully in her fourteen novels published between 1912 and 1940—she followed Miss Jewett's advice. She explored the hearts of her characters and presented her findings in spare and lovely prose.

And the secret, private Cather? She remained a puzzle even

to herself: "What I find most surprising, day after day, even after all these years, is that inwardly I am very much a lapidary, while outwardly I am rustic. Where is the person who wrote the passages that so move me? Where does she go? Who, outside of myself, sees her? While the person most often described as Willa Cather is a complete mystery to me."

She never wanted to have a book written about her and discouraged her friends and acquaintances from sharing their letters or reminiscences. Her estate will not allow any of the existing Cather letters to be published or quoted.

The excerpts that I read from her large and important body of work formed a portrait of an extraordinary human being who believed she could capture the world in words. She once said, "I have to believe my work before I consider it finished. If I don't believe it, I destroy it. If I were to publish something I didn't believe fully, it would destroy me."

When my daughter, Katharine, began her career as a writer, I remembered that Cather had said in her early twenties, "A young writer must care vitally, fiercely, absurdly about the trickery and arrangements of words, the beauty and power of phrases." I gave Katharine a framed photograph of Willa Cather taken by Edward Steichen in 1926. Her eyes look into Steichen's lens, directly out of the picture into our eyes. Her dark hair is casually combed behind her ears, the part is a bit off-center. She is wearing a white blouse and a tie like a sailor's neckerchief. Her expression is kind and wise, serious yet almost smiling.

Cather ended eight of her novels with an epilogue. In June 1995, at Merkin Hall, I too ended my presentation of her words with an epilogue, but the words were not hers. The young Truman Capote had seen her when he started to work at *The New Yorker* and years later, in an interview with Gloria Steinem for *McCall's,* he recalled the meeting. He described her as "an absolutely marvelous-looking woman. She had a wonderful open, extraordinary face, and hair combed back in a bun—and her eyes were the most amazing pale, pale blue, like pieces of the sky floating in her face."

In *The Song of the Lark,* Thea, who wants more than anything to find the artist within herself, says it was "as if she had an appointment to meet the rest of herself sometime, somewhere." I felt that for one evening the audience and I had met Willa Cather. And Truman Capote had made it possible for me to see her even more clearly than in the lovely photograph that still guards my daughter's desk.

THE QUIET CENTER
OF ONE'S LIFE

MEDITATIONS OF A

BEEKEEPER

Faith Andrews Bedford

s I sit on my porch watching my honeybees etch golden trails across the sky, I realize that I did not know how much I loved them until the year they disappeared.

In years past, as the crocus pushed eagerly through the soft earth, my honeybees greeted the arrival of the year's first flowers with excitement, diving into the deep cups of the blooms and covering their furry bodies with bright yellow pollen. Their buzzing echoed happily inside the purple chambers, and the blossoms shook. Each April, when the Andromeda bush by the back door was covered with delicate rosy panicles, the sound of the bees' quiet hum would greet our comings and goings. And as I snipped the tender new growth of thyme and rosemary, I would always find a honeybee or two already busy at work gathering nectar from her side of the herb.

But last year my bees were overcome by illness. Their disappearance left my home and gardens a quiet place. No golden haze of bees shimmered around the maple trees as their red blossoms burst open. The sky, once lively with the twirling flights of honeybees, was still. The melody of spring sounds had lost a delicate note.

I quickly called my favorite apiarist, who promised to send me ten boxes of new honeybees as soon as the weather warmed. The wait seemed endless. As robins began to dot my lawns and the bluebirds settled into their house on the fence post, I watched the thermometer, silently urging it upward. I carefully cleaned out the hives and gave them all a new coat of sparkling white paint. At last, my postmaster called to tell me my bees had arrived.

Transferring the bees from their screen-sided traveling boxes to the hives, I could see that all was to their liking. The housekeeping bees quickly set about removing the few bits of leaves I had missed; the guard bees hovered protectively at the entrance. Within minutes the recent arrivals were emerging from their new homes, rising in slow spirals to orient themselves and then flying off in search of nectar.

The new bees had arrived just in time. The peach and apple blossoms were just beginning to unfold their porcelain petals, and the early peas were about to put forth their first flowers. My gardens and orchards would bear fruit after all. With the return of the honeybees to my gardens, the harmony of nature was restored.

I may till and plant and weed and prune, but without honeybees to pollinate them, my crops would bear no fruit. These little creatures are my partners. We are stewards of the land together. In the gardens we each have our special tasks, and we treat each other with politeness. If I find a honeybee inside a cucumber blossom, I wait until she is finished gathering nectar before coaxing the vines up the trellis. She in turn carefully diverts her flight around me. The bees move quietly aside when I pluck slender pods from the bush beans whose new blooms they are pollinating. I use nothing in my gardens that would harm them.

My woods and meadows, bogs and streams are full of wild foods, free for the gathering: fiddlehead ferns and blackberries, tiny strawberries and wild asparagus. Golden persimmons dangle from gnarled branches. Both my bees and I take advantage of nature's bounty. I gather the wild foods for our table, they turn the wild nectars into honey. We work in harmony. I give my honeybees warm dry hives to live in and take care to be sure they have plenty of room and are safe from harm. For this they reward me with all the honey I need and with beeswax for fragrant candles and soothing lotions.

But harvesting nature's free sweets is only one of the joys of beekeeping. My little niece, Lily, likes to stand quietly by my side, her eyes wide with wonder, as I tend my hives. I point out the different bees going about their special individual tasks and show her the larger cells the bees build in which to raise a new queen should they need one. Sometimes we catch a glimpse of the queen herself, her slender, elegant body distinguishing her from her smaller subjects. As we sit quietly on the grass watching the bees arriving with their loads of honey and pollen, Lily peppers me with questions. How does the wiggly dance tell the other bees exactly where the source of nectar is? How does a guard bee know which bees to let in the hive and which ones to keep out? How do the bees know when the honey is ready to seal with a fresh white cap of new wax? Those are mysteries, I tell Lily, and that is the wonder of beekeeping.

In a time when science and technology have unraveled so much of what was once unknown, there are still mysteries. Why bees do what they do is one of them. My books and journals tell me much about the science of beekeeping, but they cannot explain how the queen knows just when to start raising young for the spring or how the bees keep each other warm when winter snows drift across the hives. Keeping bees creates a sense of wonder. And as I savor a warm biscuit dripping with golden sweetness, I decide that some of nature's secrets should be kept.

REFLECTING ON FOOT

Susan Minot

I grew up in a large family, and when I was young walks were group activities that occurred after Thanksgiving lunch or on summer evenings or during excursions to the beach. There was usually a baby in a carriage or someone who'd just learned to walk, slowing us down to a creaking pace. These walks were long and meandering, like the walks of lovers. On the way home a number of us would want to be carried. We lived on the top of a hill, and the road seemed so steep going up that one's nose nearly touched the pine needles scattered on the ground.

It was natural to walk on beautiful days, shuffling through brittle leaves in the fall, going barefoot down shadowy lanes. On the first warm day of spring even the stubborn and weary do not refuse the urge to walk. We would take off our shoes and socks and walk on the still-cold grass, our pale legs particularly sensitive to the new, warm breeze. But bad weather was more exciting—venturing out into a strong wind with rain drenching our faces or moving through a silent world of snow falling so thick you couldn't blink.

One walk we often took was down the driveway and along the avenue that curved along a small beach. Around the beach was a sea wall made of pebbly butterscotch-colored concrete. You could step onto the wall at one end, and as you went around the beach the wall grew higher and higher. We, my siblings and I, were not allowed to walk on the sea wall, so naturally we did whenever we could. The top was about a foot wide and we favored the beach side—if we fell, the sand would be softer. When a grown-up was around, the wall was not a place we could walk. This was the beginning of my desire for unfettered, solitary walking.

Being a lone walker when I was growing up was rare. Everyone drove; we traveled in a station wagon. On the stretches between towns we began to notice a portly middle-aged woman often out on a stroll. More and more we'd pass her on our way to the grocery store or on a different road going to pick up my father at the train station. It began to be a game as to who would see her first. She was always wearing a dress, sometimes a clear rain hat if it was raining or fur boots in the snow. After a while there was a change in her: She became a medium-sized woman. There was some argument in the station wagon over whether this woman was our walker, but there were not many people out walking, and we did recognize the plaid coat. Eventually she turned into a spindly woman, a transformation that fascinated us. Added to that was my mother's observation, "She's walking herself out of existence."

I walk to think and not to think. When walking I remember things that are important to me. If I did not walk, I would not recall a forgotten friend I knew in a Concord spring, brought to mind by the smell of lilacs in a hedge, or would forget to feel my luck, conjured up—who knows why—by the sight of reflected light on a hill.

I walk to forget. I have yet to set out on a walk in low spirits and return feeling worse than I did when I left the door. A change occurs between the gate and the porch light; walking lifts the weight off the heart. Or as the writer Jim Harrison says, "When you're out of sorts, walk a hundred miles."

In order to write, a writer needs space and time and stillness. Walker Percy, the Southern novelist, spoke of the problem of "re-entry," of going back into the world after one has been sequestered in the caves of one's thoughts. Attempting to go to a dinner party, say, in this state, can be the equivalent of jumping into an icy stream—it may wake you up but you run the risk of shock and heart attack, or of turning into a frozen block. Many writers find a cocktail effective in easing this transition. Some take naps. I am not original in choosing to walk.

Coleridge and Wordsworth were famous for their very long walks. Proust's childhood walks with the blooming hawthorns and cornflowers "constituted for all time the picture of the land in which I would fain pass my life." Rimbaud, who traveled "to ward off the apparitions assembled in my brain," was observed in Ethiopia by a man named Righas: "He was a great walker. Oh! An astonishing walker, his coat open, a little fez on his head in spite of the sun." Many of the people I know who walk a great deal are artists or writers. They are the ones who will walk sixty blocks to a movie theater in Manhattan rather than take the subway or a cab. One friend of mine who was raised in Europe, where walking is perhaps more ingrained, used to walk around New York City for hours with no destination. When asked what he had done that day he would answer simply, "I went for a walk."

The English are particularly enthusiastic walkers, with their Wellies waiting in the mud room for after Sunday lunch. A student applying for a scholarship at Oxford was worried during his final interview when he was asked by a panel what sort of sport he did. He imagined the other candidates answering high-diving or cross-country marathons and felt his chances dim before his eyes. He had no sport. "I take long walks," he said for lack of anything better, and there broke across the face of one of the interviewers a great smile. "How English," he said. The student received the scholarship.

The only way to walk in the city is fast. If you've lived in a city long enough, past lives will encounter you on those walks, dotted about like faded flags—that entranceway you once knew well, the upper window where you attended that strange party, the park bench where you sat on a cold afternoon. I have found myself walking in parts of town where it would have been safer not to be, and as I hurry past ominous alleys I promise myself next time I will take a cab. But next time comes and the night air is inviting and it's only three blocks through a dark area to a place of lights and people, and I'm once again walking, once again atop the narrow sea wall.

Walks in the city can be forlorn when you're poor or bereft, watching the warm lights in the restaurants, getting splashed by a passing bus, but there are always things to see—the dogs, the shoes, the awnings, the shine, the bags, the angry women, the shuffling men, the swaggering youth. It fills your head. Walking in the city loosens your body, but it tightens and crowds the mind. Sometimes it's just what you need.

It is different in the country. You walk and your head empties inside out, your thoughts slow down to the pace of your feet. The sound of a crashing sea takes up the back of your head, or the mountains rise up behind your eyes, a frost-crunch is felt in your feet, and the birds seem to sing in a place low within your chest. Buddha said, "You cannot travel on the path before you have become the Path itself."

* * *

Cemeteries are wonderful places to walk—Sleepy Hollow in Concord, Massachusetts, where Hawthorne, Emerson, Thoreau, and Louisa May Alcott are buried; Père Lachaise outside Paris, where chestnuts drop from great heights onto the cobblestones; a small monument for the Confederate dead in Oxford, Mississippi, hidden among ruffled greenery.

My favorite walks often take me by bodies of water. Around the island edges in Penobscot Bay in Maine the rocks are jagged and the moss is thick as velvet under the pine trees. On the North Shore of Boston at Singing Beach, where Winslow Homer set some paintings, I spent many days of my youth walking the sand, which makes unusual whining sounds when you scuff your feet. I have walked in every season the wide white beach of Bridgehampton, New York, full of ball throwers in July, empty and slanting in November. On frozen winter days the Yellowstone River in Montana bucks itself up into great greenish ice slabs along its shore, while water thick as green lead flows down its center. The forest above the St. Croix in Minnesota turns yellow in October, and as you walk above the crimson water it's like being in a lightbulb. On the Dingle Peninsula on Ireland's west coast the beaches are miles long and as wide as golf courses. At low tide, when the sand is hard, cars drive down to the water making designs with their tire tracks. Far more evocative are the prints in the sand left by feet.

The best walks are in empty places with no people around. Lately I have been spending a lot of time in southern Montana. Here walking has a pioneer aspect to it. Making one's way over hills and down gullies and along buttes is modernly referred to as hiking, but I loathe the word. "Hiking" carries with it associations of exertion and equipment. To drive ten minutes out of town, stop the car, and head for a random peak is how I would walk—wandering. One can go for hours without seeing a person or car yet there is always life: herds of antelope moving liquidly down a snowy slope undulating like a school of fish, a dozen grouse flapping in panic as they loft out of some weathered bay bushes, mule-eared deer leaping a fence.

I am partial to roads that end at the ocean or ones that take a hill and appear to stop in the sky. It is not unusual on a walk to fall in love. In thick fog you can walk and walk and seem to go nowhere. The walk itself, as Sören Kierkegaard recognized, is enough. "Above all do not lose your desire to walk," he wrote, "every day I walk myself into a state of well being and walk away from illness; I have walked myself into my best thoughts, and I know of no thought so burdensome that one cannot walk away from it. . . . Thus if one just keeps on walking everything will be all right."

GIVING LOVE A MELODY, MEMORY A TUNE

Madeleine L'Engle

"Music I heard with you was more than music,/And bread I broke with you was more than bread," wrote Conrad Aiken. With these beautiful words of the poet, Hugh, my late husband, asked me to marry him.

We met in a production of Chekhov's *The Cherry Orchard*. Hugh, the gorgeous young leading man. Madeleine, the gawky understudy. In the ballroom scene a small orchestra played one of Tchaikovsky's melodious waltzes, and whenever and wherever that is played, it is "our" music, a reminder of youth and romance and the blossoming of a love that did last until death did us part, and beyond.

Sometimes I think it is music that binds us together with harmonies that are part of all the galaxies and all the stars in their courses. Music heals, music releases emotions. Music we hear with each other is indeed more than music.

A Dohnányi symphony and a beautiful saxophone concerto by Ibert will always evoke my mother, because it was with her that

I first discovered them. The children's hymn "Jesus Tender Shepherd" makes me think of my grandmother, rocking me as we sat out on the veranda of her beach cottage. Singing that same hymn to my babies was a loving kind of continuity.

I go to a church where we do a lot of singing. I am glad of it, for the hymns give voice to joys and sorrows as varied as the arrangements of the chords. At my mother's funeral and at my husband's we sang "A Mighty Fortress Is My God." That hymn is a mighty fortress for me—it is so full of affirmation and strength that despite its associations, it does not bring tears to my eyes. Neither does "Joyful, Joyful, We Adore Thee," the hymn based on Beethoven's glorious "Ode to Joy" in the Ninth Symphony. It was my husband's favorite; we also sang it at his funeral. I can sing it now without sadness. But "Surely the Presence of the Lord Is in This Place" will bring tears, tears to overflowing, no matter how much I try to control them. Why? I'm not even sure. Perhaps because I heard it the first time Hugh and I joined up to do readings from my work, a partnership that ultimately took us round the world.

I remember the songs my mother sang to me in her sweet, soprano voice (I am definitely an alto), some of them from musical plays of the first decades of this century. My high school years were spent in a boarding school where, each spring, we performed one of Shakespeare's plays and sang the madrigals and songs of his period. These I sang to my babies, along with the nursery rhymes I knew from my own childhood. When we were bringing up our three little ones in a cold New England village, one of my favorites was, "The north wind doth blow, / And we shall have snow, / And what will poor robin do then, / Poor thing?"

I still have my grandmother's songbook of nursery rhymes, many of the melodies still familiar, several not so well known, but dear to me.

When my children were little I had a special song for each

of them. Sometimes, after we had had stories and songs, and the prayers and the good nights had been said, I would go sit with my autoharp at the head of the front staircase, so that I was equidistant from their bedrooms. I would strike my chords and sing extra songs to them as a special treat. It was a treat for me, too.

As the children grew older and began to exercise their own tastes, they did not fail to attend to my musical education. "Listen to this, Mother. You'll like the words." Often this was true, even if I didn't respond pleasurably to the music. But I tried. An unspoken rule grew up in the family. The kids played "their" music all day. At six o'clock we shifted to the classics. I learned to enjoy some of their music, though there's no way I can write to hard rock, as I can to, say, Scarlatti or Dvořák.

One day I was working in my little study over the garage and had put on some records. My son, then about thirteen, paused at the foot of the stairs with one of his friends. They called up to ask me what I was playing.

"Couperin."

"Cool! Can we borrow it?"

Margie, who was part of our summer family the year my mother died, had not been exposed to much music. Nevertheless, she played the glockenspiel in the school band. We introduced her to Mozart's *The Magic Flute* with its lovely glockenspiel solos. She played it over and over during my mother's last summer. We were all exhausted and grieved by the old woman's descent, both bodily and mentally. We groaned when we heard the record begin yet again, but the joyous melodies were healing.

When I was an adolescent I played a piano exercise called storm, and I played when I was angry, hurt, outraged. I played it stormily indeed with great banging chords, and it helped. When I need perspective in a quieter way I turn to Bach's fugues. The Seventh Fugue in Book II of the Well-Tempered

Clavier is my pretravel music, and the Fifth is what I play when I need patience in time of difficulty. Once when I was upset and showing it, my young son said, "Oh, Mother, go play the piano."

Music is, I believe, an intrinsic part of being human, as necessary as breathing and eating. We sing our joy, we sing our grief, we sing our love. The great spirituals were born of the agony of slavery. Waltzes, tangos, fox-trots come from our response to the wonderful pleasures of the body. One summer when I played in a small stock company, after the last curtain had come down we would clear the stage and then put on records of Viennese waltzes. We'd dance wildly, joyfully, with our arms around each other's waists, leaning back and waltzing our way out of the tension of the performance.

When our first little girl was learning to walk, she would stand on my husband's feet and he would waltz with her. Is this something intuitive? When I was a small child I stood on my father's feet while he danced, too.

As my mother's mind became dim, music was the last thing that reached her. Every night we would play, at her request, a violin concerto and Vaughan Williams's *Greensleeves* until we were heartily sick of them. But they were new to her each evening, and calming. They still sadden me.

One day when Hugh and I were driving back to the city from a week in the country, we heard on the radio the lovely dance of the divine spirits from Gluck's *Orfeo*. Every time I hear it, that is still "our" music.

Music defies time and separation. It gives love a melody, memory a tune. Yes, the music we hear together is more than music.

THE ROMANCE
OF OLD BOOKS

Patricia O'Toole

half hour of steady rain is all it takes for the mood to wrap itself around me. Why this should be, I don't know, but when the world's clatter disappears in the thrum of the rain, the tranquillity that settles in pulls me toward the pleasures of browsing among old books. Not rare books, and not classics necessarily, just books that have been around for a while. Books that used to belong to someone else. Books that look cherished—as if they've been read more than once and passed from friend to friend.

If my longing strikes on a busy day, I settle for a visit to the used-book establishment across the street. There is no way to keep the bell on the front door from waking the cat drowsing in the window, but the cat declines to protest. He either goes back to sleep or commences a browse of his own, in the alcove given over to architecture and opera. My own predilections are literary and historical, and with the clock ticking toward a deadline, I swear to stick to one or the other.

It is easier to diet than keep this promise. Old books beg to be read. They fall open. Their yellowed pages lie flat and are easy on the eyes. An hour goes by in a minute, and my truant self is still up on a library ladder, absorbed in a short story I've never read or a story I've read a dozen times, like Paul Morand's "Six-Day Night." Happening onto a favorite story is like an unexpected encounter with a friend too long unseen: You seize your good fortune and make time for each other. The rest of the world must wait.

The combination of a good rain in progress and a distant deadline allows for a more leisurely indulgence of my habit. On these days my destination of choice is a pair of old barns in the country, an hour away. The drive is its own reward. All sensible people are indoors, saving their errands until the rain stops, so the roads are empty and serene. Gray skies are vastly superior to blue ones for showing the lushest depths of color (which is why paintings often hang on gray walls in museums). In the rain, even the most familiar flowers and trees along my route look so new, so original, that I feel I have never seen them before.

If it rains hard enough, the barn lights come and go, but it doesn't matter. Standing at one or another of the barn windows on one or another powerless afternoon, I have read big chunks of *Fanny Kemble's Journal of a Residence on a Georgian Plantation, 1838–1839* and perused, with amazement, an old illustrated tome called something like *Night Scenes from the Bible.* As the title suggests, it is a retelling of biblical tales with nocturnal settings. Unburdened by the facts of the case, I am free to imagine the author as a gentleman of too much leisure, a fusspot who read the words "Let there be light" and then could not stop noticing its absence. Now he has me doing that. Like other writers, I often consult the Bible for apt quotations, the majesty of the prose, and a thousand other reasons. Since making the acquaintance of *Night Scenes,* I have not opened my King James without scanning the page for some sign of whether the sun is up or down.

Each winter I prune my library and lug several cartons of books to local Bryn Mawr or Smith alumnae, who hold used-book sales to raise money for scholarships. The Bryn Mawrtyrs (as they call themselves) are more punctilious than the Smithies in organizing the thousands of volumes in their charge, which makes it easy to shop from the ever-lengthening book list in my wallet. Over the four years I spent writing a biography set in nineteenth-century Washington, Bryn Mawr furnished me with at least a dozen key books long since out of print and too obscure to merit space on the shelves of my small-town library: memoirs of minor diplomats, forgotten novels of the period, an artist's letters, and a turn-of-the-century biography with its pages still uncut. This last, at five dollars, was doubly sweet since I'd passed up an earlier chance to buy it from a bookseller asking forty dollars.

The hunter and the browser are different species, and for browsers, the chaos of the Smith sale is bliss. A hunt is focused. A browse is unconcentrated. The browser's joy lies in the doing, not in bagging trophies. Only in a browsing mood could I have surrendered to the temptation to purchase volume two of Lady Murasaki's *The Tale of Genji,* an eleventh-century novel about life in the imperial court of Japan. No, I have not read volume one. But now that I own volume two, I am on the lookout for volume one—not to mention volumes three, four, five, and six.

Though not by nature a collector of anything, I have, thanks to Smith, acquired a number of first editions of the novels of John Cheever, Saul Bellow, and others. Thus launched, I am now ruled by the impulse for completion, and the titles of these authors' other novels have been added to the list in my wallet. I may never find them, and may decide not to buy them if they do turn up, but the quest for these missing pieces provides me with a sense of mission on the rainy days when I cross the street to browse with the cat.

Environmentalists despair at the tons of paper wasted by humankind, and I cannot be the only person who finishes a disappointing book and mourns the trees that died for it. But it is also true that books can be recycled almost indefinitely. The flyleaf of my faded red *Queen Victoria,* by Lytton Strachey, published in 1921, shows that it has had at least three other owners, Margaret Cunningham, D.R., and Willow Sharp. When I finished the book, I couldn't decide whether Strachey's portrait of the queen was sly but kind, or kind but sly. I wondered where Willow was, and which side she would take.

Someone once gave me a book and a card that read, "A book is a present you can open again and again." It is also a present you can give again and again. One of my most cherished books used to belong to a friend who shared many of my literary interests and did much to encourage my writing. When he died, his wife invited me to choose a book from his library. As I browsed, I understood why biographers pay close attention to the libraries of their subjects: Books can reveal as much about people as their letters do. Almost every volume in my friend's library reminded me of conversations we'd had. I picked a collection of Robert Benchley's humor, a special World War II edition designed to fit into a soldier's pocket.

I think of this gift at the Smith and Bryn Mawr book sales and invariably come home loaded with books for friends. The sight of Henry Adams's delightful *Mont-Saint-Michel and Chartres,* a perfect companion for visiting those cathedrals, makes me remember someone who is soon going to France. I pick up Stella Gibbons's *Cold Comfort Farm,* a send-up of English country life, for a couple sure to appreciate all its hilarities. If they've read it, I'll bestow this tattered treasure, all fifty cents' worth of it, on someone else. For a sister-in-law I get the four volumes of

Paul Scott's *Jewel in the Crown* and one of the best biographies I've ever read, James Mellow's *Charmed Circle,* a portrait of Gertrude Stein and her Paris salon. Could handing out diamonds be any more fun than putting a book you like into the hands of a person you like?

Although these sales always seem to end too soon, lovers of old books do need to stay home from time to time, if only to catch up on their reading. And sale or no sale, old books are seldom far away. Any town that fancies itself sophisticated seems to have a used bookstore or two, easily found in the Yellow Pages. Browsers can simply turn up and see what's there. Hunters in a particular field can check out stores in advance of a trip with the help of a reference librarian or works such as *The Used Book Lover's Guide to New England* (Book Hunter Press).

There is much left to say about the pleasures of used books— about their astonishing power to evoke another time, about my dreams of unearthing forgotten classics worth republishing, about the bashful, gentle camaraderie to be found while hunting and browsing. But those are other stories, for other times. For now it is enough to sound a warning: Once begun, a romance with old books has a till-death-do-us-part epoxy about it. At least I have never heard of such a romance coming apart. Aw, go ahead. Risk it. And keep an eye out for my missing *Genji,* would you?

CANOES: SUMMER'S
MAGIC CARPET

Judith Thurman

𝓘 used to spend my summers at a New England lake—
a cold, smooth lake with a slim neck, rather like a gourd in
shape—surrounded by the black-green of the woods. Most of
the houses on the lake were built in the early 1920s by discreet
old Yankee families, whose one ostentation was to call them
camps—even though some of them were fieldstone mansions
with ten bedrooms, and others wooden villas in the Nordic style
with handhewn balconies and gingerbread fretwork.

The founding families shared an ideal of privacy if not reclu-
sion, and the charter of their "fishing and boating" club decreed
that no trees could be felled along the lake shores, which gave
you the illusion of looking out from your front lawn at a wilderness.

Rainbows lived in this lake, as did elegant browns with coral
spots and flesh tinted pink by the tiny shrimp they fed on. No
live bait was permitted to spoil their appetites, nor motors to
trouble their spawning or their rises—or for that matter, the

peace of the solemn fisherman who emerged on the water, in full fly-casting regalia, just as the clamorous children went in for supper. When you live near a fisherman, you become strangely and finely attuned to the sounds of his canoe, so that you can almost tell—by the way he drags it onto the dock— how many fish he's caught and what his mood is.

I tried trout fishing a few times. I didn't have any luck (and perhaps I didn't want to), though I was ravished by the beauty of the gear, and in particular, of the flies, which looked like the earrings of some devoutly, even fanatically feminine little creature, such as a fandango dancer. What I liked even more, though, was watching the light dim and the moon redden before it paled and the stillness of the lake at dusk, when every sound, cry, rustle, word—even the tinkle of an ice cube in a glass half a mile away—hung like perfume in the air.

I had been going to the lake for years before I had the revelation that changed my life there: I learned how to paddle a canoe using the J stroke.

The vertical slope of the J propels you forward, while the little sideways twist at the end keeps you on a straight course. Once I knew the J stroke I could take the canoe out by myself. And it was one of those sudden jolts of autonomy that remind you as an adult what it felt like as a child to master a bike, or to take a train alone for the first time—to acquire a new vehicle of discovery.

The green canoe was our summer station wagon, training ship, lifeboat, taxi, and magic carpet. If you wanted a moment of solitude, or of intimacy with a friend, the place to find it was in the canoe. We knew that one of our housemates occasionally escaped in it to smoke a cigarette or two, unchastened by the rest of us. When the children were learning to swim, we canoed along next to them, shouting encouragement they couldn't hear, reminding them, just as pointlessly, to kick and breathe and finally hauling them up like tired and gasping fish. In July, we cruised the shallow coves where the wild blueberry bushes grew down to the water's edge, and with berry picking as a respectable cover, we managed to reconnoiter all the camps that we didn't know, absurdly hoping to find some charming, neglected place whose kindly, decrepit, and childless proprietor might sell it to us for a song.

It was always a treat to pack the canoe with wine and sweaters, and to paddle across the lake to have supper with a lively family who, like us, were only humble renters in Paradise and who enjoyed human company more than did our Thoreaulike neighbors on each side. Nothing, however, compared with the pleasure of setting out for home again after dark, of charting a course by the porch lantern, of skimming an expanse of water so black and luminous it seemed like the night air.

This is the first year in nearly a decade I've missed a summer at the lake. At the moment, all I have to remind me of it is the bottle green of the reading lamps in the great, old foreign library where I'm working. I'm enough of a Puritan myself so that I don't miss the lost leisure. What I do miss, exquisitely, is that sensation of weightless and noiseless motion—a kind of deep embryonic grace—that you take to bed with you after a day in a canoe.

Too Obvious to Forget

Madeleine L'Engle

*I*t was a gray afternoon with a light drizzle. Tuesday. Nowhere near Friday. Nearly a whole week ahead of me, a week overscheduled as usual. When someone asked me how I was, I replied, "Overworked and underplayed." A time to play, to relax, to read something I wanted to read seemed a long time away. My foot hurt. I thought how wonderful it would be to go to the seashore and walk along the oceanside, dabbling my feet in the little waves.

But here I was, on the hard sidewalks of Manhattan, in one of those blue moods that hits us all occasionally. I turned into my apartment building, picked up the mail, headed upstairs and flopped on my bed, my favorite place for going over mail. Out my big west window I can see the Hudson River and across it the cliffs of New Jersey. My view includes the route of planes for the New York airports, and I love to watch them, particularly at night, when they move like stars across the sky.

It was not yet night, and the dreary sky held no promise of

a sunset. I checked over the mail. Catalogs, a few of which I enjoy going over when I'm too tired to read. Begging-mail. Some of the requests tug at my heartstrings. No one person can help everyone in need. Yet I long to, so that is yet another frustration. At last I turned to the personal mail, a dozen or so letters, many of them intimate because the people who have read my books consider me their friend.

At a conference I was asked, "Is all the mail you get a burden?" (I get about a hundred letters a week. I answer each with a personal note or a copy of my latest epistle.)

"Yes," I replied truthfully, "but it is a burden I wouldn't want to be without. In opening their hearts, my correspondents remind me to open mine. They offer me ballast when their faith in me exceeds my own."

I unfolded the first letter, which was from a Canadian woman. "You say that you write about the obvious," my correspondent began. "Please don't stop! We need to remember the obvious, and it seems that a lot of writers are embarrassed to write about it."

I let the letter fall to my lap, feeling intensely grateful. I glanced out the window and thought I saw a streak of rosy glow in the western sky. Yes, I said silently to the Canadian woman, *you are right.* Though sometimes I have doubted my course, the obvious matters. Love and compassion and caring—these are what are worth writing about. I believe like the poet William Blake that "he who would do good to another must do it in minute particulars."

In another letter a woman thanked me for writing that my children's underwear was always streaked with pink—I usually let something red slip in with the white wash. I've made all the usual housekeeping mistakes and invented a few of my own. One time when we used to put little electric warmers in our refrigerators to defrost them, I went to my typewriter in the middle of cleaning the fridge and forgot about it. I burned up the refrigerator. Everything rubber in it was melted. The eggs, which I'd left in their places in the door, were hard cooked. I was not so much embarrassed as totally outraged that I was the first person in the household to smell burning rubber.

I care and write about the obvious problems of being a woman in one of the most troubled centuries history has ever known. I am grateful that much has changed for women—I had as good an education as any man—but sad at the anger that sometimes accompanies what I think of as healthy feminism. It is a wonderful thing to be a mother, a glory that is not given to every woman, and is given to no man.

I care about language, and I try to honor it. When did you last hear somebody saying, "I give you my word," and meaning it, seriously? Have you ever heard someone say, "I can't do this and keep my integrity"? He usually means, "I cannot do this and have my own way."

I care about the simple things in life. I love cooking dinner for family and friends. On the Wednesday before one Thanksgiving I expected six for dinner. Then several of my friends decided to drop by before going over to Central Park West to see the balloons blown up for the Macy's parade. It was the coldest night of the season thus far, and the smell of soup cooking made their thoughts of leaving vanish. I ended up feeding sixteen. For just such occasions, I always keep on hand extra artichoke hearts, mushrooms, and water chestnuts, which are good soup stretchers. I called everyone to the table and lit the candles. To me, this simple gesture is an affirmation that light does shine in the darkness. Sometimes I wonder how often throughout the centuries the candles have been lit and people have gathered together, often forgetting disagreements of the day, and been nourished in body and spirit.

It is no longer popular or obvious to say that we have or had good parents, who did the best they could, which is probably all that any human parent can do. I loved my parents, and they are still an important part of my life, though my father died when I was seventeen. My mother lived until she was ninety, and during her last years she became demanding and difficult. She was a strange, angry old woman, not the gentle, cultured mother I knew, and I was angry at what was happening to her, not so much angry at my mother, as angry at God.

Sometimes at night, when almost everybody was in bed, I would take the dogs and walk down the lane that faces our old house in Connecticut and shout out loud to God, "Don't do this to my mother!" It was not very rational, but it helped. Having written about that in *The Summer of the Great-Grandmother,* I can't tell you how many letters I've received saying, "I didn't know I was allowed to be angry." Of course we're allowed to be angry. We just shouldn't stay stuck in anger; otherwise it stops being justifiable anger and becomes bitter resentment, which is a kind of cancer of the spirit. Now that many parents are living longer, more and more of us are going through the reversal of roles: The parent is no longer the caretaker. The child is, and that is hard for us to understand.

Statistically, many women outlive their husbands, and grief is another of those emotions we need to talk about but tend to repress. Grief is embarrassing. We don't want to hear about someone else's grief, because it is a reminder that we, too, may have cause to grieve. But we need to be able to share our griefs as well as our joys. We know who our friends are when we are in pain, spiritual or physical.

Once, in the small hours of the morning when I was wakeful, I listed in my mind the people I could call at two o'clock in the morning if I really needed to. And I was grateful that I could name more than a mere handful. And I thought, too, of the people who would call me. Unless there is an unexpected and terrible emergency, we don't act on this. But it is extraordinarily comforting to know that if there is a real need, there are people to whom we can reach out for help.

When we forget the obvious, the little joys, the meals together, the birthday celebrations, the weeping together in time
of pain, the wonder of the sunset or the daffodil peeping through
the snow, we become less human. I am grateful to the Canadian
woman who encouraged me to continue to write about the obvious.

I lay back on the bed, with her letter in my lap. The flush
of color in the western sky grew deeper and more beautiful as I
let go the tensions of the day and relaxed in the warmth of
words coming to me from miles and miles away.

Hiding Out

Susan Allen Toth

"A window seat? Why in the world would you want a window seat?" asked James, my architect husband, as he began designing a bedroom addition to our house. A classic modernist, he was now consulting with someone who was secretly yearning for a cupola, turrets, winding staircases, an attic, and unexpected nooks and crannies.

A window seat, I explained, would be the perfect place to curl up and read or daydream, especially on a rainy day. It would be a hideout. James nodded—he understood. I have told him that ever since I was a child, I have always sought out secret places.

When I was still too young to venture far by myself, I escaped to a sturdy maple across the street. Swinging onto its lower branch, I climbed a few feet higher, and then, hidden in a canopy of leaves, I sat for what seemed like hours, dreaming, pretending, and twisting leaf-boats to sail down to the sidewalk below.

Sometimes my older sister, Karen, and I would look for a hideout together. If she went with me, I felt brave enough to walk to the Pine Woods, a small plantation of trees that belonged to the state agricultural college. The Pine Woods was not far, perhaps ten minutes down a seldom used road at the edge of our small-town street, but going there was always an adventure.

First Karen and I had to unlatch a heavy wooden gate that shut off the cinder road from everyday traffic. We walked carefully, crunching the black cinders below our feet and looking around at the unknown farming country that suddenly opened before us. Just beyond the first gate, we came to a high hedge of lilacs. Someone must have once planted those lilacs at the edge of the old road, but they had long ago grown wild, tangling their branches hopelessly together and struggling toward the sky.

On sunny afternoons, the lilacs beckoned us to explore the half-lit shadows under their branches. There we could always find a perfect temporary cave, just our size, from which we could spy on a rare passing car and pretend we were hiding from it. In late spring, as we sat companionably on the still-cold ground, we breathed in the overwhelmingly rich fragrance of the pale-purple blossoms that cascaded everywhere around us. We often broke off a few so we could carry them on the rest of our journey.

When we walked on, we passed cultivated fields and then a small orchard of apple trees, but we were never tempted to stop. The Pine Woods waited. As the road bent and curved, we knew we were getting closer. The plantation covered a gentle hill on the opposite bank of a shallow clear creek. As we crossed a small wooden bridge over the water, we knew we were almost there. Sometimes we ran those last few yards, as if someone were after us.

Once we entered the Pine Woods, we were in a dark green

kingdom of our own. Even on hot summer days, the Pine Woods always smelled moist and cool, with a whiff of tangy pitch. My sister, who was an ingenious builder, knew how to pile up large broken branches to form the walls of a make-believe cabin. We furnished it with pinecone dishes and a bed of pine needles. Inside our cabin, I liked to pretend we might live there for-ever—at least, until I got hungry. I was sure no one would ever find us, for grown-ups seldom came to the Pine Woods—except, I had once heard a much older girl whisper, after dark.

On rainy days, if I had to stay home and play, one of my favorite hideouts was the attic of the Miller house next door. When I appeared at her back door, Mrs. Miller, a plump and kindly grandmother, would welcome me into her kitchen, where she almost always had a spare sugar cookie or a piece of freshly baked cake. Then she let me cross the hall, open the door to the attic staircase, close it tightly behind me, and climb up to the sprawling third-floor storage room under the eaves. Since I was a careful child, I was allowed to peer into boxes, play with discarded toys, and pore through scrapbooks, old photograph albums, and yellowing magazines. Most of all, as I sat on the dusty floor, breathing in a faint odor of unpainted wood, moth-balls, and dry crinkly paper, I thrilled to the sound of rain pattering on the roof a few feet over my head.

Another favorite hideout was a neglected gazebo I discovered in someone's backyard. It was a simple picnic shelter with a door, a roof, several benches, and—best of all—a hinged wooden table that folded down from the wall. Although I did not know the family who owned the gazebo, no one seemed to notice if I stopped there, sometimes with a friend, on my way home from school. Flipping down the table with a satisfying thud, I could turn it instantly into a store counter, a desk, a library checkout stand, or the formal setting for a dolls' tea-party. Even without a tea set, tea, or cookie crumbs, I would cook, serve, eat, and pretend to my heart's content—all because I had my own small house for those few hours. I think I felt it belonged to me because I had discovered it.

Probably all children need hideouts, where they can imagine, invent, and fantasize, secure in the knowledge that no grown-up will interrupt them. But I was especially grateful for those places. Not only was I an avid reader and dreamer, but I also had an unusually close family. After my father died when I was seven, my mother, sister and I, regrouping in a tight circle, formed a kind of league of defense against a sometimes confusing and frightening world. Yet I wanted to confront and understand that world in my own way, and so I sought secure vantage points from which I could observe it.

As I grew older, I continued to search for private hidden spaces, but they became increasingly hard to find. After all, no self-respecting teenager climbs trees or burrows under lilacs. Of course I had my bedroom, but it was small, square, and unex-citing, part of a modest bungalow with nary a nook or cranny. Perhaps no one wishes for a secret and protected kingdom as much as a teenage girl. When I read about royalty, I frequently imagined queens and princesses who slept behind curtains in a canopied bed. That to me was the pinnacle of privilege. If only, I thought, I could have a four-poster bed, hung with gauzy curtains I could draw around me, I'd never ask for anything else in the world.

When, in those in-between years, I was desperate to be alone, and my room seemed too vulnerable to invasion, I'd descend to our unfinished basement, a dampish place with concrete walls and small high windows. Sometimes I'd sit for a while in an old rocker shoved near the furnace. There I'd read, scribble, or just ponder, until eventually the general gray gloominess, and a certain nervousness about spiders, forced me back upstairs. Basements, I decided, did not make satisfying hideouts.

Libraries, on the other hand, were perfect. The public library in Ames, Iowa, had a small separate cubicle for stored periodicals, and several seldom-disturbed corners. I could always feel alone somewhere in the library. In college, I retreated to the library's Browsing Room, whose glass doors effectively shut out the passing of shuffling feet. With my high armchair turned toward a window, I often abandoned any pretense of studying. There I'd sit, half-hidden behind the heavy damask drapes and burrowed deep into my cushion, looking outside at other girls hurrying toward their classes or professors stopping to chat with each other on the library path. I was quite secure, for no one ever bothered to look in.

After I married and had a child, private space became almost impossible either to find or to use. By this time I had read Virginia Woolf's *A Room of One's Own,* and I knew I wanted one, but it took years before I felt I could close a door behind me, disappear into silence, and not be interrupted. During my daughter's first few weeks, I never dared wander out of earshot. Then, when she developed lungs so strong she could cry with the range and effectiveness of an air-raid siren, I could not find a single room in the house where I was out of earshot. A close friend, whose baby was also colicky, advised me sympathetically, "sometimes when I can't stand it anymore, I just go into the shower and turn it on full blast."

As my daughter began to grow up, I, like most parents, did learn techniques of survival. After I was divorced and became a single parent, I had to hone those techniques further and quickly. In one house, I retreated (except in the dead of winter) to an unheated screened porch with only a single lounge chair. In another house, I converted a spare bedroom into a makeshift library, also furnished with only one chair. No children ever wanted to play in either of these rather barren rooms, and I could hide out there quite peaceably.

In the past few years, I have continued to cherish hideouts. Much as I treasure my current family life and value the deep companionship of my husband, I have to retreat from time to time, if only for half an hour. I may not use my retreat to solve a weighty problem. Sometimes I only sit for a while and listen to a sort of inner hum, an inarticulate melody that cannot be called anything much. If I do not find the time and place to hear it, however, my ordinary, everyday noises become a deafening roar.

Because he knows me so well, James respects my yearning for hideouts. He helps me find them, and because he is an architect, he can even conjure them up. I did get my window seat, though I actually don't use it much. Instead, I seek out a deep, soft chair just below a window in our bedroom alcove, a raised level set off by a low wall. With the door closed, I am as snug as can be, wrapped in an afghan in winter or sipping ice water in summer. A closed door, a comfortable chair, a view out a window—maybe that's all a hideout requires.

But I am always on the lookout for a new secret place. At the moment, James is designing my birthday present, a one-room studio deep in the woods near our weekend cottage. It will be a simple structure, with only a desk, a chair, and a single bed. Outside, its natural wood shingles will blend with the forest; but inside, the walls and ceiling will vibrate with color, probably soft shades of red, blue, yellow, and green.

Even though it is unlikely anyone will wander by my door, James plans on venetian blinds I can pull over all the windows. Then, in a small rainbow world no one knows about, I can read, write, think, and dream, just as I have loved to do since I was a child. Although I would never want to remain in seclusion forever, or even disappear for very long from my usual routines, I will always need a hideout. From a shadowy cave under towering lilacs to an architect's one-room cabin, these special places have nurtured my imagination and spirit, and I am thankful that my life has been full of them.

On Keeping a Journal

Phyllis Theroux

very morning just before dawn, I rise, make myself a cup of coffee, and sit quietly in a wing chair in the living room for about an hour. Waking early without effort is one of the genuine pleasures of getting older. Life has fewer days in it, but nature compensates by allowing you to greet them sooner.

I watch the light gradually turn up its strength behind the tree line, and admire how it picks out the bowls, books, and flowers in the room, read, think, and, most importantly, drop my thoughts into a journal that I have kept steadily for the past fourteen years—a period that began around the time I became a single mother.

This is not to imply that before this point my life had been entirely unexamined or unrecorded. While married, I made sporadic entries into various spiral notebooks, some of which are still extant. But the year I was divorced, I started keeping closer track of myself, for the same reason a ship's captain keeps a log:

to fix my position, chart a course, and, in times of particularly bad weather, maintain my bearings.

Now, if I am deprived of that first morning hour to myself, the rest of the day has a compromised, undirected feeling to it. And such is the value of these small black copybooks that if the one I am writing in is misplaced, I am bereft until it is recovered. Conversely, when it's found, so am I.

Some time ago, a friend of mine showed me a large trunkful of journals that had been written by his mother, the dutiful wife of a career diplomat. While she was alive, nobody, not even her husband, knew they existed. Perhaps, I thought, one of the reasons she kept a journal, as she kept to her diplomatic rounds, was to remind herself that she existed, too.

But the need to remind ourselves that we exist and have some meaning beyond our own shadow is one of the deepest of all human instincts. Journal-keeping, which is enjoying a genuine revival, particularly among women, is as old as language itself.

"Articulation is central to human survival and self-determination . . . to relieve the soul of incoherence," wrote novelist Shirley Hazzard. There are other nonverbal ways to do it. Painters, dancers, all artisans who seek to express the human spirit or objectify a vision in their work are relieving themselves of incoherence, too.

But from my earliest days, I loved everything about the sound, power, and delivery of words. I would spend hours in my room writing flowery thank-you notes, sealing the envelopes with hot colored wax and dime-store signet rings. In the convent school where I was taught a form of calligraphy, the simple act of drawing the broad, ink-filled nib of an Esterbrook pen directly down a page calmed my nerves.

Diaries did not interest me. I had the misunderstanding that you were supposed to recount everything you had done, from cleaning out the birdcage to brushing your teeth, and many days that was all that took place. Recording it only reinforced my own sense that nothing was happening. But if someone were to look over my shoulder today as I write in my journal, one would still think that my existence was confined to what I thought in a wing chair.

There is no right or wrong way to keep a journal. The mind of the writer inevitably imposes itself upon the style. My friend Richard, for instance, keeps a half-dozen journals going simultaneously, each representing different subjects he is continually pondering. My journal, like my life, is a mélange.

I write where I live, and the pages of my journal reflect my thoughts, my laundry lists of things to do, calculations of how much or little money I will be making in the upcoming weeks, conversations, stories overheard while I'm on a train.

Large events, such as leaving jobs or being sued, are often only alluded to in passing. Whether I am writing from home, St. Martin, or White Plains is rarely clear. I don't use my journal as a calendar but as an intellectual record, crying rag, and cheerleading section. The pages are full of other people's voices whose words are wiser, more inspiring, or funnier than my own:

"Life is what leaps." (Emerson)

"I can get confused in an elevator." (My mother)

"The gossamer filament which holds the artistic life is so delicate that it hardly bears analysis." (James Michener)

It is, in fact, my artistic life that I analyze frequently in the pages of my journal—either to chastise myself for not being as loyal to it as one must be if it is to flower, or to make notes for future pieces I want to write.

Upstairs in my bedroom is a large wooden box where I keep materials for I know not what: quilts, wall hangings, aprons, or curtains, as yet unmade. My journal is the intellectual equivalent: storage space for scraps of material that may or may not be usable in the future, but if I had no place to store it, the material would be lost.

Every year, I teach at least one writing seminar. At the moment, I have two going on two separate evenings. In each, I have shown students how to "graze" over their own minds, like a field, for inspiration. Sometimes I'll assign them a word or phrase, such as "My Mother," or "My Favorite Room," or "Broken Hearts" in order to narrow their focus. Then, I ask them to think, in a semimeditative way, about their topic and write down any phrases or ideas that occur to them that relate.

I have found that most people profit rather quickly from this kind of methodology. They are amazed at what they remember once their minds are instructed to search. Keeping a journal is very akin to this exercise, with the only difference (and luxury) being that the subjects your mind meditates upon can change as often as your mind.

It takes a young or inexperienced writer time to find his or her authentic voice and, of course, it changes as the writer's consciousness develops. But the pages of one's personal journal are where the least self-conscious and most eloquent (although not necessarily most polished) voice is first found, which is why so many writers often keep one.

One of the reasons people think they want to keep a journal is to trace their own progress or development in a score-keeping way. I have found this to be unproductive for the most part. Rarely do I find examining anything but the surrounding pages, going back several months at the most, to be helpful. Any further back and one realizes how consistently we spin out the same webs, only to be recaught in them. Then, too, some periods of one's life are too painful to relive.

In preparation for writing this essay, I opened up one of my first journals, begun just shortly after I had gotten separated. The pages had preserved the innocent cries of my children too perfectly for me to listen to, even fourteen years after the fact. But such is the power of the written word that when I closed the covers and put the volume back, I felt as if I were stuffing my still-weeping children into a trunk.

Just before New Year's 1993, I ran out of pages in my latest journal. Before I retired it to the chest, too, I decided to go through and pick out any thoughts that seemed valuable and bind them into a sort of rough commonplace book.

Once before I had done this, gathering up my favorite voices—William James, Thomas Merton, Florida Scott-Maxwell, my own children. But this time I found that my own voice was of equal interest to me. I had never imagined this would ever happen. Then again, "nearly all the evil in the world comes from failure or misuse of the imagination."

These are words I'd like to claim as mine—and in this case, I can.

The Deer in Springtime

Diane Ackerman

ne day, when the last snows have melted, the air tastes tinny and sweet for the first time in many months. That subtle tincture of new buds, sap, and loam I've learned to recognize as the first whiff of springtime. Suddenly a brown shape moves in the woods, then blasts into sight as it clears the fence at the bottom of the yard. A beautiful doe with russet flanks and nimble legs, she looks straight at me as I watch from the living-room window, then she drops her gaze.

Like fireworks, five more deer make equally spectacular leaps, and land squarely on the lifeless grass. But once they touch earth all their buoyancy seems to vanish, and they lumber around the yard, droopy, gaunt, exhausted. A big doe lifts a hind foot to scratch her shaggy cheek. I think that's the doe I named Triangle last year, because of a geometrical pattern in her coat. But, at the moment, the deer are in molt, which must feel itchy, and since they don't shed evenly, their usually sleek coats look criss-crossed by small weather systems. Mainly the deer seem frantic with hunger. Now they've lost their winter fat, but there's nothing in bloom. Their living larder won't be full for weeks. Desperate, they start eating the dried-up lavender leaves, whose pungent smell usually keeps them at bay; they devour the bittersweet and pull the bark from aspens and other trees they don't prefer.

I love watching the deer, which always arrive like magic or miracle or the answer to an unasked question. Can there be a benediction of deer on a chilly spring morning? I think so. Their otherworldliness stops the day in its tracks, focuses it on the hypnotic beauty of nature, and then starts the day again with a rush of wonder. There is a way of sitting quietly and beholding nature that is a form of meditation or prayer—and, like those healing acts, it calms the spirit.

Come summer, of course, the deer will ransack my herb garden, plunder my roses, and destroy the raised beds, leaving their footprints as calling cards among the decapitated flowers. They are terrorists in the garden. That's why I've planted most of my roses in a special fenced-in garden with a solid gate. Still, I leave all the apples from both trees just for the deer, I let them eat their fill from the raspberry vines, and I feed them in hard weather. Sometimes in colder months I leave apples beneath the twin apple trees where deer would expect to find them. For a decade, the apple trees have helped the deer survive winter. This year, what with the changing current of El Niño and several volcanoes hurling dust high into the atmosphere, the apple trees were sparse, and the deer found few apples beneath the snow. Despite thick, burro-like coats, they looked thin. I suppose I am "conflicted" about the deer, as the psychologically inclined like to say. But mainly I am grateful to have these emissaries of the wild so close at hand, and when they visit, all I can manage is praise.

We've worked hard to exile ourselves from nature, yet we end up longing for what we've lost—a sense of connectedness. For many homeowners, suburbanites, and travelers, backyard ani-

mals such as deer, squirrels, birds, and raccoons become an entryway to the bustling world of nature. Studying animals is easy
when they're close at hand, and there's nothing like the thrill
of recognizing individual animals with unique looks and personalities: the doe with the white half-circle beneath one eye
who stands up on her rear legs to pick apples off the trees; the
young buck who always does a small war dance before he leaps
a fence. When that happens, we lose our "us against them"
attitude, and start to feel part of a kingdom of neighbors. Deep
in our instincts and cells we remember living wild in nature,
fitting into the seamless circle of the seasons, reading the
weather and landscape, facing frights and challenges. In a real
sense we now are out of our elements, and it's small wonder we
relish rare visits to nature—picnics, jogs, and bike rides; jour-
neys to parks, campgrounds, and zoos.

We may feel cozy and safe in our homes, protected from both
blast and predator, but we pay the price with slack muscles,
weak hearts, and glum spirits. Deprived of fresh daylight, we
sink low during winter months. And yet when we search for
remedies to those distresses, only the artificial springs to mind:
gyms, pills, lightboxes. By retreating further and further from
nature, we lose our sense of belonging, suffer a terrible loneliness
we can't name, and end up depriving ourselves of what we need
to feel healthy and whole. Children know this instinctively.
When a tree stump or marsh beckons, they dive in, wide-eyed,
all hands. I suppose what we fear is loss of control, of ourselves
and of our planet; and there's no doubt, nature is chaotic, random, violent, uncontainable, no matter how hard we try to out-
wit it. But it's also dazzling, soothing, all-embracing, and
restorative. Wonder is a bulky emotion—when it fills the heart
and mind there's little room for anything else. We need the
intimate truths of daylight and deer.

Deer are such a panic species that the only way to be among
them without frightening them is to hunker down low and posi-

tively not look at them. Eye contact, even glancing, may distress them. Most often, wild animals make eye contact only when they wish to fight, eat, or mate. If you seem to be ignoring them, you pose little threat. And so I creep out, bent low, carrying a sliced-up peach, which I place on the grass near the apple trees, then, still without making eye contact, I creep back indoors. Soon two deer sniff their way to the treasure, so unfamiliar yet so sweet, and stand eating with peach slices dripping from their mouths. I've noticed that squirrels seem comforted by the sound of my voice when I'm among them, but deer require silence.

One noon last summer, I saw two fawns sitting on the grass in the shade of a large tree in my front yard. Quietly I crept out with concealed purpose—I walked easily across the yard, as if on an errand unrelated to the deer. Because I seemed preoccupied by human things, they watched me, ever alert, but didn't bother to stir as I sat down in the grass near them, averting my eyes, picking a blade of grass or two, only now and then studying them with long, thick glances. A passing car startled them and they half-stood, then settled down again. Deer don't fold their legs like dogs, but slide down over the tops of their knees like camels. As I continued my mock-grazing, they curled up and snoozed.

Where was their mother—and wasn't she afraid to leave them alone? During the first few weeks of life, fawns don't give off much scent. Small, camouflaged, and nearly odorless, they're not easily discovered, so mother might drift off without much concern. On the other hand, I might well have been in her sights, dismissed as another creature out grazing in the sun. Humans are familiars to suburban deer. By mid-summer the fawns were eating a vegetarian diet that included hundreds of species of buds and leaves, and they were roaming a wide area. But, late in the day, I would often watch them wander into open areas to nibble broad-leafed plants.

Now, a spring later, the fawns are grown, their speckles have disappeared, and their bellies look gaunt. Remembering some corncobs I was saving for the squirrel and bird feeders, I grab a jacket and hurry into the garage, returning soon with six ears of corn. Then, slipping slowly out back, I toss the corn across the yard. The deer stare squarely at them from a distance, tentatively approach the corn, realize what it is, and eagerly gnaw one cob a piece. What about the utility apples I was saving for a pie? Filling my pockets and hands with apples, I creep outside once more. As I toss apples to her, the largest female regards me solidly, eye to eye. An apple lands a yard in front of her, and still she watches me carefully, then walks toward the apple, slices it with one bite, and eats with a mixture of surprise and relish. Apples in April! She looks back at me, allows me to settle low on my haunches and watch her and her family. I try not to move.

In time, she wanders toward the others, also happily eating apples and corn. The deer will survive at least one more day because of this food, maybe a few days, maybe long enough to get to the next decent meal. Knowing that, my heart lightens. It is a moment sealed in a glass paperweight, a scene to be reflected in a gazing ball, a time of peaceful communion with nature. And there I sit on the grass until evening drops a gray screen over the air and daylight drains away. At last, the deer become startled by something real or imaginary and trot back toward the woods with the largest doe leading the way along the fence. When she finds a place she feels comfortable with, she lines up squarely and hurdles it. The others pace nervously. One stands before the fence, lifts a foot as if to jump, thinks about it again, backs up, paces, once more aborts the attempt, and then finally risks it—a from-standing-still five-foot jump straight up. Her hooves graze the top rail as she clears it. Over the years, the deer have bent the fence low between us. Soon the others follow, launching themselves from the tidy world of humans back into their familiar pandemonium of green.

Notes on Contributors

DIANE ACKERMAN is the author of fourteen books of poetry and nonfiction, including *A Natural History of Love* and *The Rarest of the Rare*. Her best-seller, *A Natural History of the Senses,* was the basis for the PBS series "Mystery of the Senses," which she hosted. Her most recent books are *Bats: Shadows in the Night* (for children) and *A Slender Thread: Rediscovering Hope at the Heart of Crisis.*

M. J. ANDERSEN was born and raised in South Dakota, where her mother and home ec teacher Alice Walther taught her to sew. During high school, she wrote a column for the *Millbank Herald Advance,* a weekly newspaper owned by her family. She graduated from Princeton University with highest honors and, after working briefly in publishing, joined the *Providence Journal-Bulletin,* in Rhode Island, where she is an editorial writer and columnist. She is married to Andrew Nixon, a sculptor. They live in a Victorian house in Attleboro, Massachusetts.

FAITH ANDREWS BEDFORD reflects in her writing the memories woven of a childhood in Illinois and New England, the experiences of motherhood, and her love of art, nature, and the traditions of family. She is an internationally published author whose most recent book is *Frank W. Benson: American Impressionist*. She writes from her farm near the Blue Ridge Mountains of Virginia and from the family home in Florida.

SUZANNE BERNE is the author of a novel, *A Crime in the Neighborhood,* and the recipient of a National Endowment for the Arts fellowship. Her short fiction and personal essays have appeared in a variety of magazines and anthologies; she also frequently writes book reviews and travel articles for *The New York Times.* She has taught writing at Harvard University and Wellesley College and lives with her family outside Boston, Massachusetts.

CATHERINE CALVERT grew up an army brat, lived for many years in New York City, and now lives in Europe. She has worked as an editor and writer on the staffs of *Victoria, Mademoiselle,* and *Town & Country* magazines, as well as the New York *Daily News.* A frequent contributor to a variety of major publications, she is the author of six books.

MAXINE CLAIR is author of the poetry collection, *Coping With Gravity,* and the work of fiction *Rattlebone,* which won the *Chicago Tribune*'s Heartland Prize. She teaches writing at The George Washington University in Washington, D.C.

SUSAN CRANDELL was executive editor of *Travel & Leisure* magazine when she visited the small city in northern England that is the backdrop for "It All Started with the Sampler," her essay in this book. "With my mother, my teenage daughter, and I all crammed into a tiny rental car rocketing around the Lake District, it was one of the more intense trips I've ever taken," she says. "But seeing the village green where my great-grandmother grew up made it one of the most rewarding." Crandell, who has also written for *Town & Country, Working Woman,* and *Food & Wine* magazines, is executive editor of *Ladies' Home Journal.*

PRISCILLA DUNHILL studied architecture at Pratt Institute in New York City and landscape history at the University of California in San Francisco. A contributing editor to *Victoria* magazine, the Long Island style magazine *Distinction,* and the Horticultural Alliance *Journal,* she writes about gardens, travel, environmental concerns, and popular culture for a variety of national publications. Her books include *Glorious Gardens to Visit Within Three Hours of New York, Glorious Gardens to Visit in Northern California, A Victorian Scrapbook, Joy to the World,* and *Nonsense and Common Sense.* Currently she is working on *The Well-Appointed Garden,* part of the Smith & Hawken garden series, to be published in 1997 by Workman.

SUSAN J. GORDON, the author of numerous essays and articles and a member of the Authors Guild and American Society of Journalists and Authors, says, "Virtually all my writing is inspired by my life." Research for her forthcoming book, *Wedding Days: When and How Great Marriages Began,* which Morrow will publish in 1998, was sparked by her sons' recent weddings and her own marriage to "a man I continue to fall in love with after thirty-two years."

ANGELINE GOREAU has written for *The New York Times Book Review, The New York Times Sophisticated Traveler,* and *Gourmet* magazine. She is the author of two books, *Reconstructing Aphra,* a biography of Aphra Ben, and *The Whole Duty of a Woman: On the Roots of Feminism.* She lives in New York City.

JANETTE TURNER HOSPITAL is an Australian who lives a very nomadic life. She has published six novels and three collections of short stories and has won a number of international literary awards, including Australia's Seal First Novel Award for *The Ivory Swing.* She has been writer in residence at universities in the United States, Canada, Australia, England, and Europe. Her sixth novel, *Oyster,* recently published to critical acclaim in Australia, Canada, and the United Kingdom, where it is being made as a feature film for BBC television. It will be released in the United States by W. W. Norton late in 1997.

JANE HOWARD was insatiably curious about why people do what they do and why relationships work or don't work. As a journalist working for *Life* magazine, she specialized in profiling writers, including Saul Bellow, John Updike, and Truman Capote. Her most acclaimed work was the 1984 biography *Margaret Mead: A Life.* Her earlier books were *Please Touch: A Guided Tour of the Human Potential Movement; A Different Woman,* an examination of how the feminist movement had changed women; and *Families.* At her death in 1996, she was working on a nonfiction book tentatively titled *Lost in the Interior.*

PERRI KLASS is a pediatrician in Boston. She is the author of two novels, *Other Women's Children* and *Recombinations;* a collection of short stories, *I Am Having an Adventure;* and two nonfiction books, *A Not Entirely Benign Procedure: Four Years as a Medical Student* and *Baby Doctor: A Pediatrician's Training.*

MADELEINE L'ENGLE wrote her first story when she was five years old, and in her long and prolific career she has written almost fifty books. Among her credits is the children's science fiction novel, *A Wrinkle in Time,* which won the John Newbery Medal in 1963 and is now in its fifty-third hardcover printing, and *A Swiftly Tilting Planet,* for adolescent readers, which received an American Book Award in 1980. Ms. L'Engle has also addressed adult audiences with books such as *The Summer of the Great-grandmother,* chronicling her mother's last summer, and *Two-Part Invention,* about her forty years of marriage to the actor Hugh Franklin. The couple met while L'Engle was acting in *The Cherry Orchard* in New York's Greenwich Village, where she went in 1941 after graduating with honors from Smith College. Her latest book, published in March 1997, is *Mothers and Daughters,* which she wrote with her daughter, the photographer Maria Rooney. In 1995 Madeleine L'Engle served as *Victoria*'s Writer in Residence.

REEVE LINDBERGH is the youngest child of aviator-authors Charles A. and Anne Morrow Lindbergh. She was born in New York City in 1945 and grew up in Darien, Connecticut. After graduating from Radcliffe College in 1968, she moved to Vermont, where she has been teaching, writing, and, with her husband, writer Nathaniel Tripp, raising a family, ever since. She is also active with the Lindbergh Foundation, a Minnesota-based nonprofit organization. She is currently working on a family memoir called *Under a Wing.*

TOVAH MARTIN, a contributing editor to *Victoria,* has been gardening indoors and outside ever since she selected marigolds as her Brownie project. A self-proclaimed "hothouse flower," she has served as consulting horticulturist for Logee's Greenhouses and White Flower Farm. In 1995, the Massachusetts Horticultural Society honored her with their Gold Medal "for extraordinary service to horticulture." She is the author of *Once Upon a Windowsill, Victoria Moments in the Garden, The Essence of Paradise, Tasha Tudor's Garden, The Ways of Flowers, Well-Clad Windowsills, Tasha Tudor's Heirloom Crafts,* and *Windowboxes.* When she isn't traveling to visit other people's backyards, you'll find her planting her own cottage garden in front of the converted cobbler's shop in Roxbury, Connecticut, that she calls home, or fiddling with the flowers in her greenhouse.

GARDNER MCFALL is a poet, critic, and children's book writer. She holds a Ph.D. in English from New York University and teaches literature at The Cooper Union for the Advancement of Science and Art in New York City. She lives in New York with her husband and daughter.

SUSAN MINOT, Victoria's first Writer in Residence, is the author of the novels *Monkeys* and *Folly* and a short story collection titled *Lust & Other Stories.* She is also the author of the screenplay for "Stealing Beauty," directed by Bernardo Bertolucci and released in 1996. Her work has been published in a dozen countries. She lives in New York City.

FAYE MOSKOWITZ is an associate professor and director of the creative writing program at The George Washington University, in Washington, D.C. She is the author of *And the Bridge Is Love, A Leak in the Heart,* and *Whoever Finds This: I Love You.* She also edited *Her Face in the Mirror,* a collection on Jewish mothers and daughters.

PATRICIA O'TOOLE became a writer because she loves to read. She has contributed articles, essays, and reviews to many magazines and is the author, most recently, of *The Five of Hearts: An Intimate Portrait of Henry Adams and His Friends, 1880–1918,* which was a finalist for the Pulitzer Prize in biography. She also teaches in the Writing Division of the School of the Arts at Columbia University in New York City.

WHITNEY OTTO is a graduate of the MFA program at the University of California at Irvine. She has also taught at the university as well as at Irvine Valley College. Her novels include *Now You See Her* and *How to Make an American Quilt,* which was on the *New York Times* Best-seller List for both hardcover and paperback books and was made into a major motion picture released by Stephen Spielberg's Amblin Entertainment in fall 1995. Her most recent work, *The Passion Dream Book,* will be published by HarperCollins in May 1997. She lives in Portland, Oregon, with her husband and their young son.

FRANCINE PROSE is the author of nine novels, including *Hunters and Gatherers, Primitive People, Bigfoot Dreams,* and *Household Saints,* and two story collections. *Guided Tours of Hell,* a book of two novellas, was published by Metropolitan Books in January 1997. The recipient of numerous grants and awards, including a Guggenheim and a Fulbright fellowship and the Pushcart Prize, she also teaches at the Iowa Writers' Workshop and Breadloaf Writers Conference. She lives in New York City.

DORIS BRYDEN RANDALL was born in Walton, New York, in 1931 and received her B.A. degree from Ithaca College in 1952. She appeared as a professional actress off-Broadway and in summer stock theater in New York and in winter stock in Florida. In 1962 she moved to Fresno, California, where she made numerous appearances in professional and nonprofessional theatrical productions. She died in 1993, leaving a husband, three children, and six grandchildren. "The Dance of Life," her essay that appears in this volume, was found among her papers by her husband, Charles, after her death.

MARJORIE SANDOR is the author of a collection of stories, *A Night of Music*. Her short fiction has appeared in *The Georgia Review, Antaeus,* and other literary magazines, and has been anthologized in *Best American Short Stories 1985* and *1988, Twenty Under Thirty, The Pushcart Prize XIII,* and *America and I: Stories by Jewish-American Women Writers*. Her nonfiction has appeared in *The Gift of Trout,* a collection of essays on trout fishing, *The New York Times Magazine* as well as the Sunday travel section, and elsewhere. She lives in Corvallis, Oregon, with her husband and daughter and teaches fiction writing at Oregon State University.

SUSAN SCHNEIDER is an editor at *Sesame Street Parents* magazine. Recently, she has also been studying and writing poetry. She is the mother of nine-year-old India, who loves to read and listen to the Beatles. Susan and India live in New York City with their hamster, Rhonda.

CAROLINE SEEBOHM grew up in England. After a period in New York City at *House & Garden* magazine, she moved upstate and wrote a novel, *The Last Romantics*. Other books include *English Country, Private Landscapes, At Home with Books,* and its forthcoming sequel, *At Home with Art*. Her biography of Marietta Tree will be published in October 1997. She has two children and lives and works overlooking the Delaware River in New Jersey.

MARIAN SELDES, a Tony Award–winning actress, was inducted into the Theater Hall of Fame in 1996. She recently won acclaim in the national tour of Edward Albee's play *Three Tall Women,* and she has made numerous appearances on television and in film. The daughter of author and critic Gilbert Seldes, she is the author of *The Bright Lights: Theater Life,* and the novel *Time Together*. Her latest films are *Digging to China* and *Home Alone 3*.

CAROL SHIELDS, born and raised in Chicago, Illinois, has made her home in Canada since 1957. She studied at Hanover College and the University of Ottawa. She now lives with her husband in Winnipeg (they have five grown children), where she is chancellor of the University of Winnipeg. She is a Pulitzer Prize winner and the award-winning author of numerous novels, plays, and story collections, and has received honorary doctorates from five universities.

MICHELE SLUNG managed a bookstore in New York City before starting her literary career in 1975 with the publication of *Crime on Her Mind: Fifteen Stories of Female Sleuths from the Victorian Era to the Forties*. Her books, among them the best-selling *Momilies*® titles, have been translated into a dozen languages, and she has written for many periodicals, including *The New York Times Book Review*, *USA Today*, and *The Washington Post*, where for five years she also wrote a publishing column. She has been a commentator for National Public Radio and a contributor to a variety of reference books, including the forthcoming *Oxford Companion to Crime and Mystery Writing*.

JANE SMILEY is the author of many works of fiction, including *Moo*, *A Thousand Acres*, which won the Pulitzer Prize, and *The Greenlanders*. She lives with her family, horses, and dogs in California and northern Wisconsin. She is now working on a nineteenth-century novel.

LINDA SUNSHINE is the author of fourteen books including *A Passion for Shoes*, *The Illustrated Woody Allen Reader*, *Lovers*, *Women Who Date Too Much (And Those Who Should Be So Lucky)*, *How NOT to Turn into Your Mother*, and *Plain Jane Works Out*. She has also written for numerous magazines. Currently, she is editorial director of Stewart, Tabori & Chang, an art book publisher located in Manhattan.

PHYLLIS THEROUX has written several books, including *California & Other States of Grace*, *Night Lights: Bedtime Stories for Parents in the Dark*, and most recently, an anthology of great posthumous tributes, *The Book of Eulogies*. Her first children's story, *Serafina Under the Circumstances*, will be published by Simon and Schuster. Her essays have appeared in a variety of national publications, including *The New York Times* and *The Washington Post*. She lives in Ashland, Virginia.

SYLVIA THOMPSON, a fourth-generation Californian, writes, gardens, and cooks with her husband, the novelist Gene Thompson, in the mountains above Palm Springs. She is a contributor to the new edition of *Joy of Cooking*, and among her other works are *The Kitchen Garden*, *The Kitchen Garden Cookbook*, *The Birthday Cake Book*, and *Festive Tarts*. Mrs. Thompson has written for *Gourmet* and *Vogue* and is presently a contributing editor to *Kitchen Garden* magazine.

JUDITH THURMAN, *Victoria*'s Writer in Residence for 1996, is the author of *Isak Dinesen: The Life of a Storyteller*, which won the 1983 National Book Award for Biography, as well as numerous books of poetry and essays for children and young adults. Her writing has appeared in *The New Yorker*, *The New York Times*, *Vogue*, *Architectural Digest*, *The Nation*, *Mirabella*, *Mademoiselle*, and many other national and international publications. She wrote the award-winning documentary on Emily Dickinson that was part of the PBS *Voices and Visions* series. She also served as the associate producer of the film *Out of Africa,* which was based on her biography of Dinesen. For the last seven years, Ms. Thurman has been working on a definitive biography of Colette, *Secrets of the Flesh: A Life of Colette,* which Knopf will publish in 1998. She lives in Manhattan with her husband, Peter Miller, and her eight-year-old son, known to *Victoria* readers as "Sweet William" and to his friends as "Cool Will."

SUSAN ALLEN TOTH is an essayist, memoirist, and travel writer whose books include *Blooming: A Small-town Girlhood, Ivy Days, How to Prepare for Your High-School Reunion, A House of One's Own, Reading Rooms, My Love Affair with England, England as You Like It,* and *England for All Seasons.* She is an adjunct professor at Macalester College in St. Paul, Minnesota, and lives in Minneapolis.

KIM WALLER, *Victoria*'s features editor and previously an editor at *Town & Country* magazine, was a contributor to *Thoughts of Home,* a collection of essays drawn from the pages of *House Beautiful* magazine. She was formerly a teacher of English and has published poems as well as many magazine articles.

ACKNOWLEDGMENTS

The Quiet Center is obviously the work of many hands. Nancy Lindemeyer, as editor in chief of *Victoria,* had the vision to create a forum for women writers. I appreciate the opportunity she gave me to invite distinguished writers to contribute to the magazine and to work with them on their essays and memoirs. (Nancy's eye is also manifest in the jacket art for this book, which she designed with the aid of *Victoria*'s art department.) Most of the essays and memoirs in this volume were edited by Mary Morris, Kim Waller, and Claire Whitcomb when they originally appeared in the magazine. Each of them is blessed with the literary equivalent of perfect pitch, and I am grateful for their help. Thanks also to Ann Bramson, Gail Kinn, and Jennifer Kaye at Hearst Books for expeditiously bringing this book to market. Finally, *The Quiet Center* would not have become a reality without the initiative taken by Daniel D'Arezzo, deputy editor of *Victoria,* who makes things happen.   K.B.R.